Chicken Soup
for the Soul®
Power
MOMS

Chicken Soup for the Soul: Power Moms
101 Stories Celebrating the Power of Choice for Stay-at-Home and Work-from-Home Moms
by Jack Canfield, Mark Victor Hansen, Wendy Walker

Published by Chicken Soup for the Soul Publishing, LLC   www.chickensoup.com

The publisher gratefully acknowledges the many publishers and individuals who granted Chicken Soup for the Soul permission to reprint the cited material.

Front and back cover photos courtesy of Susan Morrow Photography. Interior illustration courtesy of iStockPhoto.com/pinkpig.

Cover and Interior Design & Layout by Pneuma Books, LLC
For more info on Pneuma Books, visit www.pneumabooks.com

Distributed to the booktrade by Simon & Schuster. SAN: 200-2442

Publisher's Cataloging-in-Publication Data
(Prepared by The Donohue Group)

Chicken soup for the soul : power moms : 101 stories celebrating the power of choice for stay-at-home and work-from-home moms / [compiled by] Jack Canfield, Mark Victor Hansen [and] Wendy Walker.

  p. ; cm.

  ISBN-13: 978-1-935096-31-3
  ISBN-10: 1-935096-31-1

1. Mothers--Literary collections. 2. Working mothers--Literary collections. 3. Mothers--Anecdotes. 4. Working mothers--Anecdotes. 5. Mothers--Conduct of life--Anecdotes. I. Canfield, Jack, 1944- II. Hansen, Mark Victor. III. Walker, Wendy, 1967- IV. Title: Power moms

PN6071.M29 C45 2009
810.8/092052   2009920528

PRINTED IN THE UNITED STATES OF AMERICA
on acid∞free paper
17 16 15 14 13 12 11 10 09   02 03 04 05 06 07 08

Chicken Soup for the Soul® Power MOMS

101 Stories Celebrating the
Power of Choice for
Stay-at-Home and
Work-from-Home Moms

Jack Canfield
Mark Victor Hansen
Wendy Walker

Chicken Soup for the Soul Publishing, LLC
Cos Cob, CT

www.chickensoup.com

Contents

❸
~Outside the Box~

❹
~Becoming a Specialist~

❺
~Working from Home~

❻
~Ladies Who Launch~

❼
~Gender Benders~

❽
~The Dividends~

❾
~Pink Slips~

➓
~Looking Back~

Foreword

What to call the choices mothers make?

I have written countless words about parenting, and I always get hung up on a handful of those — the ones that describe the years with children at home.

If you leave a paying job to raise them, are you a stay-at-home mom? If you keep your paycheck and head to an office every morning, are you a working mom? Does any mom actually stay home? Don't all mothers work? And what the heck is a full-time mom? Is there such a thing as being a parent part-time?

When we find ourselves wrestling with words like this, odds are we are really wrestling with something else, something emotionally wrought, something with history and baggage. You don't hear medical school graduates debating whether they are doctors or physicians, or those who passed the bar exam debating whether they are lawyers or attorneys. The more secure we are, the less the words themselves seem to matter.

But while we are all pretty clear that one should never ever use the word housewife when talking about today's mothers, every other phrase feels loaded, reflecting not only how intensely personal are the choices we make, but also how certain we feel that others judge us for what we have chosen.

I first wandered into this territory when I became a mother-who-works-from-home about fourteen years ago. Neither side knew quite what to do with me back then, and it was a time when you had to choose a side. The at-home moms seemed to think I questioned their decision to leave paid work and the at-the-office moms thought I questioned their decisions not to. Fact is I didn't really question anyone; I was simply trying to find a path that brought some sense and order to my own chaotic life.

Then, five years ago, I wrote an article about all of this for *The New York Times Magazine*. Called "The Opt-Out Revolution," it told the tales of accomplished, educated women who chose to walk away from prestigious jobs in order to spend more time with their children. That article somehow made me an expert in Women and Work — an expert who still hadn't figured out what to call the women she was writing about.

The reasons women opt-out are varied, and most are a combination of things. While there are certainly women who want nothing more than to be with their baby every moment of the day, and while there are also women who are escaping the workplace more than embracing motherhood, the tales women tell me are usually somewhere between those two extremes. The pull of home and children is powerful. But in a world with a more mother-friendly workplace, more of us would find a way to meld the two. In the same way, a fulfilling job can be energizing. But were it financially possible, more of us would probably choose to leave.

Just as the reasons women leave vary, so do their experiences once they make their choice. As you will read in the pages that follow, for some it can be all they had hoped. Others admit to boredom. There is elation and regret, contentment and frustration, and those conflicting feelings can come in the space of the same moment.

In other words, mothers are a spectrum. And not a one of us stays put. The mother wearing a suit and heels in an office tower today could be planning to leave next week, or perhaps she has just returned from a few years at home. The mother in sneakers and sweats at the playground could have an accounting degree she hasn't used in years, or one that she used at the PTA meeting just this morning — or maybe she's planning to get one after the youngest starts kindergarten. The woman in the suit and the one in the sneakers could both be proud of the role models they are providing their own children, or regretting that they are not better in that department, or not really thinking about being a role model at all, because that's navel gazing and there is real work to be done.

To cram any of us into little cubbies, and to assume we know the whole of a woman just by knowing where she spends her day, that's what's loaded, not the choice of a word. What I love about the essays here is that they surprise, and challenge, and defy expectations. Like mothers do every day.

What to call a woman who makes the best choices she knows how for her children?

Let's just call her a Mom.

~Lisa Belkin

Power MOMS

Decisions, Decisions...

Why Women Take the Job

Taking the Tarts When They're Passed

In the end, it's not the years in your life that count. It's the life in your years.
~Abraham Lincoln

Six handmade pizzas were lined up on my kitchen table. It was my daughter, Emma's, ninth birthday and we had invited six friends over for a pizza-making sleepover party. The first floor of our house looked like a hurricane had swept through it: pillows everywhere; brushes, detangler, and hair ties strewn all over the floor; pepperoni, mushrooms, grated cheese and tomato sauce rubbed into the kitchen banquette seat covers.

Everything was going as planned. Except that my younger daughter, Linley, was upstairs in my bedroom with a terrible cold and cough. She was watching TV, a rare treat awarded her since she was not allowed to come downstairs and join the fun. Pizzas in the oven, I went to check on her and found her awake but having real difficulty breathing—she was taking quick, tiny breaths at a rate that I knew was dangerous. I racked my brain trying to remember what to do. I had read somewhere that if your child has croup, you put her in a hot shower to open up the bronchial passages. I got the shower running but Linley refused to get in—she just got more agitated and her breathing got even worse. I realized that I had to get her to the hospital, and fast. In that terrifying moment, I knew that something had to change. I could no longer juggle the three balls that were in play in my life: children, work, and my husband, Jim's, first congressional campaign.

To this day, I ask myself how I could have missed all the signs of what turned out to be an acute asthma attack. I was busy, yes. I'd been working as the Market Editor for a terrific regional design magazine. I loved and respected my colleagues and the magazine, didn't have to commute into New York City, and had an enviable part-time gig. I was the trend hunter, scouring the Internet and stores all over the country for the hot new design trend. The job required a good sense of design and a strong visual memory, something I developed as a child endlessly playing the memory game. It was a fun job: I was surrounded by images of beautiful objects (furniture, fabrics, wallpaper, lighting, tabletop) and when the trend I spotted also appeared in *Elle Décor*, it helped me feel a tiny bit cool, something not that easy living in Greenwich, CT.

Looking back, I can't remember the exact moment when I first started losing the deep engagement in my job, but at some point in 2008 I started asking myself why I was doing this job. Was this a meaningful way to spend my life? Was it worth all the resulting stress on me and my family? The magazine, relative to the national publications where I'd worked before, paid little and was really understaffed; I felt like I could barely keep up with all the details involved in raising two elementary-aged girls; and, my husband was running for a seat in the U.S. House of Representatives for the first time. Not only that, he was trying to unseat a twenty-one-year incumbent, the last remaining Republican congressman in New England.

My husband approached me about running for the US Congress way back in January 2007. We were sitting at the kitchen table eating dinner when he nonchalantly asked me what I thought about the idea. What did I think? Nothing, of course. I'd never ever thought about it. Who would? I tried to imagine what "running for Congress" really meant. Since Jim had never held an elected office before, he couldn't provide many details. Sipping a glass of wine, I decided that the time was right for a new adventure. This was Jim's dream and I would do whatever it would take to help him win.

Little did I know what I was getting into. Political campaigns are fascinating. They are pressure cookers. They are humbling. They are seasonal. They are exhausting. As the spouse, it was unclear what my role was except that I was in charge of the family life. Acting essentially as a single working mother was lonely, so I started attending evening fundraisers with Jim.

The sad truth about elections is that to win, you have to raise a lot of money. And in the Fourth Congressional District, part of the New York media market, a lot of money means three to four million dollars. Supporters generously opened up their homes and hosted cocktail parties to introduce Jim to their friends—Democrats and Republicans alike. At these events, I had the true privilege to meet many committed, thoughtful people whose strong support for Jim humbled me. I made new friends.

But, walking into a room of complete strangers, hoping to leave a favorable impression so that they would financially support and vote for my husband, was not an easy task. I had to watch every word I said, which was not my usual style. I had to remember names, even if I only met someone for a few seconds. I had to smile and be friendly, even when I was angry, tired, bored or hungry. (Eating at these events was perilous—god forbid I got a piece of spinach stuck in my teeth!) We did this three or four nights a week. On weekends, we attended barbeques, picnics, parades, fairs, walks and runs. We ate fried dough, Irish soda bread, tiny hors d'oeuvres (I am now an expert on local caterers) and too many hamburgers to count.

And then there were the kids to remember. We decided early on that we would try to keep our daughters' lives as normal as possible. They would still go to soccer and lacrosse on the weekends, have play dates, and go to bed on time. We would include them in events that made sense: picnics, fairs, parades. If you ask Emma and Linley what they remember most about the campaign, they'd probably describe with glee the bags of candy collected at parades or the feeling of their stomachs dropping as they swung around on the Ali Baba ride they took, not once, but five separate times this past summer.

That was the fun part of the campaign for them. Less fun was the absence of Mom and Dad. Trying to juggle a part-time job and a campaign meant that I was out many nights, unable to meet them at the bus after school or to cuddle up with them at night to read a story and tuck them in to bed. Jim was out six nights a week. In the blur that was 2008, I forgot how sensitive children are to change. I lost the intimate knowledge of my daughters that I had before work or a campaign came into my life. When friends and family asked what Emma or Linley wanted for their birthdays, I had to guess. I lost my patience and my temper and never had time to sit down and play with the girls — something my six year old rightfully criticized me for. And then there was the asthma attack.

There are moments in life when change comes banging on your door — sometimes thankfully. Sitting on the hospital bed with Linley, anxiously watching her slowly but surely regain her ability to breathe, I knew that I had to drop one of the balls I'd been juggling. Up to that moment, I thought I could be that "super mom," the one who does it all with style, humor and nary a wrinkle, always able to quickly and handily address all oncoming crises; the magician who could pull a bunny out of a hat when necessary. Well, I guess not. Embarrassingly, it took an emergency hospital visit to make me finally see and accept that I was failing miserably at the one job that was mine to do: be a mom who could raise two strong, independent, smart girls with the emotional and physical strength to live a deeply meaningful life.

So, I am grateful that I have the ability to choose to stop working to spend time with my children, support my husband and assess what it means to be the wife of a US Congressman — yes, we won! I am excited to laugh and play with my children, meet with constituents and travel occasionally to Washington, DC. I'm going to try to keep my life in balance but, knowing myself, I'll no doubt eventually grab another ball to juggle because I always have. I credit my grandmother for this enthusiastic approach to life since she gave me the advice to "take the tarts when they're passed, dear." Old fashioned and yet incredibly valuable, this advice has inspired me to accept opportunity and embrace change, chosen or not. Going forward in my new life, thankful for my grandmother's wise counsel, I trust in the undeniable truth that each and every experience, good or bad, will bring with it wisdom and learning, the best anti-wrinkle defense around!

~Mary Himes

The Path Not Taken

*It was a step forward in the passionate journey — and one made possible
by it — for educated women to say "yes" to motherhood as a
conscious human purpose and not a burden imposed by the flesh.*
~Betty Friedan

Most of my years as a stay-home mother have passed by me like the changing seasons. Busy days fold into one another until suddenly a child is in school or has outgrown his clothing. I stop then and look around, taking in the new and mourning the loss of the old, but then there are things to get done and I turn my attention back to the tasks at hand. Deep reflection is a luxury when time is short and children are calling. Still, a few years back, something happened that stopped me in my tracks and forced me to take a long, hard look at the choices I've made in my life.

When I was in college, I dreamed only of a brilliant career. I thought about children too, but in those thoughts I was kissing them goodbye as I headed out the door in my power suit. Upon graduation, I worked on Wall Street, then attended law school. Next was a big law firm in New York. The plan was to pay off some student loans before pursuing a career as a criminal prosecutor. But along the way, I met my husband and everything began to change. I was tired of the long hours and the way my life was prioritized. Soon after getting married, we moved to the suburbs. I quit my job and decided to get our house settled. I was thirty years old and it was time to have a baby.

While I was nesting, I made good use of my law degree by

volunteering at the ACLU. For almost a year, I helped research and write briefs on constitutional issues. It was a dream come true for a lawyer, even if it meant commuting back into the city a couple of days a week. The work was engaging, the people dedicated and passionate. And I decided that after I was done staying home with my children, I would restart my legal career in the non-profit sector.

When I became pregnant with my first son, I knew it was time to wind down my volunteer work. I rode the train to New York and marched into the office of the woman I worked for. But before I could break the news to her, she told me that a job had opened up—a *paying* job—and that I should throw my hat in the ring. She told me I had a decent shot at it since all of the lawyers knew me. For a second, I forgot about the path I was now on, the house in the suburbs, the baby on the way. This was my dream job. But the moment passed, as it had to. I told her I was pregnant and that I had decided to stay home with my baby. She congratulated me and a few months later I cleared out my makeshift desk and headed home for good.

My son was born that spring. Two more babies followed. Ten years passed in the blink of an eye. I was no longer a lawyer taking a short break to care for a baby. I was a fully embedded stay-home mother with a posse of stay-home mommy friends. One of my friends shared my interest in politics and law. She also had a connection to the United States Supreme Court, so we decided to take a trip to Washington to hear oral arguments. It was more to us than just a couple of nights away from our lives. It was a rejuvenation of the parts of ourselves that we had left behind years ago, and we scanned the cases that were being heard that fall like kids in a candy shop. The cases are listed by name, and I recognized one instantly. Ten years prior, I had worked on that very case at the ACLU. I was ecstatic. We booked our flights, a room at a nice hotel, massages, and restaurant reservations. And I read every brief that had been filed in the case over the years, sweeping off the cobwebs that had formed in my brain.

I was nothing short of giddy as I packed my suitcase. On the plane, I rambled on and on about the issues in the case. We arrived in DC and saw a show at the Kennedy Center. I went for a run, then had my massage. We sipped cosmos over a nice dinner, watched a movie, and went to bed much too late. We were on vacation! The next morning we took a cab to the court. We were ushered inside to a special waiting area for guests of the court, the same area where lawyers for the case gather. From across the room I heard my name called and when I turned around, my life froze all around me.

Standing with the other lawyers was the team from the ACLU that I had worked with years before. I went over to say hello. There were big hugs and explanations as to why I was there, but my mind was in a haze of realization. The only lawyer I didn't recognize was the woman who was arguing the case—the woman, it seems, who had been hired for the job I had walked away from ten years before.

We were taken to our seats, my friend and I to the visitors' section, the lawyers from the ACLU to the front table. And for most of the hour, I heard the questions that I knew would be asked, and I felt the answers form in my head. The ACLU lawyer was brilliant, but as I was admiring her, I could not help but think the words "that could have been me." It wasn't entirely rational. I may not have been hired for the job. I may not have been able to manage a baby in the suburbs and the commute to New York. I may not have been good enough to be lead counsel. Still, I was in the Court as a vacationing mommy, and the woman who filled that job was arguing in front of the United States Supreme Court. Never had my choice been exposed to such a bright light.

My friend and I headed home the next day. I re-entered my life as the mother of three little boys who were now grumpy because I'd been away. And as I lay in bed that night, I considered that life. I thought about my years with my children, and how being with them every day had given me something I had needed, a connection to life I had always ignored. And from being a mom I had also become a writer, a job I love. I felt a wave of relief that I did not have regrets. Still, I look at choices more carefully now. The feelings that erupted as I sat in the Court have stayed with me. And at every fork in the road, I remind myself to look down each path—to look long and hard. Regret did not find me this time. But it came awfully close.

~Wendy Walker

Reprinted by permission of Tom Swick
© 2008

The Award
I Truly Wanted

As a mother, you can't see the results of your work for years.
So much of it is intangible, but that does not mean that it is any less impor-
tant than any kind of job or title of any kind.
~Jane Clayson

For as long as I can remember I wanted to be a pediatrician, not just any pediatrician, but the kind who took care of the tiny babies in the plastic boxes. My sister had been premature, and I was fascinated by the fact that she lived for months in a plastic box while my parents watched her grow. Eventually, I did realize my dream and became a neonatologist.

Every time I walked into the neonatal unit I felt such pride. I loved the families and their precious babies. I loved being the one they leaned on, trusted, prayed with and cried with, and most of all I loved being the one who finally got to send their baby home. Somewhere along the line I started loving that too much and making decisions that negatively impacted my own family.

In the fall of 2001, I began caring for a baby with many problems. The more I cared for him, the more I resisted allowing other doctors to care for him. I began to work weekends I wasn't scheduled, leaving my husband and children early in the mornings while they still slept, and then rushing back to be with them before I returned to work the next morning. Mornings I wasn't scheduled to work, I begged to work, and my co-workers were more than willing to let me. My husband began to pick the kids up from day care while I stayed longer hours at the hospital making sure my patient was stable. I was off for Thanksgiving but opted to stay in town so I could look in on my patient just in case. My husband obliged.

In a passing instant I noticed how different my husband looked to me. I wondered when he decided to grow a full beard and was too embarrassed to ask how long it had been there. I noticed a new tattoo on his back of an angel with the names of our children written on each of his wings. How in the world had I missed that? I also noticed how much the kids clung to him when we went out as a family. I felt like an outsider. I wanted to talk to him about all of these things, but I was too busy to process it, too busy to give myself a chance to feel anything more than brief concern.

Then came Christmas. I was scheduled to be off again but Jared required another surgery. He was nine months old now and smiled when I came into the room. How could I leave him for Christmas? How could I leave his family? I decided to work. I don't remember Christmas that year with my husband or kids. I should; my daughter was four and my son was two—the perfect ages to really appreciate the magic. I vaguely remember a rocking horse, and a jumping Tigger. But what I remember most is carrying Jared around the hospital Christmas Day with a Santa hat on.

People asked me how my kids were.

"Baby Jones, Baby Williams? Baby Lopez?" I asked.

"No—your two at home, Stevi and Terrence."

What was I doing, spending all my time working at the hospital? I reminded myself that I was performing a great service, and that the families appreciated and needed me.

Then in January of 2002, I was called to an impromptu meeting. Annoyed at being pulled away from my patients, I went reluctantly. I found a room full of people with balloons, confetti, and well wishes. I had been voted the hospital Physician of the Year. They noted that I was the first African American, and the youngest to receive the award.

I felt elated. I thought of all those childhood dreams, fulfilled in that moment. I thought of how proud my parents would be.

During the ceremony, I anxiously waited for the CEO to read my bio. His words chilled me to the core and I remember them to this day. "Dr. Kincade is loved by all and extremely dedicated. She routinely works unscheduled weekends, stays after work, and this year she worked Thanksgiving and Christmas when she could have taken the time to be off with her family. She chose to give up her holiday to care for our patients."

I cried. I felt sad about all the missed opportunities to be with my husband and nurture my children. I felt completely offended at this person who gave up Thanksgiving and Christmas to work when she could have been with her family, the person who had raved about finding twenty-four hour day care so she could stay later at work. I struggled to swallow the lump in my throat. I thought that instead of getting Physician of the Year, what I really wanted was to be Wife and Mother of the Year.

As I walked slowly to the podium to get my plaque, tears streamed down my face. I forced a smile for the picture with the CEO. I promised myself to leave this environment where people thought it was a good thing to give up Thanksgiving and Christmas. I wanted to join the PTA. I wanted to play games with my husband and children. I wanted to know the real answer to "How are your kids?" I wanted the teachers to know who I was. I wanted to breathe again and believe that somewhere I could be a mommy, a wife, and a doctor. And that's exactly what I did.

Three years ago, I left the university, with much criticism that I was throwing my career away. I traded that career for a better career, because now I am a Power Mom. I smile as I drop the kids off at school, and return to be first in the carpool lane. I laugh at how loud I am screaming at the soccer and basketball games. I dance with the kids at the Valentine's party as they all cheer for the cool mom. I get tears in my eyes when my daughter shares how much it means to her that I came on the field trip. I finally got my dream to be on the PTA and I pinch myself because I am so excited to be on a committee. Can it get any better?

When someone asks me after a long and hot field day—"How do you have time to be so active? Do you work?"—I say, "Yes, I'm a neonatologist."

"No way. How can you be a doctor and be so active at school?"

My smile grows into a grin as I think of how I have managed to structure my work around being home for my kids. I can hardly contain my joy as I remember something said to me at the beginning of medical school. "You can have it all; you just can't have it all at the same time." And I think, "Oh yes, you truly can." When you listen to your spirit sometimes you realize that "all" may not be that far from your reach. But you have to take the first step. Sometimes that means leaving behind one big award for a million daily awards.

~Terri Major-Kincade

The Burning Bra of Freedom

*Everything that is really great and inspiring is created by
the individual who can labor in freedom.*
~Albert Einstein

W hen I was a freshman in college I had my life all mapped
out. I would graduate, get a job as a high powered
journalist, spend a few years working as a foreign correspondent, and then maybe get married, have a kid and write for an
edgy political magazine. Of course, life doesn't always follow a plan,
and before I knew it I found myself married with a baby on the way.
My husband had a good job and saw no reason for me to continue
working.

"Why not be a stay-at-home mom?" he reasoned with me. "Day
care is expensive, and besides, wouldn't you rather be home with our
son if we can manage it financially?"

Hmm. How could I respond to that logic? Yes, I knew day care
was expensive, and yes, I liked the idea of being home with my baby.
But what about MY career?

"I don't know," I told him hesitantly. "I never pictured myself as
a homemaker."

"I really think it's important for one parent to stay home," he
said.

I finally made the decision to give it a try. My maternity leave was ending soon and I informed my employer that I would not be returning to work. The next few years passed by in a blur. I grudgingly admitted that we'd made the right decision. Who can resist seeing her child's first steps or hearing his first words right as they happen? I was the one who kissed every boo-boo, nursed every cold, heard every story and saw every wondrous moment first hand.

But still, some days I wondered what it would be like to have the freedom of a career. What would it be like to not be tied down to a house and laundry and cooking?

When my second child, a daughter, was born, I had the stay-at-home mom thing down pat. By this time, my older child was in school and I had settled into a cozy routine. This homemaker thing was working out okay. I didn't allow myself to dwell on the what-could-have-beens. However, sometimes a person needs a little validation, a reassurance that she's done the right thing, made the right choices. For me, that moment came on a Thursday morning in April.

My two-year-old was napping and my son was at school. I had laid out the ingredients for a casserole on the counter. I figured I could prep everything during the peace and quiet of the late morning so that at dinnertime I could just throw it into the oven. I was seven months pregnant with my third child and experiencing the typical annoyances of late pregnancy, namely hot flashes. Every burner on the stove was on, and the kitchen was rapidly becoming as hot as the face of the sun. I was sweating, getting nauseated and about ready to scrap dinner when it dawned on me. I had the house all to myself. Not another soul was present except my napping daughter. The blinds were closed. I was hot, and in a glorious moment of inspiration I tore off my stifling sweatshirt. Reduced to only a bra and maternity jeans, I felt free.

Something came over me that morning. I cooked like there was no tomorrow. Beside the casserole, I made cornbread, a pie, blackberry cobbler and even a double batch of brownies. At one point I almost burned my bra on a hot burner and giggled. This surely wasn't the kind of bra burnings that most people would associate with a "free" woman! If only the feminists could see me now—pregnant belly, barefoot, topless, cooking over a hot stove. And I'd never felt FREER!

When everything was cooked, baked, and cooling I sat down at the kitchen table. Suddenly, my life made sense to me. For eight years, I was under the mistaken impression that I'd traded my freedom for an apron and a diaper pail. How wrong I'd been! The day I became a stay-at-home mom was the day I'd really gained my independence. Who but I (along with my husband) made all the important decisions in regard to my children? If I wanted to "take the day off" and take my kids to an amusement park, whose permission did I need? What use is "freedom" if it can only be enjoyed during two weeks of vacation?

There are those who insist that stay-at-home-moms are the backbone of society. Maybe we are, but there are days when we feel more like the packhorses of the world. Sometimes we might even resent those women in high heels toting briefcases who head out into the world to negotiate important contracts or write for edgy political magazines. But nonetheless, I secretly know the truth. I can also say with certainty that had my life followed my original plan, this jewel of a secret would have been forever lost to me. Thankfully I was enlightened on a Thursday in April when a hot flash sparked a fire in my soul. Because when everything is said and done, the real truth is this; true freedom means being able to cook topless in a hot and stifling kitchen.

~Emily Weaver

The Choice

You have a lifetime to work, but children are only young once.
~Polish Proverb

I started parenthood as a single mom at nineteen years of age. A high school dropout, I worked at menial jobs to keep food on the table. As my son Scotty grew, so did my desire to improve our lives. I completed my GED. Eventually, I managed the impossible dream of attending college — about the same time Scott entered high school. I still worked and was very busy, to say the least.

When Scott would ask me to go to the movies with him, I would mumble, "Can't... sorry." His requests for my time went unheeded and eventually he stopped making them. I was too rushed to notice. Receiving high grades was extremely important to me, as I longed to shed the shame of being a high school drop-out.

I enrolled in a business program. In addition to economics and math, many of my classes focused on motivating and understanding people. I was astonished to realize business is about people and not simply making a profit.

My schedule was a nightmare. I would wake up exhausted, yell at my son to get to school, rush to work, and then rush from work to attend a class. Then I'd rush home, throw dinner on the table (most nights) and then rush back to more classes. I'd then rush home to study and perhaps say hello to my son. Or not. Weekends meant my head was buried in a book. This treadmill went on for several months. Then came the wake-up call that would make a difference.

"Is this Helen Sayer?" An unfamiliar voice came over the line.

"Speaking." I tapped my fingers impatiently, thinking that this had better be quick. I was preparing for a mid-term exam in business law, and I was scared of failing this important subject.

"This is the Juneau Juvenile Department. We are holding your son; please come down and pick him up."

I shook my head with disagreement. I did not need a wrong number to waste my time. "I'm sorry; you have the wrong Helen Sayer. My son is at the pool. Good luck with finding the right parents. Bye." I allowed myself a moment of pity for those poor other parents. But then....

"Wait! Your son is Scott, right?" How did they get my son's name? I felt a pang of fear, beyond my self-centered annoyance at this unplanned call.

"Yes. But my Scott is swimming, and besides he doesn't get into trouble." I really did NOT want this to be my son. This interruption simply did not fit into my tight schedule. After a few more exchanges, including me receiving directions, I grabbed my car keys. I drove to the detention center, furious. What an inconvenience. I needed to be studying.

Assuming it really was my Scott, I planned my lecture, lips pursed with annoyance. And exhaustion. And fear that I wasn't good enough, wasn't smart enough for college. That I wasn't worthy enough to have a better life.

Driving, I reflected on last week's assignment in business management, where we were instructed to categorize our own priorities. What is important to me? I had written down my son as my first priority. In a flash, I saw my list did not match my daily actions. Despite great rationalizations, work and school were receiving more attention than my child. And we did not have other family around to pick up the slack.

My lips softened, as did my heart. By the time I pulled into the wintry dark parking lot, I was chastened. Did my son care if I was smart enough to go to college? He needed his mother's love and guidance during these tempting years. He did not need proof that his over-worked mom was good enough.

Entering the unfamiliar detention center, I was led to my son in a large stark room. He was slouched in a hard chair, watching television. He found my glance, and then stared at the floor. The look in his eyes was fearful and tentative. He hung back, waiting cautiously to determine my reaction.

I felt ashamed that I had allowed my most important relationship to falter. I reached out and embraced Scott. I could feel his tense body soften as I held him. Then we both scuffed our feet and looked down as the officer outlined my son's bad behavior. Fighting with another student, Scott had not been allowed to remain on school property. The school had been unable to reach me, not difficult to understand since I was on a flight to success.

My son was released to my care. He was suspended from school for three days. Back at home, I imposed household chores for him to complete, in addition to the schoolwork he would need to make up. We both fell into bed exhausted. But before I could sleep, I had a phone call to make. I called the professor who was hosting the midterm exam the next day.

"Professor, I'm sorry, but a personal emergency has come up and I am going to miss tomorrow's exam." I gulped as I uttered this distressing news.

"You know, this means you will drop a letter grade from your score?" he responded.

I winced at these words. I had taken great pride in those little letters that signified my grade. Unfortunately, my grade in parenting wasn't written out for me to see. And I would not have been proud of it at any rate.

"I understand. But this requires my attention." I hung up the phone, relieved.

Somehow a load had been lifted from my shoulders. I slept soundly for a change.

The next morning I suspended Scott's household punishment for a day. I called work to say I needed the day off. And I spent the entire day with my son. I listened as he opened his heart about the school bully and his efforts to avoid him. He moaned how difficult math was, and we both laughed as I told him college math was no easier. We ate ice cream, and sat on a park bench. I told him how hard it was, trying to keep afloat a job, a full-time education and being a single mom. I apologized for not paying enough attention. I reminded him that he was the most important aspect of my life and told him my new mission to have my life match my lofty priorities.

I dropped a class from my load. I made an appointment with Scott's teacher to get caught up on his school life. And I realized that taking an extra year to graduate was better than ignoring my highest calling, being a loving parent to my child.

This all happened many years ago. My son is an adult now and we are still a close family. And I learned a lot about what matters. By the way, it isn't a spot of ink on a report card. In the end, it took a full twenty-three years for me to obtain my four-year bachelor degree.

Though it took a few missteps to learn, I couldn't have made a better choice.

~HJ Eggers

Metamorphosis

The moment a child is born, the mother is also born.
She never existed before. The woman existed, but the mother, never.
A mother is something absolutely new.
~Rajneesh

I t was still dark and cool outside when I left the warm cocoon of our house. I walked until I got to the elementary school. Starting slowly, I forced my feet through the quicksand of my early morning run, past the cars in line at "drop-off." The kids looked like sleepwalkers dragging their small bodies into the low, wide, red brick building. My own child was sleeping peacefully in his crib at home with Daddy, his fingers curled around his soft cheeks, his chest rising and falling like the waves against the shore. Resisting the urge to turn back and watch my child sleep, I kept running. I reached down to feel my scar, the place where he was cut from me, still sore and tender.

Running down Chadwick Road, I was not like a gazelle but an elephant, heavy from the weight on my shoulders and the weight in my heart. This time at home was slipping through my fingers and I needed to make a decision about our future. Passing the school's baseball field, I noticed that the bright green, late summer grass had faded into a flat, yellow-brown. The leaves on the trees surrounding the field had turned to yellows and deep reds, while others had fallen, leaving the branches bare. I realized that I'd missed the changing of seasons. Leaving the baseball field behind, I rounded the corner onto

Rebellion Road, following the familiar route where, over the years, layers upon layers of my footsteps had been laid down.

My maternity leave would be over in two weeks. I worked in retail, and it was the holiday season, so my boss was anxious for my return. I'd been home for nine weeks with pay, and knew I should have felt lucky. My husband was working his way up the ladder but it would be years before he made any real money. We'd made plans and I'd agreed to go back to work until we could afford for me to quit. But when I thought about leaving my child in the arms of someone else, it felt like I was drowning.

Turning back onto Chadwick Road, my legs dragged, and my body was heavy from the continual lack of sleep and being full in the wrong places. My breathing was shallow and I tugged at my jog bra to allow for more air. The houses turned to buildings and Miss Karen's Day Care appeared at the end of the road. A knot tightened in the back of my throat. The bright pink walls of Miss Karen's were surrounded by a fence, which was not wooden or wicker but metal and gray. Miss Karen's white van had sat in the neighborhood strip mall parking lot all summer with a sign reading, "Open Enrollment." The enrollment form was at home in my bedside table under the notebook I filled with stories in the middle of the night when I couldn't sleep. I'd made promises about filling out the form and putting it in the mail, but it was still in my drawer.

I stepped across a divide when I gave birth and my life split in two. There was the time before motherhood and the time after. In the time before, I was a part of the world outside my home. I went to the movies with girlfriends, wore high heels to work every day, slept through the night, read books, and trained for a marathon. In the time after, I existed in a cocoon. I hadn't talked to my girlfriends for a long while, my high heels were gathering dust, I hadn't slept through the night in nine weeks, and I was too tired to read more than a chapter, or to run more than two miles. But I was happier and more filled with love than I'd ever thought possible. I didn't want to grab my shoes out of the back of the closet and wave goodbye to my child and this life. I didn't want to be a super-mom. I didn't want to juggle the demands of a career, a home, a marriage, and motherhood. I couldn't want to return to the person I'd been before.

Slowing, I stopped across the street from Miss Karen's and listened to the children playing in the backyard. I could hear crying and yelling over the sound of my own heavy breathing. My chest was tight and I fought back tears as I imagined, only weeks from then, dropping off my baby and returning to work and to the Christmas music and the messy dressing rooms and the demanding customers. A small, blond boy in overalls looked out from the playhouse, saw me watching and waved. Surprised to be caught, I turned and ran toward home. I didn't wave back. I sprinted down the wooded trail, leaving Miss Karen's behind me. A view of the marsh opened up through the trees and I stopped again, winded. It was high tide. Squinting my eyes, the gray blue of the water meshed with the brownish green of the marsh grass, and the world was liquid. This is too hard, I thought. Walking slowly toward our old brick home, I let out another breath and suddenly, I knew what I had to do.

I stuttered when I walked in the door, sweaty and breathless and told my husband we needed to talk. The baby slept soundly as I told him I couldn't go back to work, couldn't leave our child and the more I spoke, the stronger I felt.

"I'll do whatever it takes," I promised. "We'll make sacrifices. I've got the rest of my life to work."

"Okay," he said. "This is what I want, too."

With my husband's support and two weeks of my maternity leave left, I made an appointment to see my boss. I carried my baby with me to give me strength. Walking down the long hallway, my footsteps echoed on the floor. I was buzzed in through the employee entrance and checked my bag at security. My co-workers walked toward me with open arms, petting my baby and peppering me with questions.

"How is he sleeping?" asked the woman in cosmetics.

"Are you nursing?" asked the woman in handbags.

"Look at those eyes!" said the salesman in shoes.

"Can I hold him?" asked the woman from cosmetics.

I panicked, held my baby closer to my chest, and hurried down the hallway to my meeting. As I sat in a leather chair in his office, my boss asked polite questions about my time away.

"When can I put you on the schedule? We really need you back; the store is getting busy," he asked.

A painful knot formed in my throat. I reached for the cup of water he'd put in front of me and swallowed.

"I can't come back," I said. My voice quivered with tension. "I have to quit."

He was quiet for a moment and then nodded his head. Within moments it was over. Walking out of the building, I felt like a butterfly emerging from her cocoon. The sun was warm on my face and I pushed a strand of hair out of my eyes. I smiled down at my boy.

"We're free," I said out loud.

~Amy Mercer

Me, In a Handbasket

Without leaps of imagination, or dreaming, we lose the excitement of possibilities. Dreaming, after all, is a form of planning.

~Gloria Steinem

On the NASCAR Sprint Cup Series known as "after-school activities" there's a bumper sticker that pretty well sums up the condition I often find myself in: What am I doing in this handbasket? And where am I going?

If I had a minute, I'd hazard an answer. But I find it very hard to put my finger on the pause button in the middle of a typically loony "Groundhog Day" of a day when, for example, I might find myself prying Weasley, the family mouse, from the jaws of the feline carnage machine for the third time in as many hours. Let's just say if there really was a pause button and if I could find it any quicker than I could wrest the last matching sock from the puppy's teeth, I might ask: And where am I going?! But, really, where would it get me? More to the point, where would it get poor Weasley?

It wasn't always this way. Once upon a time I worked among real, live grown-ups in offices with free-flowing coffee and a desk where I could place important work without fear that scissor-wielding half-lings would fashion paper snowflakes out of it. This was a magical place where people go to the bathroom alone — with the door closed and NO audience! Perhaps you've heard of this enchanted land? I forget the name. What I remember is that it was sort of like an all-inclusive vacation—except (get this!)—they pay you!

I remember the day I walked away from Wonderland. It was as a sublimely beautiful Indian summer day in New England. You remember it. Everyone does. Before most people had poured their second cup of coffee we were calling it 9-11.

I watched the images only once, live from the newsroom where I worked, but I'll never forget the mountains of smoke billowing upward into the infinitely blue sky or the Twin Towers evaporating like sandcastles in the rain or the horrible confetti—the evidence of orderly professional lives torn to bits—drifting down among the ashes of the crippled buildings. The refrain sounded: everything's changed. For me, it rang true. A couple weeks later I put my career plan in the bottom of the filing cabinet, finished my final article for the progressive weekly I had been so proud to write for, and made my way home.

As I was bombarded that day by images of the tragedies of others, it was my own life that flashed before me, particularly my life as a wife and a mom. Sure, it's a cliché, but I knew that one day I'd be staring into the white light of the universe and it wouldn't be the work I'd be yearning for, it would be my family, and I'd hock my very soul for a millisecond more suspended in their orbit.

Who wouldn't? I'm a typical parent. But not the kind who believes that behind every snarly "whatever" is the voice of a future UN Secretary General. Like most parents, there are moments when I'm fairly certain my daughters were sprung from the loins of Zeus. The next minute I might be packing their *Little Mermaid* duffel bags and Googling "military school vegetarian meals." Clear-eyed as I am about family life, I do believe every child is a cosmic phenomenon. I know mine are.

My children aren't yet old enough to understand how precious and unlikely their marvelous lives are. You might even call them freaks of nature but, to me, they're the universe in dirty feet. I'd dreamed of children just like them since I was a girl, but lesbian mother was not prominent on any "Popular Vocations" list tacked to the guidance counselor's wall back in southwest Ohio where I grew up in the late 1970s and early 1980s. By the time I migrated East for college, I had a lot of ground to make up.

Luckily, I fell in love at first sight with the green-eyed girl with a siren's laugh and, in classic Girl Meets Girl fashion, we settled down, started careers, got married and, eventually, chose a donor from a sperm bank list that read like a Chinese Menu. ("We'll take two green eyes, athletic build, a nice family of origin, oh, and easy on the IQ. To go, please.")

Unfortunately, for my body, meiosis and mitosis were much more complicated in vivo than in the Bio text. So, after several years on the infertility roller coaster, my partner (a dangerously sleep-deprived doctor-in-training who'd witnessed enough births to surmise she didn't need one of her own) unleashed the Secret Weapon: We'd both try to get pregnant. Being former Division I college athletes, we should have known how dangerous it would be to throw a little competition into the hormonal potion.

A month later we were both craving milkshakes and toasted cheese. Nine months later we both showed up at the hospital for my partner's C-section. "Very funny," the head nurse said, shaking her head. "One of you better step up or you're both getting the needle!" Our second daughter came five weeks after. Twin daughters of lesbian mothers. Dreamgirls. My own private miracle. Before long, friends and family started asking if a third child was in the plan, to which we replied blissfully, "We're done!" Seven years later, a dear friend, whose daughter had been in our children's lives since they were all infants, died suddenly and tragically. Overnight our twins became triplets. Home needed me more than ever now.

Life might be what happens when we're busy making other plans, but I never wanted to be too busy to simply "be" with my girls. What I've learned since coming home is even without the day job there simply aren't enough hours to finish the list. I've also learned that when the office isn't beckoning, you can find time to rock your sobbing sixth-grader like a baby when her bunny hops off to the

Great Beyond five minutes before the school bus is due. And hold the wake, and make the sarcophagus, too.

Sure I sacrificed a lot to have it all. Now I'll never be Christiane Amanpour. I regret that. But I do have the family of my dreams, enough work to keep me sane and an active role in our beloved community. Every day I give thanks for my good fortune. My mother's choices were much narrower. When I was a kid and the family rodent died you flushed it down the toilet and got to the bus stop on time because Mom needed to get to work.

Not in my wildest dreams could I have plotted my own journey from lesbian feminist to intrepid reporter to stay-at-home mom. Not even Rita Mae Brown could've written this. Nor could I have guessed all that the title "Stay-at-Home-Mom" would encompass, and how busy I would be filling, pro bono, a hodgepodge of important roles—taxi driver, dog whisperer, program director, coach, league administrator—in the lives of my kids and our community.

My kids don't get it. I'm okay with that. But I do hope they're learning—if only by osmosis—the big lessons, the only rules or principles that I know from experience to be true: Time is the most precious substance on earth; and whatever road you choose, travel with love—big, red, heart-thumping love—and trust that everything else will fall beautifully into place. Just like our sweet, marvelous little clan.

~Jo Glading-DiLorenzo

The Greatest Gift

The biggest lesson we have to give our children is truth.
~Goldie Hawn

Standing on the beach alone, listening to the gentle crash of the waves, my mind drifts through the last several months and the interesting ways the Universe has gently, and not-so-gently, nudged me towards my decision to return to work. A decision that was far from easy for me.

I have been trying for four years to love being home with my kids. I really have been trying. And there is a lot about it that I do love and very much appreciate. And I am so grateful for the many special times that I have shared with my children.

But the truth is that I just don't love it. Not full time. And the more time I spend doing something that I really just don't love doing, the more impatient, and angry, and snappy I get with my children and the more depressed and resentful I feel. And being an impatient, angry, resentful mother is really not the mother, or the person, I want to be.

I know I want to make some changes in my life so that I can be the loving, present, connected mother that I've always dreamed of being. But then I think if I just try a little bit harder, or really not even try, but just relax and be present and appreciate the beauty and just stop yelling and getting angry, maybe I can start to love it more.

But I just don't love it. Not full time.

I enjoy and appreciate and savor my time with my children so much more when I spend less time being their primary caregiver. And I'm really excited now that I am finally giving myself permission to feel this, and say this, and imagine my life changing, so that I am spending more time doing things that I do love to do. I have seen over and over how this helps me to savor and enjoy the time I do spend with my children.

And yet it is still so hard.

Admitting to myself, and others, that I don't love being a full-time caregiver to my children feels scary. I'm afraid that what people will hear when I say that, is that I don't love my children.

And I really love my children. I love them more than words can express. And it is for them, as well as for me, that I am making this change in my life.

I have a quote hanging over my kitchen sink that says:

"My greatest gift to give is my happiness."

And I really believe this in my heart.

So it is for myself, and my wonderful husband, and most importantly, my beautiful children, that I am giving myself the gift of time and space to pursue the experiences that make my heart sing and that help me to be the fullest expression of who I am.

I know that doing what I love makes it so much easier to be more present and connected to the people I love, most especially my children.

And being the fullest expression of who I am, invites them to be the fullest expressions of who they are, which is exactly the kind of mother, and person, I want to be.

~Erin Goodman

The Decision

It is our choices... that show what we truly are, far more than our abilities.

~J.K. Rowling, (Harry Potter and the Chamber of Secrets)

"Mom! Mom!" shouted Steven as he burst into the kitchen wearing a grin. "We made applesauce in first grade today and Miss Shannon let me stir in the sugar!"

"Uh-huh," I grunted as I threw spaghetti into a pot of boiling water and lowered the heat under the bubbling sauce.

"Mom!" my son persisted as he tugged at my arm, "You're not listening!"

"Stop it, Steven! I'm trying to get dinner ready and you're bugging me. Go see what your sisters are doing."

"Gee, you used to ask me what I did in school," he mumbled, as disappointment clouded his eyes. "Now you don't care."

I half listened as I stirred the sauce. I felt drained from my day and the stress of teaching first-graders in a school across town. It had been a terrible, horrible, no good, very bad day. Sarah's mother was hostile during our conference; Kyle hit Andrew at recess; and I had bus duty in a downpour. I had endured twenty-one children shouting my name, pulling my arm, and demanding my attention. I couldn't stand another child—my child—doing the same. As steam rattled the lid on the pot, I felt guilty for blowing off my own steam at my innocent son. I had given the best of myself to other parents' children. I had nothing left for my own child.

After dinner, I helped my two daughters with their middle school homework and rubbed Steven's back before tucking him in. I graded papers, fell into bed, and did some soul-searching during my sleepless night.

As I trudged to my classroom the next morning, my principal stopped me in the hall. "Over the last six months you've done an excellent job of substituting for Rachel while she's been on maternity leave. She has decided to be a stay-at-home mom. Your co-workers and I hope you'll replace her... full-time."

I thought about his offer. Teaching jobs were scarce and I had heard rumors that one principal had over 200 resumes on his desk. As I considered my options I reflected on my teaching career.

I had taught before I became a mom, but once I had three children I couldn't imagine teaching full-time. Eventually, I was motivated to return to the classroom because of that dreaded question people often asked: "Do you work or do you stay at home?" If I said, "I work," it meant I had a paying job outside the home. If I said, "I stay at home," it meant I don't... work, I only—buy groceries, shop for kids' clothes, cook, clean, wash laundry, fold laundry, iron clothes, mow the yard, entertain, do home repairs, maintain a car, sew, decorate, vacuum, pay bills, teach Sunday school, work out, chauffeur kids, volunteer, take night classes, grow a garden, weed flower beds, bake bread, dust, paint walls, organize drawers, host sleepovers, support school activities... and much more.

Substitute teaching offered flexibility. I could accept jobs on a daily basis and decline work if I needed to stay home with a sick child. Plus I'd be with the kids after school. Now that I was offered a full-time position, I scheduled a family conference to help me make the decision.

"You did a test drive these past months and everything was great," said my husband. "Don't do it for the money... only if it's rewarding."

"It doesn't make any difference to me," said my daughter, Betsy. "By the time I finish band practice and run cross-country, you're already home."

"I agree, it's no big deal," said my other daughter, Lori. "We notice you're more tired when you work, but we all pitch in and help."

All eyes turned to Steven as he fidgeted and stared at the floor. "Mom, you used to laugh and be fun but now you get mad a lot," he said softly. "And we don't go fishing or bike riding anymore. I like it better when you stay home."

I hugged my son and knew what my decision would be.

When I arrived for my last day of teaching, the faculty honored me with a surprise breakfast. The principal and my co-workers presented me with accolades, gifts, and regrets that I would not be joining the staff.

As I cooked dinner that evening, Steven ran into the kitchen and thrust a small, wrapped present into my hand. He had decorated the paper with colorful flowers, a smiling sun, and a crooked rainbow.

"Open it later, Mom," he said as he dashed out the door.

On my first day as a stay-at-home mom, I unpacked the loving letters and presents from my first-grade students. I placed the red ceramic apple that read, "To the World's Best Teacher," next to the gift from Steven... a figurine of a small, smiling boy. It read, "To the World's Greatest Mom."

I made the right decision.

~Miriam Hill

Two Mothers

When you have children, you all of a sudden empathize with your parents more, you understand what it was like for them to love you.
~Laura Bush

A few months ago, during our nightly call, my mother and I started discussing a topic that we've debated before and can never agree on.

"It's the right thing to do," I said firmly. "The boys need me!"

"They already have you," she pleaded. "They don't need you every minute of every day. You have a great career where you're respected and valued. Don't give that up." Then she said with a sigh, "I would have loved to have done something with my life."

My parents left their country in the middle of a revolution and came here to give their children a better life. Raising me and my two brothers in a foreign land wasn't always easy for my mother, but she never let it show. While my father went to work during the day, she stayed home. A home that was a million miles away from everything and everyone she knew. But that didn't stop her from putting her heart and soul into creating a loving home for us.

Every day after school, I would sit at the kitchen table and tell her my tales of junior high hardships. And I had a lot of them, being the new foreign kid in school. She would listen to me while she was preparing dinner or folding the laundry and comfort me in the best way she knew how. She would tell me how lucky I was to have a good family and remind me that I should be thankful for that, instead of seeking the approval of my classmates.

Of course, at the time, I didn't see it that way. All I saw was that my mother didn't understand me. I wanted desperately to fit in with the other kids. "Why can't I go?" I would say with pre-teen angst. "Everyone goes to sleepovers here, it's NO BIG DEAL!" But she was adamant. "No sleepovers," she would say in her heavily accented English. No boys calling the house. No TV in my room. No make-up.

I was angry a lot during those early teenage years, but every day after school I would still tell her my tales and she would still listen.

I had no idea that while I was going through my life-is-so-unfair mini dramas, my mother was dealing with her own obstacles: learning a new culture, a new language, and a new way of life. Despite these hurdles, she powered through, raising three healthy well-adjusted children.

Through those first few tough years of transition, she kept the family together, the house clean, the clothes pressed, our lives organized — and had an amazing meal on the table every day. I never thought about how all of that got done or if it was hard for her. I didn't understand what it took to be a stay-at-home mom. That is, until I had my own children.

To her, I was doing it all, working and taking care of my family. But she had it so much harder than I do. She doesn't know how much I admire her strength and the way she made it look so easy. The way she sacrificed for us every single day. The way she loved us even when we didn't deserve that love. And the way she was there whenever we needed her. How could I express in words how much that really meant?

"You're wrong Mom," I finally said. "You did do something. You did something amazing. You were there for me and that meant everything."

A short time after our discussion, I decided to quit my job so that I could be there for my children like my mother was there for me. I wanted to be the one at the kitchen table listening to my sons' tales of their joys and hardships.

But being a stay-at-home mother was more challenging that I had anticipated. The feelings of isolation and paying constant attention to family matters took their toll on me and a small part of me wondered whether I had made the right decision.

Then, one afternoon, one of my sons came to me with a request.

"Read the book! Read the BOOK!" he demanded in his very loud outside voice.

As he was asking me, he was also poking me with the book. After having spent most of the day running errands, picking up after the kids, and making multiple meals, I should have been ready to spend some quality time with my son. But I was not. I was just tired.

"Not now, sweetie," I said softly with a hint of frustration. "Maybe later." My eyelids felt heavy and all I wanted to do was lie down on my bed.

"Read me a book, Mommy!" he said again. They don't give up, do they? I looked over at him ready to say "no" but he was looking straight at me with his big brown eyes, waiting for my response. I froze for what seemed like minutes but was only a few seconds. Then I snapped out of my semi-coma and realized that my SON was asking me to read him a book and I should listen to him. So I took a deep breath, sat down on the floor next to him and said, "Okay, sweetie, why don't you jump into my lap and give me the book." His face lit up and he came tumbling toward me.

As I read him the book (the same book I had read to him at least one hundred times), I slowly felt him relaxing into my arms and resting the back of his head against my chin. He was concentrating on the book with singular focus. All of a sudden, as I was reading the story, I felt his little fingers tapping against my knee as if he were playing the piano.

For a split second, I stopped reading and concentrated on his fingers. The pause was too short for him to notice. I continued reading, but now most of my focus was on his little fingers and the delicate way they were connecting with my knee. With each word, the frustration and fatigue melted away and I felt the kind of pure joy only your child can give you. Without realizing it, I was smiling as I read the end of the story. I didn't want it to end. I wanted him to keep tapping my knee with his little, soft fingers.

"Read it again, Mommy!" he said.

"Of course, sweetie. Let's read it again."

That simple moment helped me realize that I had absolutely made the right decision. And like my mother, I will make whatever sacrifices are necessary to care for and be there for my children. I only wish that some day they look back and feel about me the way I will forever feel about my mother.

~Rebecca Khamneipur Morrison

Not All at Once

Life is what happens to you while you're busy making other plans.
~John Lennon

I came of age at the time when the Snugli had recently replaced Howdy Doody as a technological marvel. "Watergate" was a household word, while "website" was merely where Wilbur found Charlotte. Women of my generation were weaving Judy Collins lyrics into wedding vows, joining the job force in record numbers, and being told, for the first time in recorded history, that they could "have it all."

I, however, wanted only part of it. And so, in the autumn of 1972, on the eve of my twenty-first birthday, I announced that I would never be a mother.

Throughout that decade, and for most of the two that followed, my husband and I watched our friends shepherd their offspring from pacifiers to prom nights. We quietly tsk-tsked each time we witnessed a parent who was too quick to dole out a cookie or too tardy with a time-out. We ate in restaurants with white linen tablecloths, watched foreign films in theaters that served espresso, and read novels on Mediterranean beaches, while our contemporaries sat through PTO meetings and all-day swim meets.

The older we grew, the more certain we became that our child-free choice was the right one. Then, in 1996, well past the middle of "middle age," I went for a walk one day with my friend, Ann. "How's everything?" she asked when we met at our usual starting point.

"Strange," I told her. "I have permanent PMS but haven't touched a tampon in two months. I can't go for a bike ride without a jogging bra, and I fall asleep on my lunch hour."

"That's the start of menopause," Ann informed me.

"I thought menopause means that everything shuts down," I replied. "I feel like it's always about to start up."

"That's how it begins," Ann assured me.

Soon it was time for my annual ob-gyn check-up. I knew if I told my doctor that I was exhausted and my period was overdue, he'd draw blood for a pregnancy test before considering another more probable diagnosis. But my health insurance wouldn't cover the fifty dollar lab work, so I scooted to the pharmacy and bought a cheap generic home-test kit instead.

The next morning, appointment day, I awoke pre-dawn and bolted to the bathroom. After I'd mimicked the drawings on the directions that came with the kit, I watched as the plastic stick in my hand turned fuchsia. I didn't think it was supposed to do that, but I couldn't read the tiny print without my brand-new, first-ever reading glasses. I was struck by the irony. Perhaps the instruction sheet should have proclaimed, "If you can't see this without your magnifiers, you're too old to need it!"

"What's happening?" asked my husband, Chris, as I roused him while rummaging through my nightstand in search of my glasses. "You aren't pregnant, are you?"

"I think I might be," I whispered.

Although my check-up wasn't scheduled until afternoon, I was in the doctor's waiting room as his receptionist unlocked the door. My long-time physician, well aware of my views on parenthood, seemed as shocked by my news as I was. Of course, he also ordered one of those expensive blood tests to confirm it, which it did.

Chris and I were not dancing on the ceiling. We spoke euphemistically of our "options," although we knew in our hearts that, for us, there was really only one. Our son, Jack Christopher Petrides, was born seven months later. He was nine pounds, eleven ounces. I was forty-five years old.

At the time of Jack's birth, I already held a mother's dream job—a part-time position writing a weekly college publication. I could do much of it at home and enjoyed enviable academic vacations. But after nearly a year of holding a steno pad in one hand and a breast pump in the other, of lowering Jack into his Pack 'n Play each time the telephone rang, and murmuring, "Mommy has to talk to the dean of the faculty," I quit my job to be a full-time mother.

Ann and my many other friends, whose children were taking Drivers' Ed and SATs, questioned how I could muster the energy to chase a toddler. I reminded them that they'd already logged their hours on the dusty linoleum floor of the downtown parents' center singing "The Wheels on the Bus," but that it was all new to me. I also told them that, although aging robs us of our vigor, it provides added doses of patience and wisdom—the two tools of parenting that may matter most.

I spent Jack's early years at home with him, doing occasional free-lance writing work and updating college admission books I'd already written. By the time he was ready for kindergarten, I was looking for ways to expand my work-at-home hours and was fortunate when my book revisions led me to a new website, CollegeConfidential.com, where I was able to utilize my writing and college counseling skills right in my own house and in my favorite office attire—bare feet and sweatpants.

Even now, as Jack heads off to middle school, I continue to resist offers to take outside jobs, in spite of their enticing salaries and ever elusive benefits packages. I've turned down consulting opportunities, too. Although the word "consultant" sounds important (and lucra-tive), I treasure the control I wield over my own schedule and the fact that this allows me to be at those athletic events and PTO sessions which I once smugly avoided, and which make my now empty-nester friends seem wistful.

Indeed, if I have learned one thing from delaying parenthood, it is that the seasons that separate diapers from diplomas will fly by in the blink of an eye. I don't want to miss them. And, just as in my younger days, I still don't want it all—or at least not all at once.

~Sally Rubenstone

Hearth Smart

Women do not have to sacrifice personhood if they are mothers.
They do not have to sacrifice motherhood in order to be persons.
~Elaine Heffner

I always wanted to be a stay-at-home mom. As a preschooler, I rocked my dolls and dreamed of the day they would be real babies. I grew older, and still the dream did not fade.

When I was thirteen, I was perusing the shelves in my favorite place, the library of my junior high school, when one of my teachers asked, "What would you like to be when you grow up?"

"I want to be a wife and mother," I said without hesitation. "I want to stay at home and take care of my children."

She gasped in unbridled horror.

"You are too smart for that!" she said.

I explained, with all the wisdom a scrawny, bespectacled eighth-grader could muster against such a formidable adult, that education was very important to me and that I did indeed want to get a degree. However, I still wanted to be a homemaker. My explanation didn't change the bewildered look in her eyes, and the drip of her disappointment permeated my sanctuary.

The years went by, and I did, as my eighth grade voice declared, get my degree. I got three of them, actually. I wrote for a small town newspaper after journalism school. Then I got a teaching degree and taught for eight years, during which time I got a master's degree. Ironically, I was often told I was very smart and ambitious, but the real ambition was the dream that never let go of me—the aspiration of caring for a family. I am sure there are many whose sentiments would have matched my junior high teacher's. The fact that someone with so much education would want to be "merely a homemaker" wouldn't be considered smart. I grew up when it was hip to be Murphy Brown or Claire Huxtable. But I wanted to be Caroline Ingalls or Donna Reed. When I was in college, I read about the biblical Proverbs 31 woman, whose primary job was to care for her household, and thought "now there's a woman with a resume."

It felt like the role of stay-at-home-mom, instead of being lauded, was becoming a dinosaur, and a simple-minded one at that. It started my own barrage of nagging, doubtful thoughts. I was stimulated by school and keeping busy. Sometimes I would glimpse myself down the road. Would I end up on the sofa, hundreds of pounds heavier in a bon-bon-and-Doritos-induced stupor while my kids from the future hit and screamed at each other? Obviously, my teacher's remark had stayed with me.

Almost twenty years after that memorable conversation, a delivery room nurse laid the warm bundle of blankets that held my newborn son, Andrew, in my arms. The reality of it was much sweeter than I had imagined, and my instincts were right. I loved everything about motherhood from the beginning: the triangle of soft, warm glances between my husband, son, and I; the way Andrew's hungry cry subsided when he was nursed or cuddled; and the sweet rhythm of his baby snores as I cradled him on my arm. I even looked forward to that dreadful deed of diapering my son. I would smile and he would coo and flail his little arms and legs with excitement. My husband was my hero when he graciously agreed that I would stay at home. I would finally learn the answer to the question that had been posed two decades earlier—would it really be a smart decision to trade in my schoolbag and life with adults for diapers and a small little being that spit up more than he talked? Would it really be wise to stop setting my watch to the workplace clock and start setting it to Big Bird time instead?

It has been two years since my dream of becoming a stay-at-home mom was realized and my "smart" research began. Here is a small sampling of all that I have learned. There is nothing "mere" about being a stay-at-home mom. It involves training a child, with emotional endurance, ten to twelve hours a day, every day. It is full of decision-making and problem-solving. Anyone who has convinced a picky eater to try a new food or trained a toddler to crouch and "go potty" on a miniature toilet knows this. Being a stay-at-home mom requires patience with little hands and feet that are slow and clumsy with tasks, but incredibly light and quick with mischief. It is having childhood rhymes and counting songs swimming around in your brain all day, and modeling manners repetitively. It's going non-stop; forget the bon-bon stupor.

Staying at home is about creativity and cleverness because there is less income for things like decorating, landscaping, and chic ensembles. My seamstress mother and aunts, former stay-at-home moms themselves, can whip up a great Halloween costume or reupholster a couch without batting an eye or spending a fortune. Being a stay-at-home mom is about analyzing finances and arming oneself with a stealth-like thriftiness that allows no bargain to escape. Staying at home requires inventiveness wrapped around flexibility and versatility. It's about being the chef of all things warm and cheesy, the baker of Elmo birthday cakes, the singer of songs, kisser of wounds, finder of all things lost, and soother of ruffled spirits.

Finally (as if the list of required skills isn't already long enough), being a stay-at-home mom is often about supplementing a husband's income. After Andrew was born, I began freelance writing from home, something I had wanted to do since journalism school but had been too afraid of failing to even try. The day I put my son down for a nap and found an e-mail with my first magazine article acceptance, I danced for joy. Being home with Andrew gave me the bravery to expand my creative outlet of writing.

In the adult world I get pats on the back followed by "good for you... you get the best of both worlds," when I tell people I work from home. I do like the choreography in this mambo of writing and meeting my son's needs, but the truth is I write so that I can spend my days with Andrew, and the job titles in his world mean more to me than a glamorous career.

I know my teacher, who was genuinely a kind woman, meant well that day in the library. She just didn't understand then what I have come to know better. Being a stay-at-home mom takes a great deal of savvy, and I am the better for it. Staying at home with Andrew has brought out traits in my personality that I never even knew existed. For me, it was at the hearth that I found my heart. I found a beautiful medley of strength and sacrifice, challenge and love, warmth and ambition, work and home. Being a stay-at-home mom is the smartest thing I have ever done.

~Janeen Lewis

Chapter 2

Power MOMS

The Daily Grind

Stories from the Office

13

Short Stack

Motherhood has a very humanizing effect. It reduces everything to essentials.
~Meryl Streep

One of the most obvious things I inherited from my father, other than the shape and length of my body, my chin, my forehead, my ears, and that highly flammable sense of righteous indignation that usually erupts in the middle of 1) the local news, 2) traffic, and 3) phone calls with customer service personnel who do not speak English, is a love for greasy-spoon diners. The dirtier the place the better, maybe because that is somehow proportional to the amount of butter they use in their pancakes.

If my father were given the choice between an expensive dinner with the former Republican president or a lunch alone at a truck stop diner that is cooking its hamburgers in a vat of bacon grease collected over the period of fifteen years, he'd say, "DO NOT FORCE ME TO MAKE THAT CHOICE."

Our favorite local greasy spoon is a place called The Blue Plate, and we often go there for brunch on the weekends, mainly because it's one of the only non-chain sit-down restaurants that has something on the menu that Leta will eat. She always orders the home fries, which are basically potatoes cut into squares and then fried. And then she eats half of a bottle of ketchup.

Is it the healthiest meal? Of course not, but we ran it by her pediatrician, who has eight kids, one who was exactly like Leta, and he said, "Look! She's getting potassium! And ketchup is sometimes made out of real tomatoes! So stop coming in here with these stupid concerns and call me when she's managed to lodge a quarter in her nostril."

A couple of weeks ago when we were on our way to brunch, Jon quietly talked to me in the front seat about how he wanted Leta to try pancakes that morning. We both understand how important it is to provide a united front when it comes to disciplining your kids or trying to teach them anything, and we're usually very good about that, except when it comes to her eating habits.

That is a battle I specifically chose to stop fighting. It was taking years off my life and making me so crazy that getting up from the dinner table and counting to a hundred was not calming me down one bit. In fact, it gave me more time to think about HOW INSANE my child was that she wouldn't eat a peanut butter sandwich. WITH JELLY. WHICH IS SUGAR. SUGAR ON BREAD. A kid who won't eat a certain type of sugar. So trying to exert any influence on that was like going, "You see that nuclear bomb over there? I think I could defeat it with this here spitball."

But I was in a good mood that morning, had slept in past eight o'clock and that made my brain a little woozy and disoriented. So I agreed to support him in his attempt. There we were whispering in the front seat of the car about how we were going to convince our daughter to eat a pancake. If that is not the dumbest First World conversation. Other ones we've had in the past few weeks:

"This iPhone is too heavy."

"Someone was using my favorite treadmill this morning, so I was forced to use the stationary bike."

"This refrigerator isn't big enough. Let's buy another one and put it in the garage."

So we're sitting there waiting for the server to bring us our food, and when he sets down Jon's plate, Jon immediately mentions that he can't wait to eat his yummy pancake. I don't say anything because I want to gauge Leta's reaction, and it is exactly what I had expected it to be: "Pancakes are yucky!"

Yes, pancakes are yucky, puppies suck, and rainbows are boring.

And the old part of me that gave up this battle a few years ago is starting to rumble a bit, and I have to bite my lip. Because I want to stand up and yell.

But I remain calm and say, "Actually, Leta, pancakes are pretty good. They taste like cake."

And in turn she replies, "But cake is yucky, too!"

Jon and I ignore this obviously misinformed statement and continue to mention the yummy pancake for the next half hour, and occasionally he offers her a bite. She continues to refuse. Want a bite of a yummy pancake? No. How about now? No. Now? No. Mmmmmm, this yummy pancake is really yummy, would you like a bite? No. How about I grab it off the plate and aim it at your head like a Frisbee? No. Are you even paying attention to me? No.

And this is where the teamwork, the united front comes in, because it suddenly occurs to me to tell her that the syrup tastes like candy, and right when I say that Jon nods furiously and suggests that she dip her finger in the syrup and touch that finger to her tongue. The mere mention of candy causes her to sit up straight, and for a second we both get the sense that she is trying to figure out if it's worth it to give in and let us win, especially if we're telling the truth. What if it does taste like candy? Wouldn't it be stupid to sit there with all that candy a few inches away, just to prove a point?

So she gives us both this look, like, you guys are so cute, look how hard you've been trying. Just this once I'm going to indulge you, but don't say I didn't warn you! And I'm waiting for the bleaaaah and yuuuuuuccck and moaning and wailing, and I'm holding my breath as she dips her finger in the syrup. And as she brings that finger to her mouth, the overwhelming aroma of AWESOMENESS hits her tongue, and without even tasting the syrup she yells, "I LOVE IT."

What?

"I LOVE IT!"

Excuse me?

"I LOVE IT AND I WANT MY OWN. MY OWN PANCAKE."

I've never seen Jon move so fast. He was out of his chair running to find the server. And in the five minutes it took for him to bring

Leta Her Own Pancake we sat there holding our breath, not looking at anything other than the table, afraid that if we moved at all that particles in the atmosphere would shift and she'd change her mind. She'd say something and we'd barely nod or shake our heads. Briefly I looked up and caught Jon's gaze, and I knew we were both thinking the same thing: that pancake would taste nowhere near as good as victory.

She ate every bite of that pancake, and she has eaten pancakes every single morning since then. It's the first thing she asks for in the morning, her own pancake, and I don't think Jon has ever experienced more joy standing over the stove. Partly because she loves them so much, but mostly because I think he knows that I am now more willing to follow his lead in certain matters when it comes to our unique daughter. Thank you, Jon, for expanding our daughter's diet from four to five things.

~Heather Armstrong

Originally published on *www.dooce.com*

It's a Phase

To be a mother is to move outside oneself,
to give of oneself in a way that is unheralded in the human experience.
~Louis Genevie, PhD, and Eva Margolies

I t is two o'clock in the morning, and a timid "Mommy?" tumbles down the hallway and seamlessly weaves itself into the dream that is giving me respite from the daytime life I lead. Perhaps a small child playing in the sand on the beach near the spot where I am lazily reading has just asked her mother for a snack or a trip down to the water to fill her bright pink bucket.

"Mommy?" The greater urgency of the plea sucks the sunny beach from my bedroom as quickly as a vacuum ingests a stray tissue. I am left blinking and confused and struggling to lift my sleep-laden body from its place of repose.

I am well aware that there is no emergency, that once I figure out which child has called and I arrive, panting and dizzy by the side of the proper bed, I will hear a small, non-apologetic, "I'm scared." I am well aware that the appropriate response would be one of two things: sit by the child's side until she falls asleep, stroking her hair and telling her there's nothing to be afraid of; or scoop her up and carry her—warm and clinging—to my bed, where she will breathe her snuffly damp breath in my ear for the night's duration.

However, after working late into the night to meet a deadline, this is the third time I have been awakened, and this night is only a small bead on a strand we've been stringing for months. Right now the appropriate response is not one that will disentangle itself from the cottony web that is my brain. In fact, I wish that I could say nothing, that by just turning and walking away, I could make this whole night-time waking issue disappear.

I sigh as I dig through the cotton in search of a solution—one that will allow me to sleep in peace until the radio wakes me to the welcome company of its morning deejays. I am stuck. I could simply tell the child to go back to sleep, but in twenty minutes, she'll call me again. Exhausted and totally lacking in parenting instincts at 2:00 A.M., I lie down next to her, and within three seconds I am sound asleep.

I don't sleep long before I startle and awaken to see that I am in the wrong bed. My own bed—big and cozy and empty—stands waiting for my return in my own quiet room, where I will listen to no one's sleepy breathing. With a conviction only realized in the lonely hours of pre-dawn, I believe my bed is calling to me. It is promising me a restful sleep if only I can quietly, slowly rise from my daughter's bed and make my way back to my own. With my every move, I can feel the bed tremble as if shaken by an earthquake. She will not wake, she will not wake, she will not wake, I silently chant as I ease myself over her sleeping body to stand, once again, on the solid floor.

The creaking floorboards in the hallway give me pause, but only for a moment. Her deep breathing remains regular, and I make it back to my room, where I slip under covers grown cold in my absence.

"Mommy?" I hear again, and I realize that I have been sleeping. I glance at the clock. Less than half an hour has passed since I re-warmed my bed. The cool air of the room is not welcoming; the thought of the walk down the hall too strenuous. I close my eyes tighter and snuggle deep into the coziness of the down comforter, hoping that my own denial is enough to lull my daughter back to sleep. But it's not.

"Mommy?" she calls once more. As the only adult in the house, I have no choice but to rise and respond to her summons. I go to her side, and in my state of sleep deprivation, I give in to her need for company. With reluctance and relief, I pick her up and carry her to my bed, where I am entertained by her snores and prodded with pointy knees and elbows for the rest of the night.

As dawn bleaches the darkness of my bedroom, I realize that for mothers, there are two universal and conflicting themes: be the best we can be for our children; be the best we can be for ourselves. In the morning, when I am awake enough to look in the mirror, I see that in the lack of sleep that defines my life, I work hard to be the best I can be for my daughter and my sons. The mirror shows me a weary, haggard mommy whose face is splotched with shadows cast by an endless string of interrupted nights, and as I prepare to get the children to the bus stop and login to the online class I teach, I know that I will have difficulty being the best I can be for myself.

This morning, I see the toll that fatigue has taken on my face, my hair, my eyes. I want nothing more than to climb back in bed and sleep through the long day, and I hold on tightly to the thought that nighttime will come soon and I will have another chance at sleep. This morning, however, the mirror is not a friendly place for a middle-aged single mother.

I have experience with my mirror, and I know that first glances can be deceiving. I have learned that my mirror often reflects a depth that even I cannot fathom—the depth within myself where I hold my strength and my purpose. Through my utter exhaustion, I recognize that as a single mother, I have done more than I ever thought I could, that I am stronger than I ever dreamed possible. I celebrate the miniscule success of making it through one more night as the only parent responding to the needs of three young children. I acknowledge that, despite my limitations, I am doing the best I can.

I see in my children the kind of stability found only in consistency. I thank God for the ability to be present in my children's lives, and I bask in the glow of my children's happy smiles and easy laughter.

No, the coming night may not be any different from the last. But through the experience, I will be. I will continue to grow and change as a person and as a parent even through these difficult nights. These nights of interruption are, for me, a phase I must pass through on my journey to becoming the best mother I can be—for my children, and for myself.

~Suzanne Schryver

15

Running on Kid Time

When my kids become wild and unruly, I use a nice, safe playpen.
When they're finished, I climb out.
~Erma Bombeck

I recently celebrated my birthday and my oldest son (sweet boy) gave me a T-shirt that says, "In Dog Years, I'm Dead." Nice.

"Ha! You are over 300 years old!" my youngest figured, with a rare burst of mathematical insight. Then he eyed the dog. "That means Chester is twenty-one.... Wooohooo! Go Chetty! You can buy beer!" Nice.

Although I seem to have a grasp of how canine time is calculated (after all, multiplying by seven, while not as easy as multiplying by five, is still fairly straightforward), I haven't been able to comprehend what makes my kids tick. The struggle for us to synchronize is a daily effort. Maybe that's because my children aren't living on Eastern Standard, Central, Mountain, or Pacific Time. They're on Kid Time.

If you set your clock to kid time, an hour of TV isn't nearly enough, nine o'clock is way too early for bed, and Saturday morning while your parents are still sleeping is the perfect time to try to cut your own bangs. On the kid calendar, Christmas is always too far away, summer vacation lasts forever, and your birthday is a national holiday. If you ask my kids, they'll check their watches and tell you that recess is too short, math class is too long, and all teachers are all really, really old. Even older than me.

In Kid Time, sitting through an hour-long church service is equivalent to being stranded on a rock in the middle of the ocean for a month. You are hungry. You are starving. "Mom, do you have any Tic Tacs? When will they pass out the little pieces of bread? I'm hungry, I'm thirsty. Will there be donuts at coffee hour? I am starving... I am fading away... I am slipping under the pews... Ahhhh...."

Likewise, a twelve-year-old boy who is supposed to practice the piano for thirty minutes will race through his piece and declare, "I'm done!" after a minute and a half. That's because a half hour of practicing the piano in Kid Time is like an adult spending three hours at a Weird Al Yankovic concert. It is interminable. Maybe we should be more understanding.

As parents, perhaps we should learn to expect a different kind of punctuality from our kids. For instance, when an adult says, "Do your homework right now," a child will say, "Okay," but she will not move. That's because in Adult Time "right now" means sometime soon, like in the next few minutes. But in Kid Time "right now" means not until your mother has asked you again and again and again, and then not until she finally stomps into the den, snaps off the television and says, "I said right now!" I try to accommodate the members of my own household who are operating on Kid Time, but it's not easy.

"Can you take me to Shawn's house?" my son asked at eight o'clock on Saturday morning.

"Soon," I said. For me, "soon" means later—after I've had a cup of coffee, after I've changed out of my pajamas and after Shawn's parents are conscious.

For my son, Lewis, who apparently has no snooze button on his kid clock, "soon" means now. Right now. "Are you ready yet? Can we go now? How about now?"

My oldest son also has a clock and it runs on its own sweet time.

"Take out the garbage," I say.

"I am," he replies, even though I can see him sitting barefoot at the kitchen table consuming vast quantities of expensive, not-from-concentrate orange juice.

Again, the fact that I am able to see him is not because he is able to bend the time-space continuum. It's because he is on Kid Time where "I am" means he will... eventually. Maybe.

Kid Time starts the second you become a parent and, apparently, just keeps on ticking. Anyone who has ever walked the floor with a colicky newborn, sent a teenage driver out with the family car, waited in an emergency room with a sick toddler, or read *Green Eggs and Ham* over and over and over knows that time with kids can make minutes seem like an eternity and the years pass in a moment. Even dog years.

~Carol Band

16

Mommies Need Play Dates, Too

Friendship is born at that moment when one person says to another:
"What! You, too? Thought I was the only one."
~C.S. Lewis

My first child, Charlie, was born in January. The winter months in Connecticut may seem a cozy time to snuggle up with your new infant, but for me they also meant long, isolating days at home. I was accustomed to working in an office all day, bantering with adults in meetings, and challenging my mind. Not so staying at home with my sweet little son. I loved him dearly and cherished our uninterrupted maternity leave together. But I was lonely.

My husband, David, and I had moved to our small, woodsy town a year earlier. With both of us working full-time, we hadn't met many other couples, let alone new moms. While I had grown up in the same town, only one old friend of mine had moved back as well and she had older kids. After a few months, I turned to Carrie for advice.

"How do I meet other moms with babies?" I asked her.

Carrie suggested I join the local Newcomers and Neighbors Club, which sponsored playgroups for mothers and their children. Because I had grown up in my town, I hadn't thought to seek out a club for "newcomers." Good idea.

Charlie and I joined the "up to twelve months" playgroup. One morning, I arrived carrying Charlie in his infant carrier. All of the other children were crawling around, mashing toys together and starting to sit up. I put him down in a corner and rolled up my sleeves to settle in with the other moms. It wasn't that easy.

The mothers in the group were welcoming but had been gathering for several months and had already bonded. I felt mismatched and awkward. I was perfectly comfortable entering a conference room and meeting new colleagues. I knew the agenda, who worked where and for whom, and how we all fit together. Entering a parenting group was like starting a whole new career right out of college. I was unsure how I fit in and had nothing more in common with the other women than motherhood and geography. They chatted easily about their kids' sleep habits and spit up, their sore nipples, and whether anyone knew a good electrician. I was more comfortable discussing strategic planning, product development, and internal politics. In truth, I was struggling to craft my social identity as a mother after years of being a full-time professional. My unease continued and I kindly bowed out of the group.

Adding to my identity struggle was my decision to return to work part-time. I'd always dreamed that when I had a child, I would stop working full-time and find a way to craft a three-day-a-week job. I was thankful that my company agreed, but torn every day I left Charlie in the arms of his sweet Colombian nanny. I lugged my breast pump to the office and booked conference rooms for regular intervals throughout the day. I'd close the blinds, lock the door, and pump milk for Charlie while checking e-mail or calling David to chat.

On the days I worked, I'd race home and find Charlie already asleep in his crib. I was blessed with an infant son who slept from 6:00 P.M. to 6:00 A.M., but my heart was broken a little bit each time I missed his nightly bath or singing him to sleep. I craved more time with him and after nine months decided to leave my job altogether. David and I planned our budget to allow me to stay home and I was relieved to put my pump away and settle in to full-time motherhood.

That January, a year after Charlie was born, I faced five days a week at home for the first time. Snow piled up in our yard as I did load after load of laundry. One morning I stood at the kitchen sink, weeping over the prospect of another daily routine of diaper changing, housecleaning, and quiet. Charlie blessed me with his giggles and grins but he didn't say, "Hey, Mom, thanks for the clean diaper. Thanks for giving me some tummy time!"

Every Thursday, I drove forty-five minutes to a music class we'd joined with a new friend, Meghan, and her daughter, Josie. It was the highlight of my week. While our babies wiggled and wailed to the music, Meghan, the other moms and I talked about our children's development and quirks. I was getting the hang of this mommy role. Soon spring arrived, class ended and Meghan and her family relocated to the West Coast.

I decided I'd better get busy. Remembering how confidently Meghan had reached out to meet me one night at a girlfriend's spaghetti dinner, I realized I would need to make the effort to meet new friends. But meeting mommies was new territory for me. I was perfectly comfortable meeting people at work, but how should I start up a conversation with a stroller-pushing stranger?

Plus, I was beginning to realize that a strong network of moms was not only crucial for my mental happiness but also critical to my success in the mommy job. Other moms had all the tried and true advice about what car seat to choose, where to get a first haircut, how to introduce solids, and what really worked for putting their kids to sleep. Without their input and listening ears, I'd be adrift in the sea of tough choices on how to raise Charlie.

So one day, while shopping for a vacation to St. Thomas, I wandered into a shoe store while Charlie was at home with a babysitter. As I tried on sandals for the trip, I watched out of the corner of my eye as a woman around my age, with a son around Charlie's age, tried on shoes as well. When she gave the cashier an address near mine, I made my move.

"Hi, how old's your son?" I asked. (A safe way to make small talk. Like commenting on a cute guy's dog in the park.)

"Fifteen months," she replied.

We soon learned that our sons were born three weeks apart and that she had also just left her job. She was shopping for a trip to the Caribbean as well. After returning from our trips, Candace and I became fast friends and our sons are best friends to this day.

Shortly thereafter, I re-joined Newcomers and Neighbors and found a new playgroup for one-year-olds. This time, I instantly clicked with the group and invited Candace to join as well. Charlie developed a group of friends and I found a network of moms.

When my daughter was born, I started a new playgroup. Soon, we had a boisterous group of toddlers and babies and mommies. We trade stories and tips and are only a phone call away should one of us need a helping hand. "You wanna talk about nursing and poop?" I say. "I'm all for it."

~Heather Pemberton Levy

Too Hot for Chicken

Sometimes the laughter in mothering is the recognition of the ironies and absurdities. Sometimes, though, it's just pure, unthinking delight.

~Barbara Schapiro

I t was a warm summer morning. I had just finished reading the grocery specials in the paper. I didn't really need anything for the next few days. Nothing stuck out as a particularly good deal except the bonus chicken packs: chicken quarters packed in family sizes. But if I drove over to the store (I reasoned) for just one item, wouldn't the gas cost cut into the savings?

Five minutes later I was headed to the store on my bike: helmet on my head, old pack on my back, and five bucks in my pocket. The temperature seemed to have gone up a little, I noticed as I pedaled the two miles to the store. Maybe I should bike more. I locked up my bike and went in. The cold air greeted me pleasantly as I entered the store. I headed straight back to the meat counter. Sure enough, there was a stack of chicken family packs just waiting for me. While the price was fabulous, the packages were a little larger than I had imagined. What the heck, I thought, as I grabbed a package weighing slightly over ten pounds, and then headed for the checkout.

"Paper or plastic," the clerk asked. She gave me a whole lot of change for so much meat and slipped the family pack into a sack, with most of it sticking out the top.

I headed outside, pleased with my purchase and with visions of fried chicken, chicken tacos, chicken and rice, stir-fry chicken, and chicken casserole in my head. Reality set in when the air hit my face. Not warm air, but really hot air. I realized I didn't have the car, so the chicken would be riding on my back. I stuffed it into my old backpack flat side towards my back as I reasoned with myself. It's only two miles. If I concentrate I will be home in no time.

Actually the partially frozen chicken felt cold against my back but the rest of me was beginning to sweat as the hot air rushed by me. It seemed as long as I didn't stop, I would be okay. The heat wouldn't really bother me. In my head I began to count the number of stop signs left before I got home. A signal light loomed just ahead at the top of the rise. As I approached, it turned yellow so I stopped. I had less than a mile left. I felt pretty good but the sweat seemed to be pouring off me from the heat. I was sticky all over. For a moment at the signal it was quiet. Then I heard a woman start screaming. The light turned green but the cars didn't move. Maybe there had been an accident? I looked behind me even though I never heard any cars crunch.

What I saw was a small herd of people coming up the road towards to me. There was a man in a suit, a woman with a beach towel, and a few others. I heard someone yell, "I'm a nurse." I looked around again and still, no visible accident. Moving faster, this herd of folks started talking loudly in my direction.

"Are you alright? We're here to help."

Who are they talking to, I wondered?

Someone put a hand on my handlebar as if to steady my bike. Another took my hand and looked me in the eye.

"Can we help you?" they all asked. I had no idea what was wrong. Out of the corner of my eye, I saw traffic stopping and piling up. Over the heads of the people now surrounding me, I saw someone directing traffic. I was baffled!

"No!" I told this little bunch of folks. "I'm fine!" It was their turn to look puzzled.

Someone spoke up. "Well, you are bleeding all over! Why don't you get off your bike and take off your backpack?"

I got off my bike and moved toward the side of the road. Willing hands held my bike and helped me get my backpack off.

"Were you in an accident? Were you stabbed?" I was peppered with strange questions.

Who are these people and what do they want from me?

Then I looked down at my backpack, sitting now on the white concrete strip of road. There was a red ring around it! I realized my arms and legs also had blood on them. I pointed to the backpack as I started to laugh—so hard I could barely talk.

"It's my chicken," I told the startled group of people.

They opened my backpack not knowing what to expect. And they found ten pounds of now seriously thawing chicken parts, which had leaked through the paper sack, through my backpack and all over me.

I looked like an accident victim. There was chicken blood all over my arms and legs—everywhere I looked.

Suddenly, everyone was laughing out of relief. Eventually, the guy directing traffic yelled "She's OKAY!" and motioned the cars through the green light. The lady with the beach towel handed the towel to me. A couple in the crowd told me they had followed me for a quarter mile thinking I would collapse.

All of a sudden I realized how hot it was! All this for cheap chicken!

Eventually I got home, showered and started supper. As my gang gathered around the table, everyone was talking about their day. Someone piped up, "I thought we were having chicken tonight?"

I smiled, not yet ready to share my adventure. "Perhaps you just misunderstood," I said. "It's just too hot for chicken today!"

~Pamela Gilsenan

Making It as a Mom

Today is the tomorrow we worried about yesterday.
~Author Unknown

My eldest daughter spun before me, as a music box ballerina would, all a dazzle in her pink dress-up gown saying, "Mommy, you are the best mom."

My eyes welled with tears remembering six years prior when I wondered if I had what it takes to "make it as a mom."

I have three girls now and each of them is individual and fabulous in her own way. I love watching how they ingest life and shine with resiliency after their failures or mishaps. I love walking them through that process. What if they could have walked me through that resiliency process six years ago when I was a curled-up ball of insecurity insisting to my husband that I was not cut out for this job?

•••

The digital clock blinked a glowing red 2:30 A.M. My head was fuzzy. Making sense of my thoughts was inconceivable. Thoughts had become like water to me during those midnight feedings, slippery and anything but solid.

It had been less than three weeks since our first child, Brooke, arrived in the world and I was doing my best to figure out how to be her mom, how to be a mom at all. Middle-of-the-night feedings turned our house into a perfect setting for a game of musical rooms. As each cry rang out, sonar-like in place of music, I'd travel between at least three different rooms to find the best place to feed Brooke. I'd go from the bed in the baby's room to our bed where my husband lay, then out to the couch in our living room. My sleepy passage through the dark house was a desperate attempt to find the most comfortable place for me to feed the barely three-week-old baby.

My memory begins when I heard the baby and bolted into her room to lift her from her crib. There had actually been nights when I was so tired that she would fall asleep on my chest while I fell nearly asleep myself. This was not one of those nights. I was systematic. I had a plan. I did all that needed to be done with the pump, formula and bottle. Feeding sessions were at times a three-ring circus between bottle, pump and breast. I tried everything and stuck with what worked.

I situated both Brooke and myself on the couch in the living room and made sure her belly was full. But her shrill crying didn't diminish. She continued calling out. In my sleepy-brained movements, I tucked her into the corner of the couch and piled three large pillows to block her from falling, before running to wash off part of my pump. I'd committed the ultimate mommy no-no. I had left a baby alone in a place where, even though the chances were slim, she could fall. I'd walked fewer than ten steps to the sink when I heard her unnatural shriek.

She'd fallen. Somehow, she'd fallen, and to this day I have no idea how it could have happened. She must have shimmied up and over the three pillows stacked like a barricaded fort, or pushed the pillows off the couch allowing her worm-like, seven-pound body to make it off the couch and land in a thud on the ground. It must have felt like a cliff dive to her. No wonder she cried with such intensity. I cradled her in my arms and panicked—yelling for my husband to come. I called the pediatrician immediately, only to be counseled that she seemed okay, that this was something that happens in some form and at some point to most moms.

I couldn't believe it. It took me the next three weeks to accept that I could survive in my role as a mom. I was terrified that every drop of formula given, every diaper changed, and every swab of alcohol to the umbilical cord was done incorrectly. I thought I was a failure at being a mom. I hadn't let the pediatrician's comforting words, or the articles I'd found about "baby's first fall," or even my husband's complete understanding, relieve me of my fear that I was not meant to be a mother.

Just the other day I took turns "flying" each of my three girls, ages six, four and eighteen months, on my shins. I hoisted their flat bellies on my legs, lifting them as high in the air as possible, feeling every muscle in my stomach constrict. I encouraged each of my girls to straighten out her arms when it was her turn. I convinced them they were flying. They giggled in a pitch unique to little girls. Something inside me felt released from that one memory of Brooke falling. I was free from castigating myself for allowing her to fall at just three weeks old. In some wonderful reciprocal way of learning, I embraced what they had to teach me in that moment. As each girl chose to put out her arms, like eagles in flight, I realized they trusted me. They knew I was doing all I could to hold them steady, to keep them from falling.

When I saw the trust in their eyes and the playful way they begged me to fly them more, it was all I needed. Their trust in me told me in kid-like sign language that I was making it. I was making it as a mom just fine. There will be times when my girls falter, times they fall, and even times they get hurt. But I know that we will make it through with resiliency—and I know that I really am cut out for being a mom of three loving little girls.

~Wendy Miller

19

Detailing the SUV

*Cleaning house while your kids are still growing is like
shoveling the walk before it stops snowing.*
~Phyllis Diller

As any Beta Mom knows, there is no walk of shame like the
one up to the office of the car-detailing place when your
vehicle is ready. I'm prepared for it now because inevitably
I get the phone call halfway through the morning from the owner.
"Um, Mrs. Wilkey? This is Bernard from Auto Shine. I know I quoted
you ninety dollars, but, uh, we've really got a lot of work to do here
and I need to have another man come in for this one." I immediately
blame my children (usually claiming I have four instead of three) in
the hopes that Bernard will view me as his partner in disgust. Bernard
has no need for such camaraderie and settles on an extra forty dollars
instead. Apparently there is gum involved.

This whole car thing makes my husband crazy. You could eat off
the floor of his car. The only extra objects in his car beside his person
are a Chapstick, an EZ Pass, and a pack of gum. Maybe a travel pack
of Kleenex during cold and flu season. All neatly tucked into the
center console, where they should be. The floor of my car may not be
clean enough to eat off of, but you'll have plenty of snacks to choose
from. Alpha Moms behind me at the school drop-off roll their eyes
because you cannot open one of my doors without something falling
out, usually an empty water bottle or a shoe. My kids, God bless 'em,

chase the rolling water bottle and chuck it back in with a "love you!" because it's all they know.

"So," you may want to know, "is MY minivan or SUV a Beta Vehicle?" Well, let me ask you this: Do you apologize when anyone but family gets in? Do your cup holders contain something resembling congealed popsicles? Are there more coats and shoes in your vehicle than in your hall closet? Does the dog consider a ride in the car "mealtime?" Have you, at any given time, had ten or more of the following items strewn about the car? Sweatshirts, soccer shoes, Goldfish crackers, water bottles, fast food wrappers, granola bar wrappers, grocery receipts, grocery lists, doctor appointment cards, dentist goodie bags, mittens, hats, hair ties, headbands, half-eaten bagels, school projects, school papers, school memos, fire safety booklets, CDs, DVDs, Nintendos, Webkinz, iPods, karate belts, ballet shoes, old fruit, juice boxes, action figures, lollipop sticks, Cheetos, Barbie shoes, Bratz feet, Bionicle pieces, Blockbuster cases, dry cleaner slips or those freakishly large Bed Bath & Beyond coupons?

(Sigh). I would like to say that I intend to turn over a new leaf. I would like to say that I never used to keep my car this way before I had children. But if I'm honest, I do recall ejecting the latest Laura Branigan tape in my '85 Mustang cassette player and flinging it behind me into the back seat, where it probably got lost among the aerobics gear and beer bottles. Chances are, if you're a Beta mom, you were a Beta girl, too.

But as I remind my husband, the day is going to come way too soon when the only trash in my car will be some coffee cups, and MapQuest directions to the kids' colleges. And that's when I'll be the one with the travel Kleenex.

~Sue Wilkey

20

Everything

What do I give my children?
A kiss on the cheek,
A bandage on the knee,
A hug when they're down.

What do I give my children?
Stories at bedtime,
Stories from my past,
Stories of their youth.

What do I give my children?
The breath from my lungs,
The blood from my veins,
The marrow from my bones.

What do I give my children?
A chance to make choices,
A reason to speak,
A voice of their own.

What do I give my children?
Everything I wish I could be,
And by the time they're grown,
Even the parts I wish I weren't.

What do I give my children?
The memories of their childhood,
Their strengths, their weaknesses,
Their future.

~Andrea Lehner

21

Wednesday Night Sanity Check

You can learn many things from children.
How much patience you have, for instance.
~Franklin P. Jones

I was in desperate need of a break. The "witching hour" was upon us once again, dinner was burning on the stove, and fights were breaking out between my two children. "Jamison, leave your brother alone! Zachary, no biting!" The whining and crying were relentless, no one napped that day, and I was at the end of my rope. My husband was in the city for yet another dinner meeting, and I was holding down the fort until way after bedtime. I was going to snap.

I called a friend who has four children the same ages as mine, and she was in a similar situation. Our husbands work together and were attending the same meeting that night. I could hear the screaming in the background, interrupted by Jen yelling, "Hannah, leave your sister ALONE!" and "No, Katie!" She kept dropping the phone to pick up the baby because he was crying. Then the pasta pot boiled over and she had to run. It seemed as if we were all suffering equally. Couldn't there be a way for us to break up the monotony, find safety in numbers, stop the fighting, and get everyone to actually eat the dinner we spent the time to prepare? Absolutely.

The first play date was at Jen's house the following Wednesday at 4:00 P.M. My daughter disappeared into the basement playroom with her twin girls and her younger daughter, and my son clung to me as did hers. We chatted about her week, described the various escapades of the kids, and crabbed about the crazy hours our husbands work. As we listened to the shrieks of glee from the girls downstairs, we both could feel ourselves unwinding from the insanity of the day. The occasional crash from the playroom would warrant a pop-in to make sure no one was bleeding, but the girls were so wrapped up in whatever dress-up fantasy they'd created that it didn't matter that a mom had invaded their space. The boys finally got down off of our laps and started exploring the toys on the first floor, and Jen and I sat just enjoying some adult company.

We ordered a pizza and salad, and ALL of the children actually ate their dinner. My kids aren't big salad fans, but if other kids are eating it, apparently it's cool. The entire large pizza was polished off, the salad was gone, and the rascals raced away for more romping. Jen and I cleaned up the plates together, wiped up the floor, and then sat back down to enjoy the pizza we'd ordered for ourselves. When we were done, we invited the gang back for some brownies (which were inhaled) and then they all danced to a music DVD until it was time to go. We left at 7:00 P.M., and my kids went right to bed when we got home. I felt rejuvenated and ready to face motherhood again. The e-mail from Jen the next morning confirmed her similar sentiments. We were on to something and it had to continue.

The following Wednesday play date was at my house, and it was exactly the same. The kids had a great time wearing themselves out, the moms enjoyed a few minutes of peace and quiet discussing the week, the kids chowed down their dinners, and all parties went home ready for bed. We've been holding the Wednesday Night Sanity Check for about five months now, and added another family with three kids to the mix. The more the merrier. Haylee has twin girls and a son, and a husband who works crazy hours, too, so she completely gets where Jen and I are coming from.

Watching nine kids from four years down to eight months interact and play together without the whining and fighting and bickering is a truly great thing, and to listen to the woes of the other moms and problem-solve together, or just listen to the funny stories of the week makes me sit back and realize that it's really not all that bad. Too many times I've felt completely overwhelmed by the constant demands of the house, the kids, and our family. Wednesday night gives me a chance to sit and really observe my children as little people. Those kids that are back-talking, complaining, whining, fighting and screaming at each other when we're at home, are actually polite, considerate, loving souls, and I rarely get a chance to view them like this. Any mom understands that you get the brunt of the abuse from your kids if you're home with them all the time, and often you don't get to appreciate the little things that you HAVE done right in raising them. This is one of those special times for us, and we all go home ready to face another week.

~Kate Munno

Reprinted by permission of Tom Swick
© 2008

The List

The pursuit of perfection... is the pursuit of sweetness and light.
~Matthew Arnold

After twenty years of working full-time, I resigned from my job as an executive assistant and tried to focus on the needs of my two children, seven-year-old Nikki and four-year-old Cobi. Both had been in day care since they were six weeks old and I never felt guilty dropping them off. Not until Nikki went to kindergarten and discovered that not all moms worked. She saw these stay-at-home moms who stood at the bus stop until their child was picked up. She envied the kids whose moms volunteered during class time and helped out with school parties. And oh boy, did she ever go nuts when she saw that some moms actually went on field trips with the class. She desperately wanted me to be one of those moms!

And so after some financial maneuvers, lots of sacrifices and much soul-searching, I resigned and became the fantasy mom Nikki had dreamed of all her short little life. I was a stay-at-home mom. However, this stay-at-home mom still operated on her executive assistant schedule.

I still awoke at 5:00 A.M. and made my "to do" list, the single item that my entire day revolved around. Rather than noting the many reports or meetings I needed to give my attention to, I was listing every single activity, craft, errand, or load of laundry I needed to do. As I had done for the last twenty years, I meticulously crossed off every line as it was completed. It was the only way I knew how to operate. I never realized how ridiculous I was being until one morning when I left my list on the table. It was going to be a very busy day, with twenty-two items already noted on my pad of paper. I needed to take a shower and get started.

Nikki must have gotten out of bed when I was getting dressed because when I came to retrieve my list and get started on my horribly busy day, I scanned down the items one last time. There, at the very bottom, Nikki had taken a crayon, and in her seven-year-old writing had added item number twenty-three:

23. I LOVE YOU MOMMY

~Cheryl Kremer

Chapter
3

Power MOMS

Outside the Box

Moms Doing Things Their Way

Super Mommy

Trying to be Supermom is as futile as trying to be Perfect Mom.
Not going to happen.
~Arianna Huffington

I stared at a black screen with the words "Super Mommy" whipping around and changing colors. My husband had at some point typed the words in so it would be my screen saver. At first, I thought it was pretty funny and liked seeing the words "Super Mommy" flash across my screen before I sat down to try to fulfill them. Then I thought about the pressure. The pressure to be everything to everybody; to make our home a beautiful home; to make our children respectful and considerate; and to keep my marriage successful. Not to mention trying to pursue my own dreams and ambitions while I was so busy being a Super Mommy! The problem was that I felt anything but super.

For starters, I was wiped out. Pooped, tuckered, tired. If I were super, I could do amazing things like fly as fast as a speeding bullet! With two young children who are always on the move, it is hard just keeping up with them. In fact, I'd be happy to be able to roll out of bed without an ache or a creak in my bones. And I wouldn't mind being thin and beautiful like all those supermodel moms that bombard us from television and magazines. I wouldn't have to watch what I eat because I would be so busy being super, I'd never gain any weight! That might help me get into the "super" category.

If I were truly super, I'd be like those other mothers who live at the kids' school. Don't get me wrong; I believe every parent should participate in their children's education. But there are some moms who always volunteer, and who always know what's going on with every committee and group. They give, give, give. I just can't do it. Well, I do what I can, when I can. But the pressure! If I were a Super Mommy, I'd be like one of those moms. Why do they seem to have all the energy? How can I get some?

If I were a Super Mommy, as my computer screen keeps reminding me, my kids would be perfect, or at least pretty darn near perfect! They would behave—always. In the market, they'd never beg me to buy them candy. At restaurants, they wouldn't stand in the chairs and sing, "I Love You," at the top of their lungs. They wouldn't run up and down the aisles at church and they would never speak unless spoken to. They wouldn't do things like pick their noses or bite their fingernails in front of other people. They would always obey me and never fight. Yeah right—I'm wishing I were a Super Mommy right about now!

If I were a Super Mommy, hot meals would be served every night and they would be balanced meals. My husband would always come home to a meat and potatoes kind of dinner. Candles would be lit and soft music would play in the background while our dog fetched the paper and the kids played quietly. Because if I were a Super Mommy, my household would be organized, cleaned, and perfect. Just like June Cleaver. Look out super June, here comes Super Mommy!

If I were a Super Mommy, I'd meet my deadlines for work, pick the kids up at school on time, get the laundry cleaned and ironed, and still make time for tea with the Super Mommy neighbors I try to be like. I wonder, are they super or just pretending to be? They seem to have it all together while I feel like a fish out of water.

I asked my kids if they thought I was a Super Mommy. At first they laughed and went off playing. I was crushed. For all I do and all I give, when asked a simple question, I get a laugh! Then one day shortly thereafter, my daughter drew a picture of me, the Super Mommy. It was a magic marker portrait with the words "Super

Mommy" above my head. (She was only five!) I asked her why she thought I was a Super Mommy.

"Because Daddy says so." This was her first answer, having seen the flashing words on my computer screen. After a somewhat lengthy conversation, I finally heard these wonderful words, "You do everything. When I grow up I want to be a mommy just like you." I felt a super wave of confidence flow through my body. I was on my way to superdom!

My son shrugged his shoulders when I asked him. His answer was, "The computer thinks so." But that retort came with the biggest bear hug I ever got from him and a cuddle. Not bad for a seven-year-old!

Finally, I asked my husband why he put that up and how I could get rid of it. He smiled and said, "Because to us you are a Super Mommy and we want you to know it every day!"

Isn't that sweet? The more I think about the words "Super Mommy," the more I think they are redundant. After all "super" and "mommy" are really one and the same. The word "mommy" simply says it all. You have to be super to be a mommy, even if you don't always get it right. You just don't need the word "super" in front of "mommy!" Besides, we moms are all built differently. We have our own priorities. Some are youthful, some help out at school all the time. Some work from home or outside of the home, while some stay at home. Some take care of their aging parents while raising young children. Some mommies seem to have it all together. The truth is, we all try hard to do what is best for our children and ourselves.

Now I sit at my computer preparing to write and I see those words "Super Mommy" doing somersaults in rainbow colors. I like them now even if they are redundant and a bit overrated. They have a "ring" to them. There might be piles of laundry on my bedroom floor, soup and sandwiches for dinner, and a deadline not met, but to my family I am the superest mommy of all, because I am their mommy. And there is nothing overrated about that!

~Jennifer Reed

If You Can

A mother is a person who seeing there are only four pieces of pie
for five people, promptly announces she never did care for pie.
~Tenneva Jordan

Becoming a stay-at-home mom once my children were born seemed to come naturally to me. I considered going to work, but couldn't fathom leaving them all day with anyone else, even family. Financially, we knew it would have its challenges, but the upside seemed to outweigh any sacrifices we might need to make.

Blessed with a girl and a boy merely sixteen months apart, I was extremely busy the first year as I coped with two under two. But I wouldn't have traded the chaos and sleepless nights for any corporate position. Reading and playing with my kids filled me with a satisfaction I couldn't have dreamed was possible. Being witness to each milestone, however small, was like watching a magical story unfold.

My husband traveled extensively and we both agreed that for my sanity and his ability to bond with the kids, he needed to find a new job. After a year of training on a measly salary, he received the news of a transfer to a new state. By this time, all of our savings were depleted and we were grateful to be sent to a rural area where the cost of living might be affordable on one salary.

My husband signed on with the promise of a lucrative bonus incentive. Unfortunately, within a few months, the company rescinded the bonus possibilities and we were stuck with a basic, low salary for at least the first year.

Once settled in our new rental home, we realistically looked at our budget. It seemed possible, but we would have to make even more sacrifices. No cable TV. No eating out. No new clothes. I walked everywhere possible to conserve gas money. And there were no vacations.

We reminded ourselves that this was a season in life and soon we would be on the other side of this financial challenge. We knew I could work and give us great financial relief and a better lifestyle, but we just weren't ready to sacrifice our plan that I would stay at home with the children.

Blessings poured into our lives in the form of gorgeous name-brand second-hand clothes, second-hand furniture, and even a few checks in the mail when we needed them. Toys were always bought from yard sales. It became my new sport early Saturday morning to peruse the sales and find the best bargains for nearly-new toys and books. Friends of ours even offered to pay for a vacation home for us to go away for a week to the beach with them.

My mother offered to tape our favorite shows commercial-free and send them to us every two weeks. We could then watch them on our VCR at our leisure. Another friend offered free babysitting so we could attend our Bible study at church. One of our dearest friends supplied us with new CDs and took us occasionally to concerts. We exchanged babysitting with friends and did lots of bartering.

Walking in the freshly fallen snow became one of our favorite outings. Strolling to the local library and participating in weekly story time became one of the highlights of our week. Going out to dinner consisted of walking to the local restaurant and sharing a huge plate of French fries between the four of us.

We finished each month with very few dollars left in the bank account, but we managed to keep our heads above water. Although I sometimes struggled with the financial stresses, I was so grateful to spend each day with my kids.

I knew people wondered why I wouldn't go back to work to get us out of our rut. They had politely hinted. But we were content and felt conviction about following through on our values. I realized one day that we never know who's watching and what they might be thinking when the wife of a high school friend of mine commented to me, "We've been watching you stay at home for the past few years. If you can do it on the little you have, anyone can do it."

Wow! I was flabbergasted. I had no idea we might actually be an example to someone. I usually felt criticized by people. Amazingly enough, this friend quit her job and went on to have two more children and is a fulfilled and zealous stay-at-home mom.

She was only the first of a few friends who followed our example and took the plunge to live off one salary and at least have one parent spend the first few years at home. Those years seem to have flown by, and when I look back on them, I vaguely remember the financial woes, but my memories of how we spent our days together are vivid and precious.

~Johnna Stein

Reprinted by permission of Tom Swick
© 2008

Staying Home

As soon as you trust yourself, you will know how to live.
~Johann von Goethe

Alex, my two-year-old daughter, cried out for "Binky." Even though I wished we could lose that pacifier forever, I began lifting throw pillows and looking under the sofa. This was my third Binky search-and-rescue mission of the day. Even worse, it was the most exciting thing that had happened to me since breakfast, rivaled only by picking Play-Doh out of the carpet and folding laundry. One month after becoming a stay-at-home mom, I was ready to throw in the diaper and go back to work as a Registered Nurse.

I thought being at home would feel like a vacation. Instead, the days were long and isolating. Time flew by at the hospital. My routine went like clockwork; I was efficient and clear about my role. But our family was stressed to the max. I desperately missed my daughter, who stayed with a sitter. My husband's job and long commute made him gone from five in the morning until eight each night. Our family was everywhere, except together. I loved nursing, but something had to give. So I resigned.

Once we found Binky, I took Alex to the playground. It was abuzz with moms and kids, none of whom I knew. Placing Alex in the toddler swing, I tried to act like I belonged. I studied the other moms, looking for clues on how to make this homemaker thing work. Every time a child approached his mother with a need, she reached into her magical diaper bag and pulled out the solution, be it a sippy-cup, bag of animal crackers, or Band-Aid.

I gazed in awe as one mother changed a diaper, never once distracted from telling her story. When done, she pulled out a plastic bag for the refuse, gracefully deposited it in the trash, and then whipped out a small bottle of hand disinfectant. I looked from her ironed clothes to my jelly-stained T-shirt. Jealous, I nicknamed her "Mommy Perfect."

While in the sandbox, Alex yanked a shovel from a boy's hand. When the other child burst into tears, I made a mental note to buy sand toys. I knew it was obvious to the other mothers; I was really a working-mom masquerading as a stay-at-home-mom. I'd expected the confidence I experienced as a nurse to follow me home. How could I be so inept managing a two-year-old, when I had effectively carried a caseload of over forty patients? I left the playground that day worried I'd never fit in.

As weeks went by, I began to accept the unhurried rhythm of my house and daughter. Slowing down gave us the time to do things like read stacks of picture books and take cuddle naps. Still, 24/7 with a toddler was exhausting. Needing a break by evening, I'd plop Alex in front of the television while I made dinner or caught up on e-mails. Ashamed at how grateful I was for my TV babysitter, I often wondered, would Mommy Perfect approve? Her son drank soy milk and ate juice-sweetened cookies. I was still too intimidated to introduce myself. Then came the day Alex gave up her pacifier.

In an effort to get rid of Binky, I suggested Alex wrap it up as an elaborate gift for the newborn down the street. My daughter smiled with delight as she decorated the box with fancy paper and bright-colored bows. She proudly delivered the package to the baby. And that, quite simply, was the end of Binky. Had I only known it was going to be that easy!

Proud of my success, I swaggered to the playground that day and saw Mommy Perfect. She looked frazzled and wore sweat pants.

"Hi, I'm Jane." Mommy Perfect held out her hand. "Excuse the way I look. Our TV's been out for three days. I'm ready to buy every kid's video ever made so I can take a shower."

"You let your child watch videos?" I blurted out in complete shock.

"Of course," she said. "How would I ever get dressed in the morning?"

Inside I was relieved. Maybe I was no different than the other stay-at-home moms after all.

"By the way..." Mommy Perfect said as she searched through her purse, "do you have a tissue? My son's nose is disgusting."

"Sure." I reached into my well-stocked diaper bag.

"Thanks. Sam has the worst allergies. He has tons of diet restrictions and is always congested. If I could just get rid of his pacifier it would be so much easier for him to breathe."

Now this was a topic I had a handle on! When the kids scampered off to play with the sand toys I'd brought, I turned to Jane and said, "It's hard to wean kids off pacifiers. But if you want, I'll tell you what worked for me...."

~Sherrie Najarian

No More Ennui

A child educated only at school is an uneducated child.
~George Santayana

Chasing away the boredom blues has been a big part of my "grown-up" life. As a young adult, I blended into a crowd of twenty-somethings who had no clear sense of direction. Many of us changed jobs, moved to new cities, and tried out new lifestyles as if we were looking for the grail of perfect-fitting jeans.

By the time I was in my thirties and married, my vagabond life-style had become a bit of an issue. I wanted adventure — my husband wanted the traditional childhood that he had missed. We moved to the suburbs. We adopted two kittens. We gardened and decorated with the zeal of overachievers with HGTV, TiVo and a Martha Stewart subscription. We updated our kitchen. We had a baby girl. We had twin boys a year later. We did a huge gut renovation while we lived in the house with our three preschoolers, our sleeping bags, a microwave oven and a ladder to access the only working bathroom.

I had tried it all — home improvement, self-improvement, yoga, tennis, golf, book clubs, volunteering, mommy-and-me classes, baby massage lectures... there had to be something more.

At forty, wandering around in my perfect house, I felt like a stranger, an interloper in this land of perfect houses, above-average children and conspicuous consumption. I tried to think of what it meant to be happy. I was happy when I was with my husband and kids. I felt authentic and accepted, and isn't that really what we're all looking for? Then I realized that I could feel this way all of the time.

After a lot of deliberation and soul-searching, my husband and I decided to home school our three kids, a daughter who is now ten and twin boys who are nine. In the last few years, I've become accustomed to people asking me all sorts of questions: "Are you a certified teacher?" (No.) "Don't they need to be tested?" (No again.) And my personal favorite, "Don't you go crazy being with your kids all day?" (For our family, it's my kids that keep me sane.)

My husband, Tom, and I have always been travelers. So when we had kids, we refused to give it up. It was a very conscious, labor-intensive, expensive choice to make, but we've never regretted it. My kids had their passports before they were finished breastfeeding. There have been trips to Europe, visiting family, summer holidays in Martha's Vineyard and Maine. We started out like all families do, lugging everything that could fit into our ever-expanding cars. Strollers, playpens, highchairs, exersaucers—my eyes roll at the memory of stuffing a Diaper Genie between my legs in the passenger seat, getting ready for a four-hour drive.

Our first "Big Trip" was a four-month-long trip through South America. The kids were seven and eight years old, and my husband would be traveling with us for the first month and the last month. I would be on my own for the middle of the trip. I spent six months brushing up on my high school Spanish. Even though I had been to South America many times before, it was a bit nerve-wracking. There was little to no cell phone coverage where I was going, and no wireless Internet. Once my husband made the twenty-two-hour trip back to Connecticut, I was on my own. Natural disasters, injuries, illnesses, and banditos: in the month before the trip I would go to bed at night pushing away the bad karma that was seeping into my mind. I took all the precautions that I could; then I just powered though. My poor kids had so many immunization shots that they looked like pincushions.

It was the most empowering thing that I've ever done, part *National Geographic* and part *Thelma and Louise*. It went amazingly well, and we all had a blast. We saw wild penguins, seals, flamingoes, waterfalls, volcanoes and glaciers. And the spectacular scenery was complemented by the unedited audio books of the *Harry Potter* series—guaranteed to hypnotize restless kids on daylong drives.

I'm convinced that I could have accomplished the same thing traveling a ten-hour radius from where we live. To me, our "travelschool" is more about creating our own destiny and embracing our choices. I no longer feel like an observer to my kids' education.

I can take their interest in the rainforest and bring it to life by taking them to the Amazon. It's much easier to put the educational pieces in context when you can have the learning be experiential. Having our local jungle guide, James, take us piranha fishing was fun, and made for a very tasty dinner! But going in his dugout canoe to his cousin's two-room hut on the riverbank was eye opening. His entire extended family lived there with no running water, bathrooms or electricity. No access road, no dentists, extremely limited medical care and schooling only for a few years to teach reading and basic math. No beds either—fewer furry friends when you sleep in a hammock four feet off the floor.

The impression left on my kids, however, was how happy the family was, even living with so little. What I took away from it was the proud independence of people with true survival skills. They meet all the basic needs of their family independently. I felt humbled and spoiled.

Friends will often ask how I can come up with a curriculum, but kids are natural born sponges; they want to learn, they shine when they get to be the center of your universe, and they like feeling smart. Every day they read, and keep a journal. We get to wander to where our curiosity takes us.

For our next trip to the Pacific, each of the kids was responsible for writing reports on two of the countries we were going to visit. Each of these led in turn to relevant science projects (coral reefs, volcanoes, glaciers). Everyone got a turn to be an expert on what interested them, from the teachings of Buddha to New Zealand's Maori warriors to European explorers.

By home schooling my kids, I can pour all of my energy into helping the most important people in my world. I taught them to read, to appreciate art, to pack luggage like a road warrior, and to be open to learning that different doesn't mean bad. I have traveled around the world with my kids, and it has made them more accepting of other cultures and customs, more patient and more thankful. Travel teaches them to be more self-sufficient, street savvy and responsible than they would ever be living in our protected little corner of the world.

~Valerie Rosenberg

27

Waiting for the Other Shoe to Drop

When a child enters the world through you, it alters everything on a psychic, psychological, and purely practical level. You're just not free anymore to do what you want to do. And it's not the same again. Ever.

~Jane Fonda

It was the shoes. Definitely the shoes that were pushing me over the edge. I caught the tiny sneaker just as it was about to hit the dirt. My son squealed in protest. I was one step away from a nervous breakdown. We were on vacation. Well, technically, my thirteen-month-old son and I were on vacation. My husband was working at a month-long conference in Geneva—the perfect opportunity for us to play and explore.

At first, I felt a bit guilty, a bit greedy even, anticipating this trip. It was quite a stay-at-home mom's coup: a month in Europe with husband, all (most) expenses paid, great apartment, my own agenda. I loved exploring new cities. It was my thing. I don't do rope bridges in Borneo, camp out for Burning Man or "summit," but I can really work an urban *Lonely Planet* guidebook. Leave no café unturned. I actually felt sorry for my husband, who would be cooped up in an office. I pictured myself at restaurants, markets, museums. I even dredged up my high school French.

So really, the inappropriateness of having a nervous breakdown while on such a glamorous escapade just seemed, well, gauche. How could this not be going well? I had a city map. I had an all-access subway pass. I had extra milk. And I was at the playground holding onto my son on the wooden rocking horse and about to cry. The added faux pas of crying at a playground just made things worse. How could anyone be sad at a playground? I guess the same way one could be sad at a carousel (yesterday), a street market (the day before), and a botanical garden (last weekend).

So, the shoes. His feet repelled them. And the socks they rode in on. I was constantly replacing them, wrestling him in his stroller to try to replace them, or worrying that his feet were going to get frostbite when I no longer had the strength to replace them. I knew things had gotten bad when I snapped at the fifth grandmother that day who grabbed my coat to reprimand me for his not wearing shoes.

It was only a symptom anyway. It wasn't the shoes. Even I could see that. No, it was also the sweater. And the jacket. And the hat. And the not wanting to be put in the stroller. And screeching on the tram. It took us longer to leave the house than it did to be out before we had to come in for a nap. Sometimes we did not even leave the house in the morning before the eye rubs and yawns started and we unpacked, undressed, and went back to bed.

I don't know why this was such a shock, not getting anything done. We don't get anything done at home. If we get dressed, have a bite to eat, and make it to the market before it closes to pick up some bananas, we're high-fiving each other all the way back. And that's when it hit me. I thought I was going to be on vacation. I needed a vacation. One appeared before me. I jumped at it. I thought it would be a nice change of scenery—that I could maybe escape the sameness of life at home. What I forgot was that I now traveled with my own little self-contained life. Which, I guess, is more or less true of everyone. Wherever you go, there you are. You travel around the world only to confront the same baggage (no pun intended) against a different backdrop.

Only this was the concrete version of that metaphysical truism. I literally had my baggage attached to my leg as I tried to cook dinner. It came with me everywhere. It made its presence known loudly and often. Obviously, the problem was that my son did not know we were on vacation. He carried on with the same attention-getting tactics that I was mostly able to ignore back home.

I could appreciate the good and the cute—the giggling, the snuggling in, the saying "nana" for "banana," the eye crinkle—as much as anyone, but it wasn't enough to get me through the day with my sanity intact. As soon as anything "less than good" happened, I immediately put forth so much energy wishing things were different that I worked myself into a funk and negated any residual good parts. Why can't he nap for more than a half hour? Why can't he eat the green bean instead of throwing it? I fought with myself far more than my son did. It started to seem as if the days were all bad, punctuated occasionally by something going well.

I think I had the feeling that if I could just get the day to go smoothly, I could have time to get back to my own agenda. But as I thought this, it was slowly occurring to me that this taking-care-of-my-son thing was my agenda. It wasn't something to get through before I could get back to my regularly scheduled day. This was it. Keeping my son safe, happy, well-fed and diapered. This was the job. This was what I was doing with my days. This was the work of parenting. That it took thirteen months and seven days for this to sink in staggered the mind a little. Was this denial a result of some latent post-post-post-partum depression?

It was like that picture-in-picture function on televisions. Your main program is running large on the screen, while the secondary program runs in a tiny box in a lower corner. If you try to watch the tiny screen all the time, it will take all your concentration to ignore the big screen, and probably give you a headache from all the squinting. It wasn't designed to be used that way. The large one is the main program. If you want to focus on the other for a while, flip the images. Otherwise, watch what you've got.

I wanted that. I wanted to appreciate what was looming large in front of me. I didn't want to fight with myself anymore over what should be on the big screen. I had two choices: denial or acceptance. Acceptance seemed more functional. The big picture could remain in focus: I was in charge of raising my son all day. Children are messy. They don't listen. Why double my misery by denying that any of the above is real or expected? I obviously had some work to do, but I was starting to get that my problems didn't seem to be stemming from Geneva, the weather, or my husband's long working hours.

As the afternoon chill settled in, my son looked up at me from his playground horse and whinnied, a big grin spreading across his face at his own cleverness. His other shoe looked up at me from the fresh mud below. My son was having a good time. I decided to join him.

~Stephanie Wolff Mirmina

28

Angels of Their Own

The fact is that child rearing is a long, hard job, the rewards are not always immediately obvious, the work is undervalued, and parents are just as human and almost as vulnerable as their children.

~Dr. Benjamin Spock

I breathed a sigh of relief today as I walked down the hallway after dropping off my six-year-old for her first day of school. Not that I didn't tear up; but I took comfort in knowing that today our whole family began a journey of trust.

My mothering has been influenced heavily by its tenuous beginnings. After spending years in medical school and consciously avoiding becoming pregnant, my husband and I were shocked when we didn't get pregnant immediately upon trying. For almost two years, nothing happened. Then, just after the passing of one of my dearest friends, I discovered I was "late." I took the test and it was positive. I spent the next three days calling everyone I knew and sharing our miraculous news. Then I spent the next nine months worrying. I worried that I wasn't getting enough morning sickness; then, when what nausea I did have mysteriously disappeared at around ten weeks, I was sure that I had miscarried. After rushing to the clinic and seeing that tiny heart beating away, I was reassured, at least for the time being.

When Lily finally arrived, we took her home, read all the

parenting books, and set out to raise this child to the very best of our ability. She must have sensed our dedication, because she decided to put us to the test. My husband affectionately referred to her as his "little Ferrari—high maintenance, but you won't find a better girl."

We didn't let her cry. If she fussed, we attended to her immediately. Of course, I carried even this to the extreme. I truly felt that no one could take as good care of her as I could; that I was completely indispensable, irreplaceable, and needed—every minute of every day. I took it upon myself to be there always, no matter the cost.

After months of getting no more than two to three hours of sleep each night, I headed to a quiet room upstairs, leaving my husband with strict instructions to page me on the walkie talkie (beyond ridiculous, I know) as soon as she stirred. When he did use the alert button, I took it seriously. I jumped out of bed and hurled myself down the stairs, practically breaking my neck in the process. What was I thinking? This is what was going through my mind: "If this child fully wakes, I'm not going to get back to bed tonight. And if I don't find a way to get some sleep, I am going to lose my mind."

I spent the first year of Lily's life keeping the car engine running while filling the gas tank during her infrequent and easily disturbed naps, and nursing her around the clock. This actually lasted until half way through my second pregnancy.

When it came time to think about preschool, we learned of a wonderful home-based program nearby. Lily attended for two years—loving every minute of it, and giving me some much needed one-on-one time with my baby, Scarlett. Toward the end of her second year, our attention turned to plans for kindergarten. When the public schools failed to meet our expectations, we found ourselves without the resources to explore private schools and made the decision to home school.

I approached home schooling much like a doctoral dissertation, becoming completely absorbed in learning all that I could about different curricula, support groups, and classes offered to home schoolers. Here I was again, living out the belief that I was the only one qualified to meet my daughter's needs. This time, though, my body had other plans. About one month into the school year, I started experiencing a series of vague symptoms—achiness, dizziness, and crushing fatigue. Now I had two children home with me around the clock—one who was ready for "something more" and really missing the companionship of her classmates, and one who was, well, two years old and in a different place all together. And somehow, I was supposed to be accomplishing what had become for me the onerous task of home schooling.

Devoid of energy many days before noon, I was panicked about the prospect of not being able to fulfill my roles as mother and teacher. I knew that I had to let up on myself and find ways to create more balance in my life. My mother's words came to me. "You have to take care of yourself so you *can* be there for your family."

I made a commitment to do just that. Regular sleep and yoga classes became priorities. More importantly, though, I began to release the idea that I had to do it all, be everything to my children. With the return of my bodily energy stores and enlightened with a new perspective, my husband and I started exploring other ways in which we could provide Lily with some of the interaction and opportunities that had been difficult for me to create from scratch the previous year. As an aside, I have several amazing friends who are able to pull off the feat of home schooling their children with seamless effort. It's a wonderful ideal; it just wasn't working for me.

We finally landed on a hope—or a dream, given our financial situation. We visited the local Waldorf School, and fell in love with it right away. We knew immediately that Lily would feel right at home there and that she'd have the chance to finally do all of the things that I wanted for her at home, but wasn't equipped to provide alone. So here it was: a group of like-minded people who were committed to helping us preserve our daughter's precious childhood. It was the community we were yearning for.

By a stroke of luck and a lot of resourceful penny pinching, we have made our first of many large payments to the school. What I see each time I hang a piece of laundry on the line to dry, or opt for the super-saver shoe special, though, is a promise. A promise to

Lily to always give her the very best I can. And a promise to me, to remember that I'm not in this alone. For try as I might to create the perfect life for my children, I cannot do it by myself. My babies have angels of their own.

~Kimberly Beauchamp

29

Every Mother Is a Working Mother

The phrase "working mother" is redundant.
~Jane Sellman

I t was the kind of splendid September day when sending kids to school just feels wrong. Fortunately, that year I was home schooling and calling the shots. Plus we were living in California, an hour from the Pacific Ocean. For all I knew, it could have been the last day of summer, and we wouldn't want to miss that. So it was off to the ocean with five children under eight—Josh, Matt, Ben, Zach, and Sophia.

Together, we cleaned up from breakfast, prepped the car, and then gathered beach blankets, umbrella, towels, swimsuits, diapers, sunglasses, sand toys, first aid kit, sunscreen, a cooler full of snacks and drinks—ay yi yi yi yi! Hello, motherhood; goodbye spontaneity. I loaded the assorted car seats and strapped, snapped, and buckled five wiggling bodies into Big Blue—the 1989 Suburban we outgrew only a few years later. We were on our way.

With everyone else in school, the whole beach was ours. I staked out our territory close to the water, hauled everything down from the car, and set up camp. For five hours I served as personal valet, sunscreen slatherer, weather advisor, recreation director, swim instructor, lifeguard, EMT, food concessionaire, manners consultant, bus boy, interpreter, peace negotiator, psychologist... not to mention keeper of the lost-and-found.

Finally, I hauled everything back to the car, strapped, snapped, and buckled five sunscreen-and-sand-coated-but-no-longer-wiggly warm, limp bodies back into Big Blue and headed for home. The sun through the window was soothing, and the car was full of contentment. It had been a wonderful day and I was pleased with myself as a mother. Then, from the back seat, I heard Zachary clear his throat, and in his deadpan four-year-old Eeyore voice ask, "Mom, when are you going to get a job?"

"This is my job," I said, somewhat amused and just a little edgy.

Homeward bound with the kids falling asleep one by one, I was left alone with my thoughts. I began to see the beauty of Zach's question. Somehow—even though it could be hard work and even though I had my testy moments—my kids didn't think of motherhood as a job.

And I decided that was a good thing because it's not really a job at all, but a calling. And callings just don't look like jobs, because they require more of a person than a job requires. This is particularly true of stay-at-home mothers whose days are spent conquering mountains of laundry, creating peanut butter and jelly sandwiches, and kissing owies.

We live in a world where success is measured by progress, as recorded on report cards, sales reports, performance reviews, pay raises and symbolized by ribbons, trophies, and merit badges. In our lifetimes, our husbands and children will bring scores of these items home and make us proud. We'll put them in scrapbooks, sew them on uniforms, frame and hang them up for all to see.

But I don't know of any special awards for teaching a child to tie her shoe or come to dinner when called. No raises or praises when a mother drops everything to drive someone out for poster board—"your project's due tomorrow? But it's almost eight o'clock!"

Every day this goes on with everyday moms doing everyday things—sometimes struggling with feelings of inferiority or even worthlessness—just being obedient to their calling.

But while motherhood can look easy (after all, it certainly is not rocket science), the irony is this: while lots of important people in important places conduct lots of important business every day, the truly most important work in the whole world is really going on at home, where the CEO is mommy.

I guess if we got disgruntled enough from lack of appreciation, we could start a Mommy Power movement with bumper stickers that say, "If Momma ain't happy, ain't nobody happy."

We could sue people who put us down at parties and maybe even become a protected minority.

But that wouldn't be very mommy-like, would it? Because there's something about mommies that should be soft where others are hard, kind where others are cruel, patient where others can't wait. We may not start out that way at all, but there's absolutely nothing like motherhood to change anything about us that needs to be changed.

At least, that's how it's been on my motherhood journey. I set out to make a home, to grow a family, and to help my children reach their potential.

The most amazing thing is that while I was helping them reach theirs, they were helping me reach mine.

~Barbara Curtis

30

The Evolution of My Anxiety Dream

I don't think that all good mothers have to bake and sew and make beds...
some of the finest never go into their kitchens at all.
~Kathleen Norris

My freshman year of college I signed up for a class that met at 9:00 A.M. The entire football team was told to take this course about the maritime exploration of the world because it was so easy. It was nicknamed "Boats." As it turned out, the irresponsible eighteen-year-old that I was found it impossible to attend a class that met "so early" so I never went. And I mean never.

When the time came to take the final exam for Boats, which was the only grade for the entire year, I prepared answers for the questions I found on the old exams in the college library, figuring that the ancient professor wouldn't be creative enough to make up new questions after decades of teaching the same course. So the football team and I took the final exam and I got a C-plus, barely surviving one of my dumbest freshman year decisions.

For many years after that, I had a recurring nightmare about taking an exam for a course that I had never attended.

As my business career advanced in my twenties and thirties, that dream was replaced by one in which I had to make a presentation at a business meeting for which I was totally unprepared. I had no

PowerPoint, no knowledge of the subject matter, and a large room full of people looking at me expectantly.

In my forties, when I worked only part-time from home, that dream was replaced by one in which I had invited a large number of people for a dinner party and I had forgotten to prepare at all. There was no food, no table set, nothing. This nightmare marked a major evolution for me as a mother, since I had spent the first four decades of my life completely unable to cook anything.

My first cooking disaster occurred when I was twelve and I obtained my grandmother's coveted fudge recipe. I carefully followed the instructions, right down to including her secret ingredient—one tablespoon of coffee. The fudge came out black, shiny, and hard. It looked and felt like a polished piece of lava. This was right around the time the astronauts landed on the moon, so there were lots of jokes about "Amy's moon rocks" around our house.

Neither of my parents drank coffee, so it was only about two decades later, when I was a full-fledged member of the caffeine club, that I realized my grandmother meant that I should include a tablespoon of actual brewed coffee, not the instant coffee flakes that I had carefully stirred into the mixture.

The next cooking disaster that stands out occurred years later, when I attempted to make pancakes for my young children. The pancakes came out so hard that the kids ended up using them as Frisbees. They were inedible, but perfectly round and aerodynamic. After playing with them all day, the kids left them in our backyard, which was fully populated with deer, coyote, raccoons, rabbits, birds, and other hungry creatures, but the pancake Frisbees were still there the next morning. It was only after another night outside—and the sprinklers running for six hours—that the pancakes apparently softened up enough to be eaten, since they had finally disappeared by the third morning.

Another time, I decided to make iced tea for my book group. It may be hard to believe, but I actually had to look up the recipe for iced tea. I diligently placed the tea bags in a saucepan full of water, with the paper tags hanging over the edge as instructed, and turned on the gas. It was good I had the water, since every one of those paper tags immediately burst into flames.

I was married to the second son of four sons, and his mother had decided that he would be the son who learned to cook. He was great at it, so I did not know how to cook anything. He even made our coffee every morning.

It was a little embarrassing—I had to discretely avoid baking or cooking assignments for school functions. I was the mother who always volunteered to bring the paper goods, spending umpteen dollars on paper plates, cups, napkins, etc. just to avoid bringing in a theoretically edible item. My downfall came with birthday cupcakes—moms really do have to make those for their kids' birthdays. One time, I tried to make cupcakes, from a mix no less, and instead of rising in the oven, they came out shaped like cups. My kids thought it was great—I had to fill in the craters with lots of extra frosting before I could even add the frosting domes on top. The poor teacher must have wondered why her students were all bouncing off the ceiling that day.

One day, my little daughter came home from school, excited about something new that she had learned in kindergarten. "Did you know that in some families the mommy cooks?" she asked, as surprised as if she had just discovered that women could be five-star generals or Catholic priests.

When the chef and I divorced a few years later, my kids learned to live on a diet of takeout food and pizza. And then I married a man who has trouble even making an ice cube.

So I learned to cook, and it turns out that it is fun and easy! I realized that what I really hated was following recipes—if I can just make up my own recipe, I'm happy, and the food is really good. As I cut back on my part-time work to focus more on my kids, my cooking got better and better and the kids stopped searching the garbage for the empty takeout containers they suspected I was hiding. I have a whole book of my recipes now, and I have successfully served many Christmas Eve dinners for twenty-five people, making almost every item from scratch. Whenever I visit my kids at college, I bring a cooler full of frozen servings of their favorite "mom" meals.

We must all have a "themed" anxiety dream of our own. I was so happy and proud that the recurrent nightmare of my forties had evolved to focus on my new prowess as a cook, instead of revolving around business meetings or college exams.

Then last year I turned fifty and became an empty nester. I went back to work more than full-time as the very busy publisher of Chicken Soup for the Soul. The kids are gone, I work every waking moment, and I haven't cooked anything in months. The other night I had a new nightmare—that 25,000 copies of one of our books came back from the printer filled with handwritten annotations and other horrible mistakes. I sure hope this isn't going to be my new anxiety dream for this decade. I'd better pull out those recipes and make time for a few dinner parties.

~Amy Newmark

31

He May Be My Boy, But He's His Own Person

*There is nothing more thrilling in this world, I think,
than having a child that is yours, and yet is mysteriously a stranger.*
~Agatha Christie

When I was pregnant with my son, my sister-in-law sent me a poem about little boys. I have no idea what it said because, in my hormone-saturated state, there was no way I was going to read something about tiny hands and tossing balls and watching my son grow into a man and then leave me. I had enough things to send me into fits of weepiness, like seeing the cat lick her paw or the commercial for cold medicine featuring a cartoon mommy and baby octopus. I hid the poem (okay, I threw it out) and figured I was safe from the philosophical ponderings of the mother/child relationship.

But of course, karma came back to bite me.

On my way to the grocery store the other day, I flipped on the radio just in time to hear Dennis Miller (yes, the old *Saturday Night Live Weekend Update* anchor) recite a poem by Kahlil Gibran called *On Children*.

As he spoke, I turned up the volume. There was no snarkiness in his voice. No drama. He read it simply and slowly, and there I was, in the grocery store parking lot, wiping my eyes with a crumpled-up Starbucks napkin.

What really stuck with me were the parts about how your children do not belong to you, because they come "through" you, not "from" you, and the reminder that they have their own thoughts, not their parents' thoughts.

Oh sure, it made me weepy, but it also made me feel a bit smug and self-righteous. "Hooray for me! I'm a great parent because I already realize what he was reciting. Henri is his own person! I will respect his decisions and let him lead his own life. I will give him roots and wings!"

It was at this point that I needed an older woman—someone who had raised ten kids and lived to tell the tale—to come along and smack me upside the head. I needed her to tell me it ain't as easy as it looks. Because just a few days later, during the play date from hell, my toddler would put me to the challenge.

To be fair, perhaps the "hell" part is a bit of an overstatement. There weren't any accidental fires and no zombies were raised from the dead. But one very out-of-control child running recklessly through my house was enough to frazzle my nerves and have me reaching for the martini shaker well before happy hour.

As soon as the boy arrived at my door, I knew it was going to be a long day. He screamed in terror when my cat slinked around the corner. He clung to his mother for a full ten minutes, then, without warning, sprang from her lap, his eyes wide with devilish mischief. He ran. He pushed the other kids. He bumped into walls, smeared grape jelly on the chair, and grabbed the cat's tail. One child whispered to his mother, "I don't like that boy!"

I tried to maintain a pleasant demeanor. While the child's mother chatted with the other grown-ups, I kept my eyes on him, ready to intervene when necessary. When he stole a toy, I gently explained it was time to share. When he jumped on the couch, I told him we don't do that and moved him to the floor. But when he gave my son a full-on body slam, I felt my patience wear thinner than a store-brand baby wipe. I rushed to my son's side and picked him up. He wasn't crying—what a trooper! But wait. Not only was he not crying, he was actually laughing.

I couldn't believe it. My little man was knocked down on his butt by this pint-sized bruiser, and he was laughing. I wanted my son to be angry. I wanted him to push back. I would've even settled for some tears, in hopes of making the other boy learn his lesson. But no. Mr. "The Sippy Cup is Half Full" was giggling, and when I released him from my protective hug, he engaged the Tiny Terror in a game of chase.

In that moment, I actually grasped the idea for the first time that my son really is his own person. Before Henri even entered this world, his father and I discussed how, whatever path in life he decided to take, we'd be okay with it. What if he decided to be a Republican, despite our decidedly Democratic leanings? What if he wanted to become a plumber instead of going to college? An atheist/pagan/Unitarian Universalist? A vegan? We were okay with anything. But those were all decisions that he'd make when he was an adult. We never once considered the choices he'd make as a child—choices we'd have no control over.

I was struck with a sudden fear of the unknown and endless questions. What if Henri turned out to be the kid who befriends the class bully? Or what if he was a morning person (which I am most certainly not), or got carsick and didn't like to travel, or hated something I loved, like chocolate? In my own fantasies about what my son would be like, I always imagined he'd inherit the best of both his father and me. He'd have his father's optimism and intelligence, and my creativity and sense of humor. But you just can't predict these things. Like his physical features (I just assumed he'd have brown hair and brown eyes, never figuring I'd end up with a strawberry blond with blue eyes), his personality would totally be his own.

And now I have to accept that I also have a son who came through me, but not from me. A child who has his own thoughts and personality. And happily, a boy who bounces back quickly when he's knocked down.

The poem contained more sage advice: *You may strive to be like them, but seek not to make them like you.* Perhaps I really should take a lesson from Henri and learn to laugh more, even when I get pushed down.

~Patti Woods

32

Some Kind of Angel's Eye View

The story of a mother's life: Trapped between a scream and a hug.
~Cathy Guisewite

I don't remember exactly what kind of ordinary disaster we were weathering that afternoon. Whatever it was, my two-year-old son needed some time alone to think about it. I explained this to him as I cast him into the horrible dungeon that was a sunny bedroom full of toys. I closed the door and held it shut from the outside.

The latch just barely clicked into position before the wood began to shake as rock-hard plastic projectiles smashed against the inside of the door. Above the racket of crashing toys, my toddler cursed me in some primal language it's probably best I don't understand. Between barrages of crashing and cursing, a sweet television voice still crooned from where it had been abruptly abandoned in the living room. The cartoon Wendy of *Peter Pan* was breathing through her familiar discourse on motherhood:

"A mother, a real mother, is the most wonderful person in the world. She has an angel voice...."

Standing in the hallway, gripping the doorknob with my hand clenched like a flesh and blood padlock of my little boy's prison, I called through the closed door, "You're not coming out until you settle down." My voice in the hall sounded nothing like the angel from the cartoon fantasy—a simpering, doting angel, beautiful but bent beneath heavily feathered wings smelling faintly like a henhouse. Maybe I was more like an angel from the *Book of Revelation* —twelve feet tall, steaming with sulfur, soaring white-hot over a two-year-old's apocalypse.

I hoped that, in truth, I was neither kind of angel.

Forehead against the door's cheap wooden veneer, I remembered a time when I was newly married, healthy, happy and—much to my surprise—not applying to graduate school. Instead, I used my university-trained mental faculties to draft a document my husband and I called "The Baby Plan." There, in blue handwriting on a single sheet of foolscap, we etched a genius plot. It outlined how we could start having our children while we were still young and poor. Even when we factored in the reality that my husband had four years left of his education, some inexplicable calculus of hope and faith held The Baby Plan together. The most amazing thing about the plan was that none of it depended on me working outside our home after the babies joined our family. I would keep collecting rent and vacuuming the dingy red carpet in the hallways of our apartment building, but other than that we would live on love—and student loans.

From the beginning, I knew the choice of a life path that wound mostly through the hidden depths of my own home was a controversial decision. Well-meaning people warned that, after my maternity benefits ran out on the baby's six-month birthday, the poverty of our student life would drive me back to an entry-level job and drive the baby into the arms of a subsidized day care. I didn't believe it. We set out to whack a divot out of the myth that careers in full-time, unpaid mothercare are luxuries young mothers can never afford.

Exactly according to plan, I celebrated our first wedding anniversary vomiting non-alcoholic wine in the bathroom of our inner-city apartment. From those first hideous moments of pregnancy to the present day, everything about mothering has been far more difficult, less instinctive, and more grueling than I had anticipated. The evening after I left the hospital with my first snuffling, suckling bundle of humanity, I lay on the shabby living room carpet and let the last of my old self run out of my eyes as tears. I finished my cry and settled down to a long career in mothercare.

Some days I knew it would be easier to leave my spirited son and the four brothers who followed him with strangers than it would be for me to stay home and care for them myself. And I missed my old self—her briefcase full of bar graphs and airplane tickets, her uninterrupted nights of sleep. I'll always be grateful for the choice she made to trigger this maternal nuclear fission—the constant exploding and expanding inside me, as I divide myself over and over and over again among my children. I think my old self would agree that a career in mothercare was the best possible evolution of her original feminism and humanism.

I went home to stay within arm's reach of my children over eleven years ago and I'm still here today. I stayed here during every moment of my husband's education. I stayed here even when we lived in a boomtown notorious for its outlandishly high cost of living. It was frustrating when people tried to tell me how "lucky" I was to be here. Luck is not the same thing as finding the faith and fortitude to stick by the hard choice to sacrifice comforts and aspirations in favor of caring for one's own children all day, every day. I believe our family was blessed for our faith in mothercare, and two weeks before my oldest son's tenth birthday, our onerous student loans were repaid in full.

Though the angel mother from Wendy's song seems as distant from me as ever, my dedication to full-time mothercare has given me something like an angel's eye view. I walk the fuzzy line where what begins as ironic becomes miraculous. It doesn't take very long before the bedroom door stops shaking and my little boy is sitting miserably repentant in an empty toy box, ready to come back into my arms again. Especially on days like these, I know it's from here at home, better than from anywhere else I've been, that I see the world as it really is—a family badly in need of forgiveness, sharing, and unconditional love.

~Jennifer Quist

Power
MOMS

Becoming a Specialist

Stay-at-Home Mothers in Special Circumstances

33

Teaching Them to See

The most beautiful things in the world cannot be seen or even touched; they must be felt with the heart.

~Helen Keller

My mom has eyes at the ends of her fingertips," my then four-year-old son blurted to his friend.

I chuckled, but then marveled at his insight. He was absolutely right. After losing my sight, I used my hands to feel my surroundings, find items in the kitchen, sort the family's clothing and pick up toys from the floor. In reality, my whole world became "seen" by my fingertips. When I touched something, the image was immediately transmitted to my brain, allowing me to see with my mind. Eventually, I learned to use my other senses so I could still be a mommy to my little ones.

But initially, my adjustment to blindness was not easy. The hereditary retinal disease struck like an unexpected storm, rumbling with rage, viciously destroying my retina and with it, my family's dreams.

In a brief, eighteen-month period, those dreams of being a stay-at-home mom to my three-, five- and seven-year-old sons halted with a horrifying screech. At first, my field vision reduced to the size of a keyhole. And with desperation, I pleaded and begged God to allow that vision, though small, to remain so I could still see their smiles.

While my youngest son slept, I'd stare at his features, attempting to memorize every detail — his long eyelashes against his chubby olive cheeks and his curly hair framing his round face. With tears blurring my diminishing vision, I engraved those images in my aching heart. Uncertain of the length of time I'd have that tiny amount of sight, the rope of anxiety and worry choked me. Tormenting thoughts of my sons bearing scars of shame from having a blind mom invaded my sleepless nights.

Ophthalmologists offered no hope. One told us that if there should ever be a cure, we would know first because it would be all over the news.

With my husband's support, I entered the waiting stage. A forced smile masked my face, hoping my children wouldn't see the turmoil that rumbled within me. Just a few months later, my vision closed in completely. The gray nothing before my eyes shoved me into a dark prison surrounded with bars of anger, bitterness and resentment.

Weeks later, the very desperation that burned in my heart forced me to look up. God then eased peace into my soul and wisdom into my thinking. My sons needed me more than I needed my sight.

Armed with a new attitude, I resolved to still be their mommy and to use my commitment to care for them and my love to nurture them. My ears became tuned to their every sound, alerting me to their antics or whimpers of pain.

I quickly learned that whenever facing obstacles, opportunities usher in — to learn acceptance, increase creativity, deepen determination and above all, choose optimism over gloom. And with that renewed attitude, I accepted the adjustments in all aspects of our family's routine.

Within that busy schedule, learning Braille dropped to the bottom of my list of priorities. Without sight, the daily tasks of running the house took twice as long to finish, eating up most of the day and leaving me drained by evening. By bedtime, rather than practice reading those dots on a Braille book, I listened to cassette tapes for inspiration from the Bible and thus, drew courage for the next day.

In each one of those days, creativity became my best friend. I swept and mopped the kitchen floor barefoot, so my feet picked up any crumbs or sticky spots I'd missed. My memory also developed like a muscle after long workouts. I memorized lists of phone numbers. In a moment's notice, I'd call a friend for a ride for my sons or to ask about school details, which other moms read from the notes their children brought home.

I also made my own mental notes of dates and times for my sons' activities and commitments at school. And though some mischievous behavior might have gone unnoticed, I gathered confidence to discipline them.

"Come here young man," I ordered my six-year-old. "What are you eating?"

"Nothing," he said, his voice muffled, no doubt trying to hide something.

I drew closer as the smell of chocolate wafted even stronger. "Give me those M&Ms." I held out my hand. "It's dinner time."

Once he obeyed, he ran off with a distinct dragging sound on the floor. "And tie those shoe laces, you're going to fall."

They soon learned Mom was still in control. Often I wondered if they truly knew I saw nothing. But I knew what my heart saw—a lesson my sons would learn from their mom who couldn't see. I'd teach them with my attitude, common sense and most of all, a sense of humor.

We played games and tricked each other. During bedtime one evening, I stepped in my youngest son's room and noticed it to be more quiet than usual. I tiptoed toward his bed, felt for the pillow, and leaned down to kiss him. But my lips met a surface quite different than his round cheek. Knowing I'd be coming in to kiss him, he'd gone headfirst under the covers, and my kiss on his toes evoked a muffled laughter under the blankets.

That laughter replaced sadness and a renewed attitude replaced self-pity. Looking back, dreams I'd crafted, uniquely tailored according to my plans, had shattered and expectations of how our lives would be had vanished. But, to my delight, different dreams became reality, with a richer lesson, a deeper sense of appreciation and a more profound love. I'd become a mommy who could do—not because of what I possessed or lacked, but with what I chose to give.

I'd planned to teach my sons about life's beauty, its wonders and its adventures. But rather than teach them to see what the world holds for them, I taught them what their hearts should hold for the world to see.

~Janet Eckles

34

Yes, I Am

There is cool water in being a mother, there is steam;
there is salt, there is sweetness, there is bitter, there is utterly delicious.
~Anne Lamott

I never wanted to be a traditional mother. I was far too cool for that and besides, my own mother and grandmother made it look un-fun. My life plans included being a superhero, savior of the universe, doctor, lawyer, and actress. Definitely not a mom.

Fast-forward thirty years. Do I need to tell you that I'm a mom? Of course not. And until very recently not even an "also" mom, meaning "I'm a mom, but I'm also a (fill in the blank with the profession that legitimizes your existence in small talk at cocktail parties)." By the way, where are all these wonderful cocktail parties I read about people making small talk at? Anyway. I stay home. With my children, who have never been to day care (give or take a few months). Pretty conventional, right? No one is more surprised by this than I am. Me. Founder of WOW in high school—that's Women of the World, which in my teenage mind meant the beginning of gendered mutiny across the globe.

After college, I worked at various jobs, from social worker to bookseller. I got married, went to graduate school, worked in corporate America, traveled, taught English as a Second Language at a posh private academy, and got a Ph.D. from a top twenty-five school. All so I could be a mom. It's a head scratcher, but wait... it gets even more astonishing: I wouldn't change a thing.

Somewhere around the age of fifteen, I had an epiphany. My version of the epiphany story is that I saw my best friend Ginny's list of goals for her life on her closet door. Number four was to adopt a child. My self-absorbed fifteen year-old heart burned with shame when I read it. I was wholly and entirely focused on me, me, me. But Ginny was like that, mature beyond her years. Her goal became my goal. If I ever wanted a child, I would adopt. What's funny is that Ginny swears she had no such list and no such goal. But my epiphany stuck and five years into my marriage, I was working on my dissertation on the obscure Virginia Woolf book, *Three Guineas*, and ready to start a family. And so we adopted.

Coursework on gender inequality and sexism led me to China, where more than one million baby girls were reportedly stuck in orphanages, without homes or families, simply because of their gender. I had a little first-hand experience with that type of gendered rejection, so off I went to collect my perfect baby girl. Clearly, there is a God and she is kind, because I was given a calm baby who could sleep anywhere. In other words, the beginner model. Mothering didn't come easy. The planning and responsibility of having to pack a bag and strap another being into a car seat before I could hit the road weighed on my flighty free spirit. My daughter was easy; I wasn't.

It all got better with practice. As my daughter thrived, I finished my dissertation, survived my husband's eleven-month layoff, and away we went to a new life in Providence, Rhode Island—home to the Rhode Island School of Design, Brown University, and really old money. We were fish out of water, but we made do. With our daughter now five, we were lonely for another child and so was she. We adopted another little girl from China, a toddler, who had complications from cleft lip and palate, was Hepatitis C positive, and at age three, was already considered "old." I'd integrate her into our family and jump back into the world of work without even breaking a sweat. Ready, set, whoa!

Our new addition had a difficult transition into family life. She'd lived in an orphanage all her life. Family life in a house in America was stressful for her, and sometimes she'd just spin out of control, running into brick walls head first (on purpose) or trying to jump out the second story windows. Constant supervision was required. No work for now. On we went, becoming a family of four, dreaming of a time when things would be simpler.

Our second daughter did integrate into our family and became a delight to be around. Always happy, she sings and dances her way through the day, draws and makes books, and dreams of a future filled with her own store, church, restaurant, four children, and a light green van. She is magical. When she hit age five, she was a fully adjusted member of our family. Life had gotten easier. The kids could bathe themselves, they spent their days at school, mealtime was less messy... you can guess how this turns out. Yep. We got another one. But this time, things turned out very differently.

Eight years old, from Ethiopia, daughter number three was shell-shocked when we met her and remained shell-shocked three months later. She didn't adjust and her behavior spiraled downward. Her terror was so palpable I thought I could reach out and touch it. We took her to therapy and received lists of diagnoses, most of them just polite ways of saying she was mentally ill.

Sounds like a nightmare, right? It was, at first, before we knew what was going on. But once she was diagnosed and medicated and under the care of a therapist five times a week, things returned to normal. But there is no more talk about me returning to the world of corporate work. Our newest requires more tending than a work schedule would allow. And more energy. So here I am, nearly nine years into parenting, still at home. A full-time, stay-at-home mom, the last thing I ever imagined I would be. And I enjoy it!

Being a mom is both what I thought it would be and the opposite of what I expected, all at the same time. Sometimes, my day is about the mundane: stain removal, pushing vegetables into disinterested children's bellies, and stimulating their minds. Other days, it is sublime, like when we sit, my daughters and I, at bedtime and talk about the hard things, the things I want them to hear from nobody else but me.

If I'm conventional, so be it. Four days a week I blissfully enter my upstairs office and write. I paint and meditate and read in order to maintain my sanity. And on occasion, I do imagine a time when others do not occupy the bulk of my energy. Yet even now, I appreciate it. Sometimes it's fun. Other times it's difficult. But it's never dull. Motherhood is one of those jobs with that tricky clause at the bottom of the job description that says, "...and other duties as required by employer."

What would I tell my teenage self now? Relax. Motherhood will allow you to re-visit your childhood, to do all the things you wished you'd done more of as well as the things you were never comfortable doing. It will bring you magnificent joy, deep fulfillment, and a sense of pride and confidence in your very womanhood. Parenting satisfies me in a way little else does. It'll be a tough act to follow.

~Robin D. Hayes, Ph.D.

I Am Loved

Husbands may desert their wives and wives their husbands.
But a mother's love endures through all.
~Washington Irving

On a sweltering hot Wednesday in July, 1999, I became a first-time mum to a tiny, perfect baby girl, Sophie. Since that day motherhood has been my priority. Whatever else happens, I put my children first. It is this belief that got me through the hardest years of my life.

My second daughter, Jane was born on the last day of March, 2002. I was determined not to have an April Fools' baby, which might explain why she came quickly. Within hours I was home, another beautiful daughter in my arms, the luckiest woman on earth.

I had all the ingredients for happiness—detached home in the English countryside, two healthy children and a clever husband. I gave up teaching to become a full-time mother and devoted myself to making my children and my husband happy.

That's what the outside world saw. But I was so lonely that it hurt. I cried myself to sleep most nights. I felt like running away and letting somebody else deal with the demands of my life. I had trouble with simple jobs like making a sandwich. I did ridiculous things like putting the laundry in the oven, and I had no idea why.

I went to see my doctor. She diagnosed Postnatal Depression and organized a home appointment with my health visitor.

I remember that day. I remember sitting in the kitchen, listening to my options. Medication, group therapy, or more home visits. I didn't want any of them and decided on a fourth option—to snap out of it.

There are moments that change your life forever, flashes of realization that show you how things truly are. One of those moments happened when the health visitor gave me a leaflet explaining how my husband needed to be patient, understanding and supportive. Just as I was skimming this information he came into the hall and ran his finger along the skirting boards.

"Look at the state of these," he said.

My husband said this kind of thing a lot, but on that occasion I heard the meaning behind it.

You see, over the years I had known about, but never faced, my husband's Obsessive-Compulsive Disorder. He didn't suffer badly, but it was enough. Magazines should be parallel with the edge of the table, sofas ought not be sat on in exactly the same spot or else they would wear thin, all toys must be put away, the dishwasher should be emptied as soon as the cycle finishes, the children must be scrubbed from head to foot every night, the kitchen floor must be swept each day, the sinks ought to be as shiny as our neighbor's... I was tired of it. Tired of trying to be perfect, tired of never achieving perfection, tired of knowing I never would. Yet I battled on because I loved my family and didn't want to hurt them.

Things improved. I began to feel better and, by the time Jane was a year old I had started a pre-school music workshop and had become chairperson for our local playgroup committee. These roles helped me to feel that I was worth something, but there was still an aching loneliness. My husband was away with work a lot. I felt like a single mum.

Over the months I fought and fought to make our family right, but nothing worked and I began to run out of energy, and will, and hope. But then something happened to change everything.

It was the day after Halloween. My husband seemed angry because I didn't want him to go to London without us. I was fed up with being left behind week after week. It became an argument and in the heat of it he admitted he'd been having an affair over the past six months. He told me she had recently moved into a house just around the corner. He declared that he was in love. And he said it all in front of little Sophie.

True emotional anguish is hard to describe. It is as if an invisible hand pulls and squeezes and tears at your insides. Every thought has a spiteful sting, and tears are in your eyes even when they are dry. You think you will never be happy again. You are afraid and defenseless. You feel worthless.

I told my husband to leave, to go to this other woman and never come home. I phoned everybody I knew to let them know I was alone. I tipped every drop of alcohol down the sink so as not to be tempted, and I dismantled everything that represented our marriage—his belongings, family photos, every memory was removed from the house so that I could concentrate on moving on. Although I was in pain, I was free, and I knew I had not failed. He had.

For several weeks I lived on adrenaline. I ate hardly a mouthful and slept very little. But everything went on as normal for the sake of my girls, especially Sophie, who had just begun her first year at school. There were times when I broke down, but always by myself. They never saw the tears. They were washed and dressed and fed and cuddled just like before.

I look back at myself in 2003, so thin, so vulnerable, so tenacious, and I am amazed by my achievements. I organized my own divorce—went to the law courts alone, collected the forms, deciphered the legal jargon without a solicitor. I sold the house and bought a small property with the equity, and decorated it and moved into it within a year. I went to visit my husband in his new home, met his partner, shook her hand and introduced her to Sophie and Jane as "the lady Daddy loves now."

On an icy evening in late February I went on a date. It began snowing so heavily that we almost cancelled. It is good that we didn't because I met somebody very special. The following week he took me, Sophie and Jane for a walk by the lake, and he brought bread to feed the swans. Over the following months he was there for me, even though I clung to him one minute and pushed him away the next.

It took a whole year for me to realize he wasn't going to bully me, criticize me, change me, or make me cry. I stopped living in fear. I no longer flinched when touched. I stopped being paranoid about mess and cleanliness; the children could be noisy, use glitter and get muddy and it didn't matter. I could be me. We could be a family.

In January, 2006, we bought a house together and in 2007 we had a baby girl, Pippa.

Sophie and Jane call him Daddy. I shop, I cook, I clean, I wash, I iron, I write, I paint, I teach, I garden, I wipe bottoms. I am in love, I am loved. And I am happy.

~Isla Penrose

36

Sean

The beauty of the world has two edges, one of laughter, one of anguish,
cutting the heart asunder.
~Virginia Woolf

Never did I imagine that my introduction to motherhood would involve seven in-vitro procedures, three D&Cs, and the death of a child.

I am a typical wife and mother in many ways; I had a career in banking before I married at the age of thirty-six. After two years of trying to start a family on our own we got pregnant with our first IVF try and my son Ian was born in 2003. Having him was, of course, wonderful, but a huge life change for me as I was used to doing what I wanted to do when I wanted to do it, and now my whole life was this little boy. The second time around we were not so lucky and it took six IVF cycles to have our twins. I found out during a level two ultrasound at twenty weeks that "Baby A" had a heart defect. Our world would never be the same.

My children give me a reason to get up every day and here I am, still breathing, a year and a half after burying my seven-month-old son Sean.

I struggle daily to come up with reasons why this happened to my family. I feel fortunate in the way that Sean died because I know that his death will make a difference. My perspective on being a mother has changed since his death. Instead of being an over-protective mother when my five-year-old climbs up the jungle gym, I ask myself what would be the worst thing that could happen if he were to fall? He may have to go to the emergency room for some stitches or a concussion, but he won't die.

When I hear my two year old crying out for me in the middle of the night, half of me says, "Ugh. Please go back to sleep." But the other part of me relishes that I have the privilege of tucking her back in, stroking her hair, and kissing her face. When the dreaded bedtime routine starts after a long day, I remind myself that I would give anything to give Sean one more bath, to caress his soft skin and hear him laugh with delight. His last solid food was a jar of carrots and I can't help but see his face as I stroll down the baby food aisle at the supermarket.

My husband has become a softy with discipline since Sean's death; he can't stand to see our children unhappy. When the dreaded "I hate you" is screamed when a privilege or toy is taken away, he doesn't want these to be the last words he hears his child say, so he gives in. A photo of Sean is a reminder that he will never see him again in this lifetime; the finality of his death is anguish.

Sean's congenital heart defect was diagnosed as Hypoplastic Left Heart Syndrome. In layman's terms, his left ventricle stopped growing and he would require a series of three surgeries over the first two years of his life to reroute his blood. I read up and realized that this heart fix would be good for about twenty years and then my son would need a heart transplant, that is if he made it through the pregnancy without going into cardiac arrest before he was born.

My son Sean and daughter Delaney were born at thirty-six weeks; Sean's fight to stay alive in the womb is the reason my daughter just celebrated her second birthday. Sean had his first heart surgery at five days old and came home six weeks after he was born. He was home for four months before he was to undergo his second surgery, which was a great success, but the day before he was to come home, something devastating happened. He had a heart attack in my husband's arms.

Sean was revived, but his heart was severely damaged and could no longer function on its own. He was placed on life support and our agonizing wait for a pediatric heart began. If this had happened at any other age my son would be alive today. The hardest organs to come by are pediatric ones. Babies are not supposed to die. When a family is approached while their child is dying, and asked to think about "harvesting" the organs, it seems barbaric and an invasion of privacy. It is incredibly difficult to be in such an agonizing situation, to think about saving dozens of other lives but only with the organs of your precious baby.

No amount of money, connections, prayers, or networking could help us help our son. We had to depend upon the tragedy of another family to make the heart wrenching and incredibly selfless decision to donate their brain-dead infant's organs to keep Sean alive. We needed an infant heart.

I was told Sean might tolerate the heart and lung machine for up to two weeks before problems would arise. Sean was placed number one in the country on the donor waiting list but it took twenty-nine days to get a heart.

I want to thank the family who donated their infant's heart to Sean. The heart was healthy and strong; it functioned wonderfully when all of the clamps were released, but twenty-nine days of life support had taken a toll on Sean and they couldn't stop his bleeding. He never woke up from the surgery.

I have been an organ donor ever since I checked off the "yes" box on my driver's license application, but had never thought about organ donation for my child. Not that I wouldn't have donated, I just never thought I would outlive my children and the concept had never crossed my mind. I'm hoping that Sean's death will help other parents consider the idea of organ donation for their children before they find themselves in a situation when it's impossible to think clearly.

All we can do to honor Sean's memory is to stir up awareness about donation, particularly pediatric organ donation. We have set up a foundation in Sean's name so that perhaps one family can be spared the tragedy we went through. And, of course, we can love our surviving children with all our hearts.

I love and miss you my sweet blond haired blue-eyed smiling baby.

~Victoria Marsh

37

I Am a Mom, but Writing Won't Quit Me

Writing is the only thing that, when I do it,
I don't feel I should be doing something else.
~Gloria Steinem

Five kids banged through the door after school.

"Mom, I'm hungry."

"Mom, I need help with my essay."

"Mom, my best friend doesn't like me anymore."

"Mom, I don't want to do my chores."

"Mom, I have a science project due tomorrow."

I muttered, "I'm changing my name."

But then I wouldn't hear, "Mom, I love you." "Mom, come cuddle with me." "Mom, I had the best day." "Mom, take a walk with me."

These were the thoughts and feelings I wanted to jot down so I wouldn't forget them, if I only had the time.

Later, while I prepared dinner, the toddlers hung onto my legs. I finally picked one of them up while stirring a sauce on the stove. Then the other one wanted to be held too, so I sat them in their high chairs with a snack so I could use both hands to dice vegetables. Because I am partially blind, I carefully gauged with my fingers where to slice beyond them with the knife.

As I worked, the phone rang. I grabbed the bright red receiver off the wall.

"Are you busy? Dumb question," my friend Jenny chuckled.

The boys started pounding on their trays. I dragged the phone with a long cord around the kitchen and handed them each a piece of cheese.

"I'll only take a minute," Jenny continued. "I heard a profound quote just for you."

I balanced the phone on my ear.

"Here it is," Jenny said. "I might want to quit writing, but it won't quit me."

"I can't quit writing! I never got started," I complained.

"You won a contest at age ten and wrote for the city paper in high school. You've got what it takes."

"I figured I'd write when the kids grow up."

"Writing is a good career for a mom like you who wants to stay home."

"Dream on. With this mad house, I couldn't put two words together."

"Well, think about it," Jenny encouraged.

During the rest of meal preparations, I thought about what Jenny said. I need to write down these precious family memories to inspire others. Maybe I could earn a little money to help my struggling family of seven children.

Later when all the kids were in bed, I pondered some more. I longed to write. The ideas and emotions had to come out. They say who I am. I realized if I didn't begin to write now, I would keep putting it off with the excuse that I'm too busy with my large family.

How would I do it, being visually impaired? I had never let my disabilities get in the way of achieving anything. For example, with my kids, I found rides instead of being their taxi driver. They read ads to me for grocery specials so I could be frugal in shopping and buy in bulk.

My imagination wandered to lessons learned and situations I could write down—lively conversations at the dinner table or night talks when I tucked them in. I told them a story because I couldn't read one to them. Often, they told me one or listened to a story on tape. I hoped to write down all the firsts in my kids' lives that I would observe since I was lucky enough to work at home.

Even though I felt overwhelmed, I needed to find a way to fit writing into my schedule. I wanted to make a difference as a writer as well as a mother.

The next day the boys took a nap together, a novelty. Because of my processing about writing, I thought, "Why not?" I dragged out the typewriter and my feelings poured out. This is how I started a journal that would capture those moments and events with the kids.

I made an effort to write every day. It was one word, one snatched quiet moment at a time while the younger ones napped or rested and the other kids tended them or when they were all preoccupied. If I tried to create while having a toddler sitting on my lap, he did the freelancing, not I.

Sometimes inspiration would hit as the kids came through the door after school. They respected my busyness and would holler, "Hi! Mom, I'm home."

I would call back, "I'm here."

They didn't always need to talk. They wanted to know I was there.

When I typed, editing was tedious. I had to look closely to see the words and be careful the arm carrying the key that struck the roller didn't hit me in the nose. I used a magnifying glass to correct with Wite-Out, a taxing job for a partially blind person.

Persistence paid off. I was published by the time the last of my kids went to school. Now I had peace and long breaks to write; however, nothing stopped the flow of words quicker than a call from school stating that my child had punched someone on the playground.

Soon the rehabilitation worker saw my potential as a writer and purchased a computer with large print software. This made word processing easier. I could insert or erase by pressing a key command.

When my youngest children were almost through grade school, my partial sight started to deteriorate so I couldn't read large print easily. Because of my success as a writer, rehab gave me a computer with not only large print, but also speech capability. After that computer quit, I earned enough money on one article to buy another system with speech and large print.

Diminishing sight caused my work with word processing to be more difficult. My nose dusted the computer screen as I tried reading the print. With clear vision in only one corner of one eye, I leaned over the keyboard to see the page, ending each day with a backache.

One afternoon, while editing, my eyes ached from squinting. I squeezed them shut to rest. I noticed my daughter watching me.

"Mom, it really is harder for you. Let me help." It took her five minutes to do a task that normally takes me two hours.

I hugged her when she was done. "Thanks honey, that helped a lot."

The reason I kept writing comes down to celebrating slices of my life with others, especially my children. I gave each of them a scrapbook of my writing achievements, a legacy for them that shows a lifetime of experiences they can treasure and share with their children someday. My story lives on forever through them.

The sacrifice I put into creating a piece of writing was an accomplishment and well worth the effort. It's like having a baby. I forgot the travail I went through when I touched the pages of the magazine with my published article in it. I had a sense of satisfaction, just like the contentment I felt when holding my newborn infant. They are both a labor of love, only I realize being a mom holds the greater reward.

~Pam Bostwick

38

When the Path Chooses You

Children are the anchors that hold a mother to life.
~Sophocles

Tuesday, June 17th, 2008, marked the beginning of my first summer as a stay-at-home mom. It is a strange feeling not working. I enjoy it, but I also feel a little guilty. I know I am still working but having "home" as my only responsibility is foreign to me. My days are now filled with dishwashers, laundry and bike rides. It's almost like I'm cheating the system. Until I remember what put me in this position.

When my younger daughter, Alexa, was six months old, I returned to work full-time. I took a position that was thirty-two hours per week, teaching morning and afternoon preschool classes. I did my job poorly and I was deeply depressed. It wore me out.

There were two key reasons for my depression: Alexa had recently been diagnosed with encephalopathy (a disease similar to Cerebral Palsy), plus I had the sickening cost of day care to deal with. I barely made ten dollars an hour and I was paying almost three hundred dollars per week for childcare. Most months I brought home about two hundred bucks after childcare and taxes. There were a couple of months when I was in the red on payday. Suffice it to say, I was a mess.

Then came Alexa's sixteen-month check-up at the end of

February. I told our pediatrician that her left eye was floating. On closer examination, he agreed, wrote down the description in medical terminology and told me to mention it when we saw the neurologist the next week.

Neurologist check-ups always began with a chart review. He noticed she had undergone an MRI the previous July and that he had never seen the report. This was likely caused by a glitch in the radiology system. For some reason the films he ordered had been sent to Alexa's plastic surgeon. I could tell from the look on his face that the report was bad. I began to panic when he said, "I can't believe I haven't seen this until now."

If I was struggling before, I was drowning now. Did I mention my husband was working two states away? And I was in the middle of parent-teacher conferences at work. My mom stepped in and got Alexa to her MRI that week. I took calls from the neurosurgeon between Kindergarten Readiness meetings.

Alexa has an arachnoid cyst in her brain. Arachnoid cysts are pockets of fluid that form in the lining of the brain. Hundreds of babies are born every year with them and many never know about them their entire lives. Alexa was not so lucky. It is the educated guess of medical professionals that her disabilities are directly and indirectly related to this cyst. The cyst was originally found at eight weeks of age on an MRI. Her neurologist at the time sent us directly to a pediatric neurosurgeon for a more detailed evaluation. At that time, the cyst was small but precariously positioned. He felt that the risk of surgery far outweighed the current minimal dangers.

Now all of the risks were real. The cyst was pressing on her optic nerve. It was located in the operation center of the brain. Apparently, when she had a growth spurt, her cyst did as well. We were now dealing with a huge potential for debilitating sensory and motor function loss. The cyst was on the right side, thus explaining the left eye issue. To make matters worse, she had increased hydrocephalus (abnormal accumulation of fluid in the brain).

It was on a Friday afternoon as I was finishing up the conferences when I received the call I had been dreading. Our neurosurgeon told me quite plainly that the danger was high and that he had scheduled her for surgery the following Monday. "Wait!" I shouted, "Her dad is not here." After a few moments he said that as long she was not showing any signs of distress we could postpone it until Dad came home, but not a moment later.

Those three weeks between that call and her surgery were pivotal. It was at that time every year that I received my intent form for the next year of work. My poor performance as a teacher was noted and it was made clear to me that I was welcome to continue my morning class or take an opening in day care. Under no circumstances would I be hired to teach two classes.

This hurt my feelings, because in the past I had based my self-worth on my job. When I did well at work I felt good about myself as a person. I knew I was a productive member of society. Now all bets were off. My value was tied as much to my kids as it was to my job. I knew being a wiped out zombie everyday after work was not quality mothering. I engaged in heavy-duty soul searching. Then came marathon late night phone calls to my husband about our budget. It took us seven days to make a decision.

I checked "I do not plan to return to my position at this school for the 2006-2007 school year" on my intent form, and signed on the dotted line. I was both relieved and frightened. I knew that I was not surviving the limbo. I knew it was best for my girls for me to not be perpetually stressed. I knew Alexa needed to be in a more loving environment during the day.

Her surgery came and went. Alexa is a tough kid and she improved overnight. Her therapists noticed better coordination and her unexplained fussing ceased. She could sit up longer. Her left eye settled down. She was happier and so was I. I stayed at the school through the summer. I worked a tiny part-time job the following year so Makayla could take swimming and gymnastics lessons at a reduced rate. I left in August of last year.

I became a full-time stay-at-home mom shortly before Labor Day, 2007. It hasn't been easy but it has been worth it. My girls know where I am most hours of the day. We can splash in the pool, we can bake, and we can cuddle whenever we want. After all that we have been through, I think I will easily get used to seeing the rewards of my work on the faces of my children.

~Astacia Carter

Change in Plans

A bend in the road is not the end of the road... unless you fail to make the turn.
~Unknown

I had heard the expression, "There is one beautiful baby in the world and every mother has it," and when my son was born, I knew I had that baby. That is until things began to be not so perfect, and, eventually, my "number one son" was diagnosed with autism. Thus began the life I hadn't bargained for.

My parenting philosophy changed entirely with the diagnosis. I had always imagined myself as a mother who would push for my "number one son's" individualism, supporting any direction his nature took him. Now, I work hard to make him just like every other kid. He has things like Transformers, Pokémon and SpongeBob shoved down his throat, with the hope that they will help him connect with his peers. When we walk through a toy store, I watch what other little boys are begging their mothers for. When they drop to the ground in a temper tantrum, I step over their kicking feet to reach for that very item. If that is what typical boys desperately want, then that is what my boy shall have.

After four years of undergraduate study, a two-year master's degree, three years of law school and a year of articling—I imagined my credentials would land me a hot job downtown. I could picture it before it happened: swanky suit, power lunches, lipstick dabbed to perfection, Blackberry reminding me minute-by-minute how important I was as I sashayed in my Manolo Blahnik heels—cute and clever, heading into court!

Present day reality check: I just had my fifth baby, and my eldest, who recently turned eight, has autism. My lifestyle standards have adjusted, to say the least. Now my measure of a successful day is to get through it without smelling like baby pee or toddler puke. The vision of Manolo Blahniks has transformed into the reality of my favorite pair of fuzzy bunny slippers.

It did not take me long to realize that a legal career does not particularly accommodate women with small children, especially children with special needs. This is not to say that I don't have the opportunity to use my finely tuned legal skills—the definitions have just been altered. "Advocacy" now means being an expert on school board policies. I know what rights the law provides, I write to Members of Parliament, and I protest in the rain on the front lawn of our government offices for autism funding. And at home with five children, my skills in "negotiation" are constantly put to the test!

There is a fantastic poem by Emily Perl Kingsley called "Welcome to Holland" about life with a special needs child that was given to me when my son was first diagnosed. The poem compares having a child to planning a trip to Italy. You and all your friends are planning a trip to Italy, so you buy all the gear you'll need, learn some Italian and make plans to visit the Roman Coliseum. Everyone is going to the same place and seeing the same things. Then you have a child with a disability. You become separated from your friends, who made it to Italy. You instead find yourself in Holland. Now you have to learn a different language, become part of a different culture, and meet different people. But once you get used to Holland, you see that there are tulips, windmills and Rembrandts. It's not where you wanted to go, but you are there and it's not so bad.

When we have kids, there are no guarantees. I am not working in a swanky office downtown, but I am in Holland. My "number one son" brought us here and it is a place I love because I am here with him. It's not as glamorous as Rome, but I couldn't imagine being anywhere else.

~Julie Cole

I Never Wanted To Be a Supermom

Everybody knows that a good mother gives her children a feeling of trust
and stability. She is their earth. She is the one they can count on
for the things that matter most of all.
~Katharine Butler Hathaway

I never wanted to be a supermom. I just wanted to be a regular, run of the mill mom. You know the kind that is part nurse, part chauffer, part toy truck mechanic, and part nutritional and financial counselor. I didn't want to be the kind of mom who juggles career and family. I was content just being in charge of the home and family.

I will admit there were times when I felt judged for my decision. There were also times when finances dictated I do something to earn a little extra money. I was thankful for my college education because it did allow me to earn money from home as a freelance writer. I was the new June Cleaver, and very happy. I didn't know just how happy I was, though, until I was thrown into a new role.

At first the choice was just that: a choice. My husband had been ill with a chronic but manageable illness. We felt that if he could take some time off from his crazy manufacturing manager shifts, we all would enjoy a better quality of life. I went back to full-time work and he became the full-time stay-at-home dad while he took courses to help him find a career conducive to better health.

It was a struggle at first. I felt like I was missing out on all I had enjoyed for the last twelve years as a stay-at-home mom. I felt I was missing the day trips to the beach in the summer and having the time to decorate the house for the holidays. It literally took me nine months to adjust to the fact that I was gone twelve or thirteen hours a day, including the commute, and had only weekends to accomplish what I used to do while the kids were in school.

I only had to endure another year of that schedule until the company restructured and my job was eliminated. Even though I was happy to be free from a job I barely tolerated, I worried about many things. I had provided the health insurance for my family and a little more than half of the income. I was hopeful at this time, too, though. My husband was truly happy for the first time in many years, working toward a career he loved and one that would provide well for our family. His health had improved greatly by being home and able to stop and rest when he needed to.

We enjoyed this for three short weeks. Then life changed in a way we never imagined and one that would leave us redefining each role in our family. My boys suddenly needed a supermom the day my forty-eight-year-old husband died from a heart attack.

The boys are fourteen, twelve and nine. They need a father and a mother. I find myself wondering how I can be all things to them. How I can be their driving teacher, catch partner, nurturer, and just mom, the person they go to for warm cookies and hugs? How can I provide for them? I struggle with the roles because I never felt like a great mom. Can I be a better dad? Certainly not. I feel like I was really good at being a wife, but that role no longer exists.

What is a supermom then? To me a supermom is someone who recognizes her shortcomings and asks for forgiveness of her children without the guilt trip. She is someone who tries a little harder each day to have more patience than the day before. She is someone who strives to end each day, no matter how hectic or chaotic, with a good-night kiss and an "I love you" that is heartfelt. With this definition, we can all be supermoms.

~Kim Wierman

Reprinted by permission of Tom Swick
© 2008

Meeting Isaac

Before you were conceived I wanted you. Before you were born I loved you.
Before you were here an hour I would die for you. This is the miracle of life.
~Maureen Hawkins

I could point to the fact that Benjamin was ten pounds, four
ounces when he was born as the reason for my tunnel vision
when he didn't grow. I could excuse myself with the fact that
he was my seventh child, and our home was a teensy bit chaotic.
Perhaps it was my borderline cocky attitude about how healthy my
breastfed babies were. But in the private corners of my heart, I know
the real reason it took me five months to wake up to the shocking
realization that he had not grown. Let me explain.

When a friend had the courage to tell me that something was
terribly wrong with Benjamin as we were camping, it all came crashing in. Why hadn't he smiled yet? Why were his eyes so sunken?
Why did he never hold his head up or look around? Was his lack of
crying really a sign that he was content, or something much more
frightening?

I threw all the sleeping bags and clothes into the car with my
children and drove home in a panic. I was in his pediatrician's office
first thing on Monday. And although she tried to hide her alarm, she
sent me directly to the hospital. I do not know what she told the
emergency room staff, but when they ushered us in by name and
escorted us quickly to a room, the gravity of my failure to care for this
child threatened to crush me.

For the next eleven days, Benjamin was studied by a dozen doctors as they searched for clues as to why he had not grown. One doctor was famous enough to have a syndrome named after him. He reminded me of Santa Claus, with his white beard and little spectacles. He had a bow tie and rang a tinkling bell by Benjamin's head to see if he would turn to the sound (he didn't). The geneticist interviewed me for some time, using up several pieces of paper for the dozens of aunts and uncles and hundreds of cousins on both sides of our families. I was amazed to see her full and expectant belly, and pondered what kind of inquiries a woman with her knowledge would make when choosing the father of her own child. But the endocrinologist who changed the history of our family did not arrive until three days after the hospitalization began.

In completely losing myself in the care of my baby, so precariously perched on the brink of survival, I had neglected my own appearance for the past seventy-two hours. So when a woman appeared at Benjamin's bed at six in the morning, my first thought was, "how could anyone look that great at dawn?" Her hair was beautiful, she had heels and make-up. I wondered how far she lived from the hospital and why she cared this much about a little boy she had never met. She soon found the clues she was looking for—a fat tongue, an outie belly button and pudgy toes. She suspected congenital hypothyroidism, and sent him for a nuclear scan on his thyroid.

Waiting for the test, my weary mind drifted to further levels of astonishment. How does this doctor keep track of all the subtleties of this momentous treasure hunt, where children depend on her to know the answers so that they might win the prize of life? What's more, the really substantial rewards, the ones I get every day in my job, like slobbery kisses, and a small hand in mine when we take a walk up the road, or a story fresh from my child's imagination—these compensations are mine to enjoy. This life-saving doctor said goodbye to Benjamin long before he could form the words "thank you," or throw his arms around her neck.

The test confirmed what she already had sleuthed—Benjamin's thyroid was completely ornamental. She started him on growth hormones, a small, inconspicuous pill, and we watched for signs of growth. It was an excruciatingly slow process.

In those early, sleepless nights during our time at the Cedars-Sinai Medical Center, I was in earnest conversation with God. I wanted to know, desperately, if He was taking this child back from me. I knew that I was being greedy, that I had six other children at home, but I wanted THIS one. I remembered the story of Abraham being told to sacrifice Isaac, his beloved son, on a mountaintop. I felt as if I were climbing that mountain, in a hospital named after the mountain that Moses ascended centuries later, and waiting for an answer.

One evening, a man came, as many had, to do therapy on Benjamin. I started a conversation by asking where he was from. He said he was from Africa. I started to perk up. "My husband went to Africa. Where in Africa are you from?"

"Ghana," he answered.

"Ghana! My husband loves Ghana!" We launched into a lively discussion about the country, and I felt some excitement after days of churning anxiety. When he turned to leave I asked, "What is your name?"

"Isaac." The door slipped shut and he was gone.

The name felt like a billboard saying, "You get to keep your son!" The tears came afresh, and I wept with gratitude — gratitude to the people who immerse themselves in textbooks and memorize symptoms, gratitude to the quiet flock of therapists and nurses whose faithful vigil keeps children warm and breathing, and gratitude to the God who placed this precious child in my unworthy arms.

That is the real reason for my selective vision early in Benjamin's life. If I had never come face to face with losing him, just like Abraham did, I might never have known the vast expanse of my love for him. Then in a few years, when tantrums, or slammed doors or broken promises clouded my vision, I would not have had that crystal memory to yank me back to that which will never change, my love for my son.

~Lori Odhner

Maggie Mae

*Mother love is the fuel that enables a normal human being
to do the impossible.*
~Marion C. Garretty

Maggie Mae, named after Margaret Thatcher and the Rod Stewart song, was my first "child." Not just an English bulldog, but to my husband and me, our first joint attempt at parenting. When we took the long drive to Enfield, Connecticut, from New York City to choose our baby, Maggie literally ran from the security of her mother and siblings and seemingly chose us. Years of fun and adventure raising her in New York enhanced her naturally friendly and outgoing temperament.

Later, with a move to the suburbs of Connecticut, she settled into a calmer life, one where she graciously stepped out of the limelight to make room for our two children, Ben and Sarah. She was always a part of the scene, however: annual holiday photos, car trips to the Berkshires, long walks, and later, when she became tired and more stubborn, "drags" around the neighborhood.

You could always count on Maggie to cuddle up next to you on the couch and snore away contentedly, head on your lap, with her tongue, too long to be contained, stuck out and dried up over her lower lip. We joked about "kissing her on the lip" as she really only had a lower one! The kids called her Scoobie or Scoo-scoo for short, and she taught them how much work, respect, compassion, and responsibility it takes to be a pet owner. She was always much more than just a pet, however, as she gave us all the gift of unconditional love.

After twelve and a half wonderful years of life, Maggie died on a Wednesday. I know it was a Wednesday because it happened to be my "crazy day." I needed to get up by six, get the kids up, semi-nourished, dressed and ready for school, the dog walked and fed, then myself transformed from morning mommy into some sort of presentable shape. I also needed to get my son to the bus by 7:39 A.M. or he required a twenty-minute drive to school with my daughter in tow. She needed to get to her school by 8:00 A.M., a physical impossibility if we missed the bus. Every Wednesday the kids referred to me as "Rushing Mommy," because despite my best intentions to remain calm and collected, I inadvertently morphed into a clock-watching, neurotic creature who I often could not even recognize.

Although Maggie's general health had been deteriorating, she was holding her own. So, on that particular morning, as I was beginning the "walking Maggie" portion of the morning routine, it seemed that she was not at all herself. She could hardly make the walk to her special bathroom area of the yard, and once there, lacked the strength to even hold herself up to urinate. With my assistance, she slowly made her way back inside where the children were watching television, and then immediately collapsed on the carpet in front of them. The children shot up from the couch and we all huddled around Maggie, unsure of what to do to help her as she lay there panting. My seven-year-old son burst into tears, my three-year-old daughter sat petting Maggie's head telling her, "It's okay Scoo-scoo," while I just felt overwhelmed and in shock at what was happening.

Within moments, while I had my son in my arms and all three of us were massaging Maggie's side, she very gradually shut her eyes, stopped panting, and in her final moment, released her bowels all over the carpet. "MOMMY!!!" screamed the children in unison. "Did Maggie just die???" wailed my son. "Can we get another puppy?" asked my daughter. So here is one of those moments: our beloved dog is dead on the soiled carpet, the children are distraught and trying to understand what just happened, and mommy is feeling completely traumatized and overwhelmed.

I believe that there exists within all parents an untapped emergency resource that somehow enables us to cope. For better or for worse, we are able to put aside our immediate needs in order to do our best for our children. So, perhaps with such thoughts skirting the edges of my consciousness, I told the children that I wasn't certain that Maggie was dead, but she was definitely sick and in need of help. We had to get her to the dog doctor.

This was followed by a blur of activity; I scooped up Maggie's accident, threw on some clothes, and somehow coaxed the children into the car. Leaving the passenger door open, I went back in for Maggie, and with strength I didn't know I possessed, managed to get her fifty-five pound body into the car. At that point my son, who wasn't buying the Maggie-may-not-have-died line, tearfully informed me that there was no way he was able to take the bus to school that day. Unable to argue with his logic, I drove the twenty minutes to and from his school, while poor Maggie slid back and forth on the car floor.

When the children left the car at their respective schools, I encouraged them to say goodbye to Maggie. Ben stroked her back and whispered, "I love you" and when I finally pulled into my daughter's school, Sarah gently kissed Maggie on the head and ran inside.

Maggie and I were suddenly alone in the car and all the sadness over the loss of my wonderful girl began to take hold. Through tears, I stroked her soft head one last time and silently thanked her for years of love and devotion. Somehow, I phoned the vet and was instructed to get her to their office as soon as possible.

I was escorted to a private office where Maggie's vet very gently informed me that I could take her ashes home, or that they could keep Maggie's ashes and distribute them in a "special dog place." Too dazed to decide on the spot, I asked if I could contact her later. When I returned to the car, I phoned my husband in tears and told him the horrible news.

As the day progressed, thoughts of Maggie, my family, and our years together that were at first blocked, eventually came out. Home together that evening, gathered around pictures of our beloved companion, my husband, Ben, Sarah and I held hands and talked about Maggie and our fondest memories of what made her so special. As we went around the circle, sharing our stories, I could truly feel Maggie's spirit, and was comforted by the certainty that she would always remain a truly special part of our family.

~Diane Powis

The Moms' Club

A mother's love for her child is like nothing else in the world.
It knows no law, no pity, it dares all things and
crushes down remorselessly all that stands in its path.
~Agatha Christie

I saw her at the hair salon. I knew her baby was in the intensive care unit at Georgetown University Hospital. Tears streaming down her face, she talked quietly to another stylist. I knew then she had joined my club.

My club is Moms of Chronically Ill Children. No one ever wants to be in the club, but once you're in, you have a unique perspective. It's the ability to walk around thankful for every day. When others are tired of child care duties, the moms in my club are thankful to have child care duties at all.

When you meet another club member, you instantly recognize her steely determination to keep her child alive and functioning. You know that, like you, she gives up most of her personal time, her carefree moments with friends or spouse, and her ability to parent effectively the siblings of that child. You know that this mom is wary, she is hardened, and she is bewildered. You see her in doctors' waiting rooms and in cafeterias of hospitals everywhere, where she sits and wonders, "How did this happen? Why am I in this club?"

For years, my husband Eric and I tried to avoid the inevitable; our daughter Allison needed a heart transplant. That time consisted of dashed hopes and failed efforts to find an alternative to what doctors said was "trading one disease for another." Transplants are not a cure.

The early days are the most shocking, when the diagnosis is fresh and the reality of the situation has barely broken through your wall of denial. You keep wishing you would wake up from the nightmare. But as time passes, the duties of caring for that child become more routine. You begin to program yourself to do things that health professionals are well trained to do. Although you are baffled at the prospect of administering medicines and using whatever medical equipment might be required, you learn to do these things in a sleepless state.

The nights are the most difficult, when you're alone with your thoughts, your questions. Did I cause this? Did that glass of wine I had when I didn't know I was pregnant lead to this? Why is it my child who must suffer? Why is it my family that must endure separations, isolation and endless medical appointments?

Soon, you discover there is no answer to these questions. You are reassured by friends and loved ones who promise it's just bad luck, or maybe God's will. You lose your faith, just when you needed it most. How could a benevolent God sanction this attack on an innocent child? Then you flop to your knees with guilt and pray feverishly for forgiveness, for tolerance, for second chances. Sometimes when you get it, you can't tell if it was God, the doctors, or that four-leaf clover your cousin mailed to you and is now taped to the hospital bed.

Allison barely survived the waiting. During the weeks in intensive care, I watched cartoons with her, horrified that someone else's child had to die to save mine. The daily landing of the helicopters made her wonder, "Is that her heart?" Was it today that her new heart would arrive on the roof of the Children's Hospital of Pittsburgh while we waited below? That's what Allison believed. We couldn't tell her the truth. I said, "Somebody didn't need their heart anymore. They will give it to you."

After a three-month stay and the placement of a healthy heart into the tiny malnourished body of my four-year-old, we gathered up the items people had sent to us. She sat in the midst of twenty new stuffed animals and crowed excitedly, "I've got a zoo in my room." I turned away to hide my tears from her wise eyes. I will never forget who sent her those cuddly friends, the only ones she had for many months, because we named them after the people who sent them. We still have Peyton the monkey, Mary dog, Aunt Carol doll and Mr. Maloney bear. Although my growing-up girl, now a teen, no longer craves the company of her old friends from her zoo, I can't bear to give them away.

With these memories as vividly preserved as my first kiss, I never forget to send a soft and funny stuffed animal to a child with an illness. It may seem unimportant, but only moms in our club understand their value both to the sick child and the mother. In times of grief and stress, the smallest things can offer the most comfort.

Life after a long hospital stay is like re-entry for an astronaut. Walking in the light of day on a street with trees feels like a religious epiphany. The world went on without me, while I lived in the cocoon of the hospital, with its beeps, crying babies and nighttime interruptions. With time and reassurance from the nurses, I learned to administer her medicines, swab her mouth, and change her bandages.

Those last days at the hospital, we lived for our release papers; the time away from fresh air and birds singing feeling endless.

Then it arrives. The day and the hour and the minute you and your child leave the hospital and walk into the sunshine. As relieved as you feel, a new panic takes over, when it's only the parents and their girl. Confusion is the state of normal. Did you give her the right medicine, and what happens when she spits it out, or refuses to eat? How will she survive the fever or the fluid in her lungs from exposure to other kids during one blessed hour playing in the park? Was it worth the fleeting laughter, the minutes of joy? Perhaps it was. Her doctor says, "We don't give a child a transplant so she can live in a bubble."

Back in the real world, you discover that the club continues to add new members. You watch when the new mom is initiated with a shake of your head. You know what's coming and it isn't pretty. She catches your eyes in a new way. Now she understands why you've always looked so panicked and afraid. Of course, club members envy those other mothers with healthy kids. When one complains of an ear infection or strep, you feel like laughing in her face.

So that brings me back to the mother from the hair salon. Will she look at me with a new appreciation for my badges of courage? Not yet. It's too raw, and you feel so alone in the beginning. Down the road, she'll be the one who remembers to call when my daughter goes into the hospital for tests. She'll bring dinner over afterward. Often the love for your child drives you to do more and be stronger than you ever imagined. Some, like my friend Jillian Copeland, who founded a school for children with special needs, make a difference for other families too. Now, her son will have the education of her dreams.

And though you don't want to join us, you will find solace in your fellow members. We are there to back each other, with compassion and understanding. So that's the small consolation in this life of worry. You are not alone.

~Renee Sklarew

Power
MOMS

Working from Home

Or at Least Trying....

The Second Shift

Fill your paper with the breathings of your heart.
~William Wordsworth

Recently, I tried to explain to my four-year-old son that our caregiver, Sue, was leaving. We talked about Sue's new job, and I reassured him that he could still draw pictures for her and call her on the phone. I sat down on the bed, intent on making this transition easier for my son, and asked if he understood what this meant. "Sure," Kyle told me. "From now on, *you're* going to be the nanny."

It was true, but his words still startled me. Yes, I was becoming a nanny, or more precisely, a stay-at-home mom. After four years as a professional working mother, this would mean a significant change in my life-style, not to mention my kids'.

Let me first say that no mother I know is entirely happy with her current situation. Women who work a nine-to-five job often worry about leaving their kids in day care and dream about the simplicity of a world where the biggest time constraint centers on scheduling play dates. Stay-at-home mothers might sigh at the thought of a workplace where everyone is potty-trained. As a writer, I'd had the best of both worlds. I worked full-time from an in-home office, which let me sneak hugs when I wanted them, then disappear into my room and lock the door. I would hand my three kids—Kyle, his brother, Jake, age two, and Sammy, the baby—to our nanny every morning and go off to do what I was paid to do.

Then my husband and I decided that, finally, we were going to make our dreams come true and build a new house. Day care, one of the largest line items in our budget, began to look like a very nice down payment. We agreed that I'd take care of the kids while my husband, Tim, was at the office. When he returned home at six o'clock, my own workday would begin. Granted, we'd never see each other. But we'd have a new house in a year.

At first, I was thrilled with my new role. After hearing about — instead of witnessing — Kyle's first toddling Frankenstein steps and Jake's timid forays into English, I would actually be there for my daughter's first smile. But, a niggling voice reminded me, I'd also be there for the whole miserable time that she's teething or Jake is giving up his naptime. Suddenly, I panicked: I would be present for my kids' formative moments but also for everything in between. Would the new arrangement prove to be too much of a good thing?

My first week on the job was a sobering one. The children's initial glee over having Mom available on a twenty-four hours basis quickly wore off. *Sue* had let them eat breakfast while watching television. *Sue* had made them whatever they wanted for lunch. *Sue* was never talking on the phone when my four-year-old desperately needed to know how clouds were made. In my defense, Sue's only job had been to take care of the kids, whereas I had cleaning and errands to attend to. But when the kids held me up against the gold standard of their former nanny, they found me lacking. Throughout those first few weeks at home, I was haunted by one refrain: *She made it look easy.*

Some of the biggest challenges of being an at-home mother come simply from being tied to your home. I clean up the toy room at least five times a day, and each time I'm stunned by how much damage a few very small people can do in fifteen minutes. There is some comfort in being the drill sergeant and voice of reason, until you realize that you are the only voice of reason. Also, the only one that isn't high-pitched, doesn't lisp, and can string two coherent thoughts together. Indeed, I had forgotten how isolating the experience could be. By the time Tim comes home, I'm starved for conversation, dying to hear sentences that contain multisyllabic words.

The antidote to feeling isolated, of course, is to get out of the house. This is no small undertaking. It takes fifteen minutes to locate coats and negotiate who gets the red hat and who gets the blue. Another five minutes to pack up snacks that will keep the peace during the drive. Three minutes to struggle with car seats designed by childless sadists. And one minute to retrieve the infant in the car seat that I've inadvertently left on the kitchen table.

Some things you just can't do with three young kids who are all awake. You can't drink a cup of hot coffee—someone's always tugging on your leg to be picked up or wanting a sip. You can't complete any banking transaction that can't be managed at the drive-through window. You can't get your own hair cut or your teeth cleaned.

You can shop for groceries, but it becomes an Olympian event. We usually begin in the parking lot with a bribe: those who behave get M&Ms at the checkout stand. I unlatch Kyle and Jake and have them place both palms on the side of the car like little victims of arrest. This keeps them from darting into traffic while I wrestle the infant carrier seat free. Jake then throws a tantrum until I get the exact cart he wants, and Kyle crawls into a second cart. Then I push one cart and pull the other, my body a swivel hitch in a caravan that Jake has likened to Thomas the Tank Engine. We stop at the deli counter regardless of whether we need anything, because the kids are given free cheese. We spend most of our time in the cereal aisle with me trying to turn their heads the other way, knowing that health food is less seductive than a rabbit with 3-D glasses. At last, we pay and stagger back to the car for another round of loading.

Food shopping notwithstanding, there are highlights to being at home all day. I was watching the other day when Jake chivalrously shared his sandbox bucket with the preschool love of his life. It was into my arms that Kyle sprang when he got off the kindergarten school bus for the first time. I got to see my boys push their little sister in her stroller, leaning down to call her "sweetie pie," like I do.

Most memorable are those moments that sneak up on me when

I least expect them. One day we were cleaning up paper left behind after a cut-and-paste free-for-all. Kyle had gathered all the clippings into a pile on the table. "Okay," I said. "Now let's get the stuff on the floor." My son looked at me, surprised, and then dutifully swept the pile over the edge. Then there was the time I had just collapsed on a couch, exhausted after a particularly difficult morning, when my two-year-old crawled up beside me. "I lub you," he said. "My pick my nose?"

At the end of every day I retreat to my office at 6:00 P.M. to start my second job. Sometimes when I write, the results come out sounding like Dr. Seuss. Play, I now realize, is very hard work. I've had to gain endurance and patience. I've become an expert at arbitration; I've developed a professional voice of authority. And I've learned to see my old career anew. Handling a demanding editor pales in comparison to negotiating with a toddler in the throes of a full-blown tantrum.

After several months at home full-time, it still isn't easy. Occasionally, to reinforce my confidence, I have to remind myself that Mary Poppins is a fictional character, not a benchmark to measure myself against. I tell myself that not everyone has the imagination to make a sea monster out of an egg carton as I did last week, or to pick Play-Doh out of the carpet and nurse a baby simultaneously.

There are other gains worth noting. Because I am on duty around the clock, I've come to know my kids with a thoroughness I did not possess before. Likewise, I am no longer a mysterious woman who does God knows what on a computer they are not allowed to touch. I am now someone who senses a crisis even before a lower lip trembles; someone who knows the right moment to call attention to a bulldozer out the window and avert a sibling war. We may still fit the broad roles of parent and child, but now we also see each other as complex individuals, and we've learned what makes each other laugh, hurt, and heal.

Even now as I'm writing, I hear the sounds of an escalating fight outside my office. The baby is screaming, and my husband is slowly losing patience. *See, it's not just me*, I think, glad to be out of the fray.

And then I recall naptime, which for the first time in a while, came without a squall. I remember how easily the kids crawled into bed and how beautiful they were. I stare at my computer, where I am supposed to be mulling over the plot and characters of a new novel. Instead I find myself considering whether tomorrow will be the day Kyle reads aloud his first word, or Sammy sits up by herself. I try to shake my thoughts back to the matter at hand. But I find myself thinking instead of my children, characters who have taken the story of my own life and have given it twists stranger and far sweeter than in any fiction.

~Jodi Picoult

First printed in *FamilyFun* Magazine, February 1997

45

Mamá Está Trabajando

At work, you think of the children you have left at home.
At home, you think of the work you've left unfinished.
Such a struggle is unleashed within yourself. Your heart is rent.

~Golda Meir

Y
ou know she's a monkey. I mean, at least part monkey. She's two years old and becoming obsessed with the space between her big toe and second toe. She tears off her shoes and socks to examine it closely. She'll pull out a piece of lint and ask herself, "What's that?" But then she transforms.

Something about the way she walks makes her seem like a little elf. She thinks no one is looking and she stealthily makes her way into the innocuous oven that comes with her kiddie kitchen. She's just the right size to sneak inside. She likes to hang out in there and wait for someone to find her. This is tremendous progress from her hiding by shielding her eyes while she sits in plain view.

Suddenly she's out of the oven and again she is transformed. She's a fairy sprinkling magic dust around the family room as she visits with her toys and dolls. Or are they cookie crumbs?

It's easy to be spellbound by this creature. Dalia Maria. She changes all the time. Excited and jumping one moment. Small and snuggly the next. Her index finger strokes her nose as she enjoys her delicious thumb. I want to just take her and hug her and drown her in kisses. But while she is full of magic, I am cursed with a headset and laptop that keep my fingers typing. I have this wonderful consulting job that allows me to work from home so that I can be with her, but I'm seldom really with her. I have to have my eyes on the monitor at all times, my ears perked to hear the special bell that indicates someone is sending me a message on IM that I need to respond to. My phone is either on or recharging as I jump from conference call to conference call.

Dalia lives in a netherworld of playing games, dressing dolls, discovering ants, reading books and watching *Sesame Street*. I live in an alternate universe of connections and being connected, responding to a never ending stream of e-mails and listening to what seem like interminable "virtual" meetings discussing the same issues, challenges, risks and mitigations day after day after day. The daily grind is shaken often by critical messages that need to be sent out, urgent meetings that need to be arranged to discuss essential topics that cannot wait until Monday. You would think we were saving lives and not creating software.

I have slacked off and left my computer to go play with Dalia. It is so blissful to get down on the floor with her and make the Little People dance and sing, or color in her Diego coloring book. But when my time is up and I return to my computer, she cries and screams and the chastising eye of the babysitter makes me understand that sometimes it is better if I just stay in my office and not "torture her" with Mommy's presence. So sometimes I sit behind a closed door and listen to her laugh and sing, hear her ask for water or beg for a cookie and I have to stand my ground and not let her in.

Our babysitter is Colombian and speaks almost no English. She has taught Dalia to say that "*Mamá está trabajando* (Mommy is working)." My daughter now understands this to mean, "Mommy can't be with you because she is doing something else, something more important that has to take precedence." And it kills me that this is the case.

I am blessed to be able to have the flexibility to be at home — if my daughter is sick, if we are leaving that night for a trip and I need to pack during my lunch hour, if I have to throw in a load of laundry—I can do those things. I can dial into a virtual meeting and have my laptop ready and connected to a wireless Internet. Not everyone has this option.

But sadly, the picture that other working moms have of me sitting with my child on my lap typing, happily running around in our yard or visiting the park, is just not a real one. I am the mom waving goodbye as a babysitter takes her away to do those wonderful things. I tried visiting her at the pool to see her splashing and having fun but once she laid eyes on me, there was no turning back. Either we all had to go home together or I had to stay. There was no way she would let me leave. And a conference call was planned so we all had to head home. Mommy seems to take all the fun out of everything.

Until 5:00 P.M. Until the laptop closes, and dinner calls, and Dalia and I put on our aprons and make dinner or play a game or go for a walk and then we are free. At 5:00 P.M., I'm like every other working mom who is so happy to be done with my day and so happy to spend time with my baby. Working from home isn't the same as being at home. It's a subtle difference I've learned to accept.

~Cristina T. Lopez

46

Mom Wrote a Book and All I Got Was This Lousy T-Shirt

Writers will happen in the best of families.
~Rita Mae Brown

Did you do your reading?" I ask my children this every night, almost as often as "did you brush your teeth?" According to them, moms who are writers are not at all "chill" about reading. According to my children, moms who write are uptight, always fussing about book reports and grammar and telling a story with a beginning, a middle, and an end. Moms who are writers make terrible suggestions, like a mother/son book club. Or writing camp. In the summer! Moms who are writers are also, according to my own three children, obsessed with dental hygiene. They call me the Teethinator.

Until a few years ago, they knew I was a writer only because that's what I told them I was doing in there on my computer. And because I always say things like "writing is re-writing," when they're ready to hand in a book report after a single draft. And "don't forget your book" when they go anywhere, even to a friend's house. And "reading for pleasure is life's greatest joy." That's when they give each other the look that says, as clear as words on the page: Help! Our Mom's crazy.

Having a mom who's a writer stinks. But they'd never actually seen—or read—anything I'd written.

Then, one day, all of a sudden, it seemed, there was to be a book. Mom's novel was being published. They didn't know what it was about but they knew it was fiction—"fiction's the stuff that's made up, right?" they confirmed nervously—and they knew they should be proud. They knew this because people kept asking them, "Aren't you proud of your mom?"

They didn't want to be proud of their mom. They wanted Mom to be proud of them. But they were excited. Their joy at the news was pure. It was the kind of happiness only children are capable of expressing so genuinely. Their glee—Mom's novel is being published!—was unadulterated with envy.

The enthusiasm from my children—I'll never forget the way their faces lit up so spontaneously when I first told them—made the experience so much more poignant for me. It made me believe there was some kind of divine plan at work. God, was that you? In a burst of clarity, I knew, the way you just know these things, there was a reason it had taken me so long to publish my first novel. It was so I could share it with the three of them. This realization touched my heart.

It took twenty years. It sounds almost quaint now—I came to New York to be a writer—like saying I went west to seek gold, but as so many aspiring novelists before me, that's what I did after college. In my original plan, if I had one—I was not, nor have I ever been, one of those "planning" types—I would have already written and published at least a few novels by the time I had my children.

I worked at day jobs in the magazine world and I took classes and workshops. I scribbled bits of things, short stories, and a chapter or two, even a bad screenplay. When my first child was born I was fortunate to be able to leave full-time work to focus on my writing. But I had a baby, and then, quickly, another one, and then a third. There seemed to be so little time. Yet the urge to write would build up inside me until I would feel like I was going to explode if I didn't do it. And so I'd write, a few pages here, a few there. My inner censor was particularly foul-mouthed and loquacious and there were times when it seemed like an exercise in futility. But the creative process is powerfully addictive and I kept writing because I loved it.

I would tell people I was a writer and then suffer the inevitable follow-up question. Trust me, nothing induces more eye rolling at a cocktail party than being an unpublished novelist. At least if you say you're "just a mom"—and yes, I hear women using this exact phrase all the time, "just" a mom—it smacks of commitment and devotion and home baked snacks. But a still-yearning-to-be-published aspiring novelist in her thirties with three children? Please.

I shocked everyone, even myself, when I finally produced a novel. As I had my moment of epiphany—my children's joy was the reason it took me so long—I imagined they were experiencing similar epiphanies. There's a reason their mother is the way she is, always nagging about reading and re-writing and "the creative process," whatever that is: She's a writer.

At first, they were patient. A photographer came to do a picture and invited them to sit in on one or two (so I could get the holiday card photo done.) In past years my husband and I would have to wrestle them into position for one half-decent shot of the three. Now they posed and smiled tolerantly.

This was the price of fame, they were telling themselves. Yes, the joy I thought I'd seen on their faces? It was because they thought I was going to be famous. And then, naturally, they would be famous. Weren't all writers famous?

Now, sharing the excitement with one's husband and children is not the only good thing about publishing your first novel later in life. Another is that you no longer suffer any illusions that a book will dramatically change it.

I know I'm not going to be on *Oprah*. (I was amazed at how many people seemed to believe that must have been written into my contract. "When are you doing *Oprah*?" they'd ask.)

I don't expect that anyone will have actually have read my book or even heard about it. "I didn't read it," people love to tell me. "But I don't read."

And I'm not anticipating hanging out with George Clooney at Bungalow 8 instead of walking safety patrol at the kids' school. I've never been to Bungalow 8. Is it still a nightclub? Does George Clooney even go there?

But my children were looking for the dramatic change. Fame is so much more interesting than boring old books. They waited patiently, those first weeks after the novel came out and there were articles in magazines and parties and readings. There was even a good review in *The New York Times*. It was only a matter of time, surely, before they were discovered.

And then it was over. The book was still in the stores. But their mom was not famous. Neither were they. And their mom was still obsessed with reading. And teeth. Nothing had changed. Nothing at all.

Now, my daughter finds me at my desk, wraps herself around my neck and mutters with disgust, "you still working on your book?"

"My sentiments exactly," I say.

She doesn't find this funny. My children don't want me to be funny.

"You already wrote the book." One book is enough, her tone implies, wavering between impatience at being forced yet again to point out the obvious to her dimwitted mother and suspicion. What was I doing on that computer when The Book had already been published?

"I'm working on another book," I remind her.

She buries her head in my hair and sighs. The whole mom's-a-novelist thing is so over.

And then, because I can't help myself, the words come out of me. "Did you do your reading?"

~Danielle Ganek

47

Finding a New Voice

Far from depriving me of thought, motherhood gave me new and startling
things to think about and the motivation to do the hard work of thinking.
~Jane Smiley

I stand in the library, in my hand a book—red Moroccan leather, with gilt-edged pages, and gold embossing. A rich book that warms to my touch, my hand reverently placed on the front and backboards. Its slightly moldy smell suggests its age. I am surprised to find that I am unconsciously swaying back and forth, rocking, as if I were trying to rock it to sleep. At that thought, I look up quickly at the clock on the wall.

Time to get home. My first day back in the library has come to an end. I'd been home full-time with my daughter for two years, and I am beginning to establish myself as a professional again after a divorce. I feel like an imposter in the grand row of books, as if the books can tell I am now primarily a mother and not living the life of the mind I had imagined when I completed my Ph.D. I put the book back on the shelf, my fingers lingering on the raised letters of the spine. I go home to put my daughter down for a nap, to try to write in the space created by her sleep.

The need to write has become a physical ache, like needing the touch of a loved one's hand. After Sarah was born and I left my original job as a professor, I thought at first I would be lost, not know who I was or what I would do. Who was I if I wasn't Dr. Hudock? Instead, I filled pages of my journal, sometimes writing only in the dim glow of our nightlight, with my daughter snuggled beside me. When my infant girl fell asleep in the car, I drove to the Berkeley Marina or Point Isabel and parked close to the water so I could look out over the bay while I wrote furiously until she woke up. I wrote with all the passion I had felt for words when I was a child, with the same abandon as someone new to language. Childlike myself, I began to change, and to grow.

One day I sat, watching my daughter play with a golden flower, pollen spread across her face. Her face was rapt with attention, with energy, with focus. Sarah was living completely in the now, with no concept of before and after. I lay down beside her, picked my own flower, and looked at it. As I sat with her, I gained a new sense of the motion of time. Being outside deadlines, schedules, and appointments allowed me to feel the spaces between activities for the first time in my life. Being required to sit still and simply be with her retaught me the value of silence, of being still.

Nursing also helped me relearn how to be in the moment. When I was younger, I learned to avoid anything uncomfortable with my body through my imagination. However, I learned to use my skill too often, rarely sitting with the difficulties of the moment. But nursing changed that. Instead of spinning off into new mind adventures, I needed to focus on her, and, therefore, stayed more in my body. I began to see more, feel more, experience more. Like a yogi in training, I sat in a position that would eventually become uncomfortable, willing myself to not disturb the sleeping child. And I held this position, sometimes for hours, as she slept and nursed. I felt every muscle, every tendon, every nerve. My mind also became still, watching thoughts come and go. This stillness of body and mind allowed me to hear myself in a new way and, later, to write in a new way.

Most important, however, was the new sense of wonder I experienced in the presence of my child. I looked into her eyes and knew that I needed to write of her, of me and her, and of all that came before and will come after. Infinity is not enough for her, and all I had to offer her were halting words. She taught me new phrases to speak each day as I grappled with the distance between my feelings for her and the poor job words did when I tried to convey the power her spirit and beauty had over me. Ultimately, my longing to describe her in words sent me to my journal, frantic.

And when I looked back over what I had written, I began to see a shadow behind the ink blots the pen made on the page. And it was moving, becoming more substantial, coming into the light.

It was me. Years of academic writing had taught me to obscure my existence behind the printed words. Writing in the academy needs to be more objective, careful, sanitized. Less personal, subjective, real. The rawness of life doesn't appear in scholarly journals. But after my experience as a new mother, I felt that I could come out from behind the edifice of words I had built to hide myself, and I began to reveal myself to the reader in a new way, in a way my academic writing would never allow. After giving birth, I felt anything could be. Even that. Even me. I birthed a new voice as well as a daughter.

But now, books wait for me in libraries, leading me back to the echoing sounds of the academic voice. Can I hear it without letting it overwhelm me? Without it silencing me with its assumed authority and pretend objectivity? Will my voice begin to sound shrill and trite in comparison, as I try, once again, to speak the language of the academy? Or can I bring back what I have learned from full-time mothering?

As the books to be read wait for me in the library, so do the books to be written. They live in my imagination, in my file drawers, in my notebooks. But I know births of the new are not easy. I will work to bring my voice into the world, but in a way that makes sense to me, that is organic and whole and beautiful. That reflects my body and spirit as well as my mind—the all of me. My new writing will not look like the academic prose I once wrote, and now, I can live with that. I know I can write books deserving of fine bindings, of gilt, of leather. Ones that fit in those library shelves. Ones deserving of me.

~Amy Hudock

Originally published on *LiteraryMama.com*

How I Became an Author in the Back of My Minivan

I can't tell my children to reach for the sun. All I can do is reach for it myself.
~Joyce Maynard

One day not too long ago, I was at my son's preschool to help out with a class party. As I waited with the other moms for the party to start, one of them looked at me strangely and then pulled something from my hair. It was a Goldfish cracker. She asked me how I managed to get a Goldfish stuck in my hair and I drew a long breath. Then I told her. I'm a mom. I am also an author. I do most of my writing from the back seat of my minivan, and on this particular morning while I was waiting for party duty, I got a little tired and had a nap. In the car. On the back seat. Where the Goldfish live. This all sounded absurd, of course, and I suppose it is. But it came about through a series of events that are entirely sane.

The story begins over a decade ago when I became a mom in the suburbs of Connecticut. In spite of my four years at an Ivy League school, two years working on Wall Street, and three years of law school, I jumped at the chance to "opt out" of my career as a lawyer and raise my kids. For me, it was a simple decision. I could use whatever talents I had helping corporate clients, or I could use them to nurture my own offspring. There were millions of lawyers, but only one mother for my son. It didn't occur to me that by leaving the life I had worked years to create I was also leaving a piece of myself behind.

As it turned out, I had joined masses of former-professional-women-turned-moms whose talents were now being directed at their children. My job was my child; my child was my life. My schedule became a maze of baby groups, mommy-and-me classes, nap schedules and brain stimulation exercises. There were baby birthday parties, massage classes, post-partum Pilates, and, of course, a vast array of discussion groups. At every turn, my small accomplishments were replaced by new worries. Why isn't my baby sleeping through the night? Why isn't he crawling yet? Is his baby food really organic? Should I make it myself? Yes! Suddenly I had a freezer full of kale and broccoli ice cubes. The piece of me I had abandoned became fully embedded in this new job of mothering, and the drive for perfection began to overshadow the small moments of joy that all of this was for.

By the time my baby was a year old, I was deeply unsettled. I had become a case study from Betty Friedan's epic work *The Feminine Mystique*, and I knew that it had to stop; I needed an outlet that transcended fabric samples and lunch dates. I had never thought of being a writer. But this was the dream I discovered when I reached inside myself for something to save me from the trap of perfecting motherhood. For the next two years, I wrote a little bit here and there, stopping and starting with morning sickness and again when my second child was born. I wrote during every babysitter hour that I had, during naptime and the other stolen minutes in a mother's life. And as I became more committed to this dream, I also became a more efficient time scavenger. When my three-year-old started nursery school, I decided to skip the long drive home and instead work somewhere in town.

On the first day of this new plan, I swallowed my guilt, left my baby with the sitter, dropped my older son at school and went to Starbucks—suburban mommy Mecca and home to my favorite dark roast. I got a coffee and a table in the back, then pulled out my laptop and some notes. Taking a sip of the coffee, I instructed my brain to focus. *Focus.* An alternative rock band I had never heard of was playing in the background. *Focus.* A woman I'd met at a playgroup came over to chat. *Focus.* The two *baristas* were discussing their body piercings. This was NOT working and time was slipping away, precious time I was paying for with mother guilt and cold hard cash. I packed up my things in frustration and went to my car. But instead of getting in the driver's seat, I slid open the side door and ducked into the back. I moved the boosters, sat down and started to type. It was brilliant! No one could see in through the tinted glass. It was quiet. And there was nothing to do after I swept the Goldfish crumbs to the floor—nothing to do but write.

This became my new office. I stocked it with blankets when the weather turned cold. I bought an extra battery for my laptop and a coffee reheating device. I wrote and wrote, telling no one for fear that the slightest discouragement would break my resolve. When I was overcome with morning sickness again, I stopped writing. When it passed, I dusted off my laptop. Then came the third baby and another interruption. But the need persisted, and so I started again. Through these years, I began to make small concessions to buy myself more time. I gave up the gym and ran with the kids in a jogger. I turned down any social invitation where I couldn't bring them along. Every minute of school or sitter time was devoted to writing in the back of my minivan outside the nursery school, YMCA, or back at the Starbucks. My life had taken on a frenetic pace. But I was happy.

I finished my first novel, *Four Wives*, when my youngest son was nearly two. It is a story about women, about the choices we make and the lives we forge as we muddle through the inherently conflicted worlds of work, marriage, and motherhood. I wrote it because these were the issues that had been living inside me and so many women I had come to know. And, ironically, writing about this conflict gave me my own personal resolution.

Four Wives was published in the spring of 2008, marking the beginning of a new career that actually fits in with my life as a stay-home mom. My days have become jigsaw puzzles—baking muffins at 6:00 A.M., driving the boys here and there, cleaning up toys, making dinner, and writing in between. I am settling into a reality that was once a crazy dream, born of inner conflict and executed in the back of my car.

Just this year, I have set up shop at a desk in my home. All of my boys are in school now, giving me time to work in the mornings. It is an odd luxury to no longer worry about battery power, warmth, or finding a bathroom. But there are times when I get stuck, when the house is calling out to me or my thoughts are frozen, and I find myself parked outside that Starbucks, nestled in among the Goldfish. Sometimes the best part of a dream is the journey that makes it come true.

~Wendy Walker

Reprinted by permission of Tom Swick
© 2008

Tomorrow

If someone wanted to paint a portrait of my mother,
he would have been wise to paint her at her desk. Where she was happiest.
~Mary Gordon

The gritty, acrid taste of coffee grounds assaults my tongue as I gulp the dregs of my morning coffee. I revel in the quiet — the time to read the paper, jot down a few words. The rest of the morning routine's activities; feeding the dog, letting her out, clearing the countertop drain board and making the coffee, are interlopers on my time alone.

I stare out at the redwoods and San Francisco Bay. The azure-colored water of the pool mimics the color of the sky and of the bay beyond. It shimmers silver and reflects the deep greens and browns of the redwoods overhead. So beautiful and so inspiring. Only today, I'm stuck. The words aren't flowing. I feel a tightness in my chest, a familiar feeling that I'm in a race against time. I hunger for, and am nourished by, this quiet hour alone. But today the sands of time are swiftly sifting down. The hour's end is near, and I have little to show for it. I've been robbed by my own inability to focus.

And now, alas, another intruder on my time. A distant door slams and I hear the familiar thump, thump, thump of little feet as they make their way down the hall from the bedroom. Disappointment softly settles over my body. It will be another twenty-four hours before I'm once again alone. For this privacy-seeking introvert, that's far too long.

"Mama, you're always here in front of the computer," Caroline whines as I turn half way to see her outstretched arms. "Up, up," she commands. I struggle to lift her four-year-old weight as she shifts first one way, then the other. Encircling each other with our arms, we sit and face the distant water—and I close up the computer. "Mama, I want you," she continues. "You have me," I assure her. I want you. I need you. I want my mama. I love my mama best of all. Sweet nectar for this mother's soul—and such an awesome burden.

There are never enough hours in the day to get it all done: the dishes, the bed-making, the laundry, room pick-ups, pet feeding, cage cleaning, car maintaining, gardening, pool cleaning, dinner cooking, drink fetching, e-mail answering, car pooling... the parenting, the playful part of it, is lost in the edges of the day.

And since it is not my strength, I pass the play baton to my husband whenever he is home and rush to the desk to busy myself with the endless number of tasks that can be accomplished on the computer: bill-paying, communicating with family and friends, photo editing and archiving, writing for volunteer positions, vacation planning, life planning, and, last but not least, my own personal writing.

So there I am, in my own private place, every morning in a pursuit to accomplish as much as I can before I hear the oh-too-recognizable pitter-patter of sweet little feet marching the well-worn path from the bedroom to the office, and to the chair in front of the computer. She knows that this is where she'll find me.

And it's where I'll be at the end of the day when she again needs me most. After her hour of hilarity with Dad has been interrupted by his need for sleep, she runs, milk cup in hand, to sit again on my lap at the upholstered taupe chair in the room with the golden colored walls that is my refuge, and the computer's resting place. "I need you Mommy," she says—as if I didn't know. She sips away at her milk.

I resolve every morning that this will be the day of change—the day she won't come in search of me in front of the computer. It will be, rather, the day she will find me with her always—on the floor of her room performing the role she is directing, wearing the costumes sewn by a devoted grandmother for a four-year-old. Or I'll be reading her a book as we sit together in the warm, welcoming embrace of the deep purple couch in the living room. It will be a day when we bake cookies together and create new works of art. We will go to the park AND the zoo. We will use chalk to transform our driveway into the yellow brick road. I won't raise my voice or whine back. Caroline won't have to say, "I need you Mommy. I want you Mommy." Instead, she'll simply smile, pleased that she has finally taught me to play—as she has so often cautioned me she would do.

I won't feel the silent reproach of my husband, who can't understand how much there is to be done; how behind I am. That day of play will happen... tomorrow. Right now, I have a couple of deadlines approaching. Caroline knows where to find me.

~Marian Brown Sprague

Working Against the Odds

The quickest way for a parent to get a child's attention is to sit down and look comfortable.

~Lane Olinghouse

Your kids can disrupt your work even when they're not physically in the room with you. I wasn't really aware of this early in my career as a stay-at-home mom and writer. In those days, they intruded on my career mostly by their actual presence in my so-called office.

According to a plan optimistically hatched when I was still pregnant, I went back to my telecommuting job as a staff writer for a publisher of health-care magazines when my first baby (colicky) was just three weeks old. Friends gave us an old (no, an antique) wind-up baby swing, into which I would strap my red-faced, bellowing baby the moment she was fed, changed and burped. I'd wind up that crank until it was stiff, then set her off swinging as high as she'd go without flipping over. In haste, I'd shoot out e-mails to people I was supposed to be interviewing about tricky subjects like irritable bowel syndrome (could this be my newborn's actual problem, rather than the mysterious colic?) and Alzheimer's disease (could I be suffering early onset?). With half an ear, I'd be listening for the sound of the swing running out of steam. If I didn't catch it in time, the baby would open one eye, realize she wasn't in motion, and go off like a smoke alarm.

When the time came to conduct an actual interview, I'd go through an elaborate ritual of preparation. About half an hour before the scheduled call, I'd make sure the baby was fed and changed. Then I'd squeeze her into a sling I wore round my middle, and begin The Soothing Walk. This walk—a high-energy jig with a bit of a shimmy thrown in—was soothing to nobody but the baby. In fact, I'd lost fifteen pounds since the day I invented it. But if I stopped the walk for even a second, the baby woke up and yelled herself puce.

Jigging and shimmying, I'd check my recording equipment, a spaghetti of wires that could mysteriously let me down at any moment. At the introduction stage of the interview, I'd warn my subject that a baby might scream in his or her ear at some point. Since the baby was practically on the phone with us, a fair amount of heavy breathing and the occasional hiccup could also be expected. Then I'd race through my questions, jigging and shimmying like crazy.

By the time the third baby came along, we had a nanny and I was writing a novel. This was when I realized that a child could disrupt work without being anywhere near me. All it took was a distant roar of pain or rage to send me pounding down the stairs to see for myself that my son hadn't lost an arm, leg or tooth. And whenever the phone rang I felt obliged to check out who was calling, in case it was the school or pre-school to announce a bout of vomiting or a playground fracas.

Now that they're all at school, my mornings are my own. And yet at any moment a child can still interrupt me. I'll be in the middle of a challenging plot snarl-up, and quite unbidden the face of my eight-year-old will flash before my eyes, and I'll realize I didn't remind her to wear sneakers for gym. Or I'll catch sight of a violin case and slap my head, knowing that my eldest should have it with her at this very moment. Or I'll remember that I didn't put in a note about a play date, and I'll have to stop and phone the teacher.

Despite these occasional setbacks, I can't believe how far we've come. Every now and then I take a moment to remind myself that when he was three, my son's favorite way to get my attention was to stand behind me on my chair, put both arms around my neck, and gradually apply more pressure.

And as it turns out, the interruption I'll remember forever wasn't even caused by the children; at least, not directly.

I was in South Africa, visiting family and doing as many press events for the release of my novel as my publicist could throw at me. The most challenging of these were the radio slots, mainly because I had to handle them from my parents' farm in KwaZulu-Natal. Anybody who calls my parents on a regular basis knows that the sound of the phone makes the dogs howl. They howl with passion and conviction, and for quite a long time, drowning out whoever is trying to say hello to you. Obviously, this isn't the way you want to greet a producer from a national radio station.

Even more perturbing, South Africa was experiencing almost daily power outages at the time. A timetable of scheduled outages was published in the papers, but it had a tendency to be wrong. So every time I spoke to someone on the radio I half expected to be cut off mid sentence and plunged into darkness.

The children were the least of my worries, to be frank. My mother was excellent at distracting them.

In spite of all the opportunities for disaster, I fielded a few radio chats without incident. By the time the last radio interview rolled around, I felt like a pro. I was installed in my parents' study with a cup of tea at hand, waiting for the call, when my father came in and solicitously set up a digital slide show on the computer to help me pass the time as I waited.

The phone rang, and the interview began. The talk show hosts, a trendy, upbeat pair, asked easy questions about my novel. It was bountifully clear that neither of them had read it, but we were having fun. And then, suddenly, a burst of sound exploded from the computer. Acting on pure reflex, I leapt from the chair, dived out of the room, and shut the door, squishing but not severing the coiled phone cord. On my way out, I caught sight of the screen. The silent display of snapshots had abruptly given way to a video of my son at a kindergarten soccer game. The air absolutely rang with cheers, claps, groans, and loud exhortations from the sidelines.

I stood outside the study door, trying to ignore the muffled roar of the soccer crowd, somehow or other still babbling on about who knew what, even while monitoring the corridor for dogs and children. I wondered what my hosts thought of the sudden sports-fan outburst and my equally sudden incoherence. I hoped they concluded that I was talking from a sports bar, although even there I don't think you'd hear a spectator shout, "Turn the ball around! Other way! Other way!"

There is, of course, another way to look at all this. And yes, there are days when I think with guilt and sadness of the ways my work interrupts my time with the children. But, let's face it—not that many days. I don't often work in front of my children any more, you see. They can always find a way to make me wish I hadn't.

~Elise Chidley

51

Tales of a Power Mom

Now, as always, the most automated appliance in a household is the mother.
~Beverly Jones

Since the day I had my first daughter and made the decision to work outside the home, I have felt like the man on *The Ed Sullivan Show* who used to do that crazy thing with the spinning plates. For those of you who are not old enough to remember, the man would start out at one end of a long line of thin poles that resembled cue sticks, and on top of each pole he would place an ordinary dinner plate. By gently rotating the pole, he would set the plate precariously spinning on top. He repeated this process, quickly moving down the line of poles, setting each plate spinning. Of course, the idea was to have all the plates spinning simultaneously, but as he would reach the end, a few of the first plates that he had set spinning would begin to teeter and the man would run frantically to the beginning of the line to rectify the situation.

To me, this is what motherhood, family, and career represent—a series of spinning plates, all of which appear to be teetering on the brink of falling at any one point in time. And, of course, I am the frantic person trying to keep them from crashing down and splintering at my feet into a million pieces!

This really wasn't what I had envisioned at all. I started out as an idealistic twenty-one-year-old teaching for the New York City Board of Education. As an elementary school teacher, I worked until three, had holidays and summers off and really didn't have much work to take home. I had always been told that this was the ideal career for someone who planned on being a wife and mother someday. Unfortunately, I soon learned that this was not the career for me and began the search for something else to do when I grew up. My fiancé, Bob, encouraged me to go into the business world, which seemed to me like a scary foreign country. But with his urging and a few missteps along the way, I found myself in the financial services industry working for a large Wall Street brokerage firm. We got married and a few years later decided to start a family.

Alexandra was born and I couldn't have been happier staying at home, watching her grow, until the day I realized that I was singing *Sesame Street* songs in my head when people were speaking to me. Don't get me wrong; I love my children. But I knew that I would be a happier person if I resumed my career. The spinning act officially began when I went to work part-time back on Wall Street. Leaving my baby with one of my sisters, getting on the train at 8:00 A.M. and most days returning home at 7:00 P.M., started to wear on all of us, and I eventually decided to find a position that would keep me on Long Island, closer to home with less travel time involved. At first, this decision meant working four half days a week. The motherhood, family and career plates were spinning quite nicely. As time went by, I worked more and more hours until it became full-time, five days a week. Organized day care came into my life then and there were many days that I felt like the worst mother in the world—leaving my child with strangers, watching her little face through the blinds as she held on to the day care director's hand and waved goodbye. The motherhood plate was starting to seriously teeter!

As Alexandra grew, I lamented the moments that I was missing. I couldn't even think of volunteering to go on a class trip, and being class mother was totally out of the question. I kept telling myself that I had to keep that career plate spinning and I tried to do my best to maintain a balance. Of course, I then compounded the potential of a motherhood plate crash when my husband Bob and I brought our second daughter into the world. And what a serious balance shaker she turned out to be! Due on June third, she arrived on April twenty-second. Samantha was an absolute joy, but for anyone who has given birth to a preemie, you know that not a day goes by when you don't worry about their every breath and think about the potential future consequences that you may face as they develop. Well, thankfully, she's absolutely fine and is now a teenager, but having two children made me realize that the motherhood plate in the spinning game was about to come crashing down if I didn't make some changes to the velocity of the career plate.

That was when I decided to become an independent financial advisor. Freedom! My schedule was my own. I wasn't working for someone else, subject to their schedule and demands of "9 to 5ism." I could make my own schedule. I could see clients when I wanted to, or had to, but it gave me control over the speed of the spin. This meant that I could go on class trips, or I could be class mother; things that I could never expect to be able to do working for someone else and away from home. The balance that I was looking for finally seemed like a reality. I wasn't having the pangs of guilt and constantly worrying that I was neglecting one part of the plate chain for another.

It's been a little over a decade since I made this change. Challenges still present themselves. Adding the "teenager" factor to the spinning game certainly brings an unexpected element to the wobbly equilibrium of motherhood, family, and career. I have always tried to keep things in perspective and make sure that I am paying attention to everything that needs it. Of course, there are days when I am completely overwhelmed by this task and am not above a meltdown here and there. I have found though, that modern technology helps when you are trying to keep these plates spinning. Unlike that poor man on *Ed Sullivan*, I can use my electronic calendar to keep track of where all the plates are and where they are going, use e-mail and instant messaging to answer any emergency that may come up during the day, or to send a message to my girls letting them know that even though I'm not with them I love them bunches. I can keep the plates spinning even when I'm not watching them like a hawk. Or, at least, that's what they think!

~Donna La Scala

52

Remembering Who I Am

The true way to render ourselves happy is to love our work and
find in it our pleasure.
~Francoise de Motteville

When I was thirty years old, I got married. For a while, I thought I had married the wrong man, but it is more true to say my ex-husband married the wrong woman.

He had, I think, a very clear idea of the type of woman he wanted to marry, and I had a very clear idea of the type of woman he wanted me to be, the type of woman I really wanted to be: a woman to make my parents proud, to finally settle down, grow up.

I had had disastrous relationships throughout my twenties. Had dated a string of unavailable men, either physically or emotionally, and wondered if it was possible to find love without pain, without getting my heart broken all over again.

Here was a man who seemed to be everything I should be looking for, and if he didn't make my heart beat faster, surely that was more sensible. So I married with my head rather than with my heart; told myself that this was a different kind of love; this was doing the right thing.

I had grown up assuming I would have a similar life to my mother. She didn't work, and I think that somewhere, deep down, I had thought I wouldn't either. But she had me at twenty-four, and I didn't have my first child until I was thirty-one. Things were clearly going to be quite different.

I had already published two books by the time I got married, both bestsellers, and it never occurred to me not to work. Perhaps if I'd been in a different field, or been part of the corporate world I would have stopped, but I worked for myself, and it seemed unfeasible that I wouldn't carry on. And financially, it made no sense for me not to work. I was paid too much to justify not doing it, and it was clear, very early on, that I was going to be the breadwinner.

I had four children, quickly, and kept writing throughout my pregnancies. *Bookends* while I was pregnant with my first, *Babyville* immediately afterwards. It never occurred to me to not work, for working helped me hold on to a piece of myself when I felt the rest of myself disappearing. Working helped me cling to sanity.

When my life felt like a haze of sterilizers, baby bottles, breast pumps and screaming. When I could barely get out of my pajamas for the day, or put my colicky baby down long enough to take a shower, working helped me remember who I was.

When I lost myself in a haze of post-partum depression, went to bed every night resenting my husband for being able to escape, to go to work and be with adults, working helped me remember who I was.

I continued to work, pouring everything into my novels. *Swapping Lives*, about a woman trapped in a life she didn't want, and finally, after we passed the seven-year mark, *Second Chance*, about Holly, who finally finds the courage to leave a marriage that is entirely wrong for her.

Writing has always been a catharsis for me, but in writing *Second Chance*, it became life-changing. I knew, without a shadow of a doubt, not only was I trapped in the wrong life, but that it was possible for me to be happy.

Making sense of my feelings through my writing, together with the fact of my financial independence, allowed me to leave. The fact that I hadn't just supported myself throughout my marriage, I had supported my entire family; the freedom of knowing I could continue to support myself, and my children, gave me the courage to walk away and start again.

It wasn't easy. If I thought being a working mother of four was hard, it was nothing compared to being a working single mother of four. I wasn't on my own for long—I met Beloved soon after I separated—but he is not the father of my children, and to all intents and purposes, I still consider myself a single mother, for I am the one who runs the lives of my children, and when the buck stops, it inevitably stops with me.

Now I work not just because I have a family to support, but because it gives me choices, because it helps me be as whole a person as I can be, and honestly, because it helps me be a better mother. For I am a better mother when I have time for myself. I am a better mother when I am stimulated, emotionally, mentally and spiritually. I am a better mother when I have time out to remember who I was before these small people took over my life.

I adore my children. My children are the very best thing to have happened to me, and certainly the best result from my first marriage, and I love the fact that I have a tremendous amount of balance in my life—in many ways, the perfect job.

I get up with my kids every day, make them breakfast—eggs, waffles, pancakes, toast—round up their homework, stuff it in the backpacks, pull out fifty-seven crumpled up pieces of damp paper from the bottom of the backpack, (mostly permission slips that were due in the week before) yell at the top of my lungs because all four children's shoes have clearly walked themselves off in the middle of the night because THEY ARE NEVER IN THE MUDROOM WHERE THEY BELONG, walk, bleary-eyed, to the bus stop with them, and kiss them goodbye as they clamber up the steps of the school bus.

I then get to shower, dress, waste half an hour looking at gossip websites, realize the time, grab my laptop and run down to my local library where I sit, resisting—mostly successfully—the urge to play computer solitaire for three hours, and instead write my novels.

I am always finished by lunchtime, and aside from the odd book tours, I am always at home when the children get off the bus, and get to be "Mom" for the rest of the day. It is the perfect balance, and I love that I am defined as so much more than a mother. Being a mother is a gift, and a joy, but it is not all that I am. I am a wife, a friend, a writer, a blogger, an artist, a cook, a gardener, an amateur pediatrician specializing in skin complaints, and an agony aunt.

(No wonder I'm permanently exhausted...)

I work not because I have to prove anything to anyone else, but because it makes me more of myself. Working makes me whole, and I couldn't imagine a life without it.

Having said that, if you offered me a stress-free life on a beautiful Caribbean island somewhere, no deadlines, no book tours, no interviews ever again, I may have to seriously consider it....

~Jane Green

Power MOMS

Ladies Who Launch

*Stay-at-Home Moms
Create Their Own Jobs and Give Back*

Ladies Who Launch

There is no comparison between that which is lost by not succeeding and that which is lost by not trying.

~Francis Bacon

Even before I had my own children, I was inspired by the beauty of the lifestyles created by women entrepreneurs. For years I had been working in the corporate world, first as a lawyer and later, after obtaining my MBA, as an investment banker. I felt desperately uncreative and I kept thinking that there had to be more to the real world of work. Having come from a family of business owners, and being a lover of academics, I felt completely let down. After working for a few start-ups, I began to notice how different work was for women who ventured out on their own. Rather than compartmentalize their lives, they were building their passions, lifestyles and businesses together in a holistic way. So I decided to start my own business—a magazine that would showcase these courageous women.

I began putting together the pieces and learning the media business as I went along. But then I became pregnant with my first child. My husband and I decided to move to Cleveland, Ohio, which made the chances of launching a magazine that much more difficult. So I went online. On my own, and full of doubt as to how I was going to do this and make money with a small child, I started slowly—building my subscriber base by word of mouth. Most of this was done during nap time, those few precious hours when I could work on my passion, adding layers into my life beyond being a stay-at-home mom.

Ladies Who Launch was a one-of-a-kind website when I started it in 2002, which amazed me. Women were launching businesses at twice the rate of men, were making choices based on their need for freedom and flexibility, and were reaping excellent returns by redefining traditional business models. I was floored that no one was addressing this astonishing fact. There were so many female success stories out there that my entire goal for Ladies Who Launch at the time was to showcase these triumphs as well as the passions that brought them about.

The concept for my weekly e-mail success story was simple. It highlighted women who built businesses on their own terms along with the off-the-beaten paths they took to get there. Some women went to business school, others had no experience whatsoever, some started on a hunch, others wrote elaborate plans—but the bottom line was, there was no single foolproof process that worked. My newsletter, with its sincere words of advice, inspiration and shared stories created momentum among women far and wide, encouraging them to give their dreams a shot!

As the weekly e-mails continued to circulate and the website grew in scope, it became clear that women were craving community, tools and education. They wanted an outlet for sharing information, ideas, experiences and resources. Ladies Who Launch quickly evolved to offer local and worldwide workshops in addition to an enhanced array of accessible tools online. My mission evolved as well—making entrepreneurship a viable option for every woman became the main goal.

I am and will always be personally invested in this goal. I know that by providing solid roadmaps, start-up and growth packages, workshops and access to expert seminars on everything from phone systems to online marketing, my company can make women's dreams reality. The truth is, every woman has a project, a passion, a dream or a creative outlet that she would like to explore more deeply. By removing the intimidation, fear and hardship from the process, we can make it fun by connecting women with each other and giving them tangible tools and resources they can really use.

Now, six years after I started Ladies Who Launch, women are still driven by the same lifestyle desires and still derive as much pleasure from picking up their kids at school as they do from running million dollar businesses. The idea of working from home, growing a business organically, taking small steps and testing plans as they go, still outweighs for many women the security of a corporate job, the perks that go with it and the chance to enjoy predictable financial rewards.

As the mother of two small girls, my life is never easy, but never dull. I'll admit there are times when I wonder if I'm doing it all wrong and missing out on something special. Am I there when it matters, am I having fun? Do I feel joy on a regular basis? Can I define joy by the moments in between the planning and executing? Am I in the "flow" of my life, my work, my family and love? Rather than let myself be consumed by guilt, I have learned to let go of it and live in the moment.

One thing I know for sure is that every day I demonstrate commitment, hard work and passion that make me an unparalleled role model for my little girls. It is my hope that they will find their own joys and passions and develop self-esteem by trying things, failing, succeeding and overcoming. I have failed many times in my life but my motto is "never give up on your dreams." Whether you want to build a multimillion dollar business or take up gymnastics in your forties, anything is possible, and often we learn more from failure than success.

Each of us has a purpose. Interestingly though, as the Founder and CEO of Ladies Who Launch, I don't think mine is to be a leader. I'm more of a master facilitator and communicator. I believe that I was meant to inspire and awaken possibility in others. However, for one person to inspire another she must first be inspired herself and be actively living her dreams, parallel tracking both, which I am.

Every day I try to be aware of my choices then decide how I want to live my life and adjust my strategies accordingly. The only constant in this world is that everything is always in flux. The sooner we realize this inevitable fact, the sooner we can play the game of life the way we want, taking full responsibility for our choices and diving head first into them with enthusiasm.

I have many more ideas and passions up my sleeve and many more dreams to play out. I would like to try opening a restaurant, buying a ski house or traveling with my girls and my husband to exotic and fresh, new places. I feel optimistic about the future both personally and with respect to Ladies Who Launch. Optimism, I believe, is the ultimate mindset for success!

~Victoria Colligan

Reprinted by permission of Tom Swick
© 2008

54

Paying It Forward

There are some things you learn best in calm, and some in storm.
~Willa Cather

August 28th, 2005, was a day that would change my life forever. That morning, after arriving home late at night from the hospital with my third baby girl, Abigail Gage Boyle, I could hear my two other daughters (Mackenzie, age four and Chase, age two) anxiously waiting for us to wake up so they could meet their new baby sister. There was a nervous sense of excitement for all of us, wondering how our family dynamics would change. Would things be that much different with three children vs. the manageable two? I heard the pitter patter of feet and giggles heading towards my room and soon after the introductions were made we spent the morning taking photos, laughing, kissing, and rolling around in bed.

My mom and dad were visiting from Florida to shower their two older granddaughters with affection, making the transition much smoother. I was sleep deprived and thrilled to be home in my own bed. We live on a river and the water views are medicinal for me. Just looking out my window relaxes me with nature's artwork. My father and husband decided that the only way to give me some peace and quiet was by physically taking the girls out of the house on a fishing trip.

It was a picture perfect summer day, with clear blue skies. There was a warm, salty smelling breeze caressing all exposed skin that morning. The fishermen made their way down the dock to unload their gear before heading back up to the house for a quick lunch. As

I casually glanced down to the dock from my bedroom window I saw Mackenzie trying to scoop up jellyfish with a net and I saw Chase sorting through the trays of her daddy's tackle box. My dad was on the dock involved in some project and my husband had his head in our anchor well. Chase must have hooked herself on something, letting out a yelp, so my husband decided to lift her onto the boat, putting her out of harm's way... or so he thought.

Chase is a very independent child, and at that moment she wanted to be doing exactly what her big sister was doing, netting jellies. Within the blink of an eye she tried to get off the boat backwards, thinking that her feet would land on our floating dock... but she never made it. She slipped six feet down into the water between our dock and boat without a splash or a sound. Mackenzie screamed to Daddy that Chasey was in the water and wasn't swimming. She pointed to her exact entry point, a tight space where Patrick and my father would not have looked first. My father saw her floating towards the surface underwater with her eyes and mouth wide open. I casually glanced back out my bedroom window and saw the panic chaos. A chill ran up my spine and I knew in my gut immediately what had happened. I left Abigail in the middle of my bed and bolted downstairs and out of the house.

When I arrived on the dock I saw my beautiful, precious Chase, blue, convulsing with lifeless, wide open, catatonic eyes. I screamed for my mom to call 911. I don't remember dropping to my knees and begging God to spare us, to please not take my baby, to please bring her back. In slow motion I saw Patrick administering CPR and the Heimlich Maneuver while Mackenzie and my father stared on in quiet shock. Somewhere in my head I heard sirens but my entire life was flashing before me. How could this be possible? I had just come home with a beautiful new life. How could I lose one?

I felt a rush of different emotions ranging from extreme sorrow and pain to anger, guilt and blame. I tasted how a family can fall apart after losing a child accidentally. As suddenly as those emotions came I witnessed the life come back into my child's eyes as she screamed "Mom!" while violently beginning to vomit. I didn't know if there would be any lasting repercussions, nor did I care. At that very second, I knew she was back on the planet with us. In the ambulance, the attendant told me to do anything I could to keep her conscious and awake. They wanted to check her short-term memory. I had given Chase and Mackenzie their own kittens (Sebastian and Serafina) for their birthdays a month earlier so that they would also be "mommies." The paramedics were asking Chase her name and age and she was not responding as she vomited in and out of consciousness.

I asked Chase what her baby's name was and she said "Sebastian" with conviction between sputters. I knew my child was not only back on the planet but she had her wits about her too. It was at that exact moment that I decided I was going to give back by making a positive out of a negative. I learned that day how crucial time can be. From the minute an accident happens until someone calls 911 the clock is ticking. How one reacts in the first five minutes of a crisis is crucial because the average ambulance response time in the U.S. is between five and fifteen minutes. Most people do not know that brain damage occurs due to lack of oxygen to the brain in five minutes. Brain death is probable after six minutes. Unintentional injury is the leading cause of death in children under the age of fourteen.

Recognizing that we had been spared and that we were given a second chance, I created C.H.A.S.E. for Life (CPR-Heimlich-Awareness-Safety-Education) hoping that our experience would inspire others to get educated so they too, could have a happy ending. My mission is to educate anyone involved with children in the basic lifesaving skills needed to sustain a life until help can take over. C.H.A.S.E. was created to change the statistics in this country, with prevention, education and resources along with national awareness campaigns. We created an eighteen minute animated instructional called *How to Save a Life* with the intentions of it being shown nationally. In less than two years time we have become a nationally recognized tax-exempt nonprofit.

The C.H.A.S.E. initiative is currently being piloted in fourteen hospitals in New Jersey along with five hospitals in New York City. Our goal is obtainable and we have the remedy for a global social problem. I am grateful we were able to save our child that day, and I hope my experience will help save other children.

~Farley Boyle

55

You Can Have It All

What is sad for women of my generation is that they weren't supposed to work if they had families. What were they going to do when the children are grown—watch the raindrops coming down the window pain?

~Jacqueline Kennedy Onassis

When my first baby, Veronica, was born I felt that I had it all—the loving husband and the baby I always wanted and waited so long to have! I just couldn't get enough of her—I couldn't wait for her to wake up so that I could play with her; I wrote her songs and letters; made hundreds of pictures and videotaped her every progress.

When Veronica was two years old something strange happened. As I was hanging out the laundry I felt tears running down my cheeks. And then I felt a deep yearning inside of me for something else, for something that was not a part of my life at the time. As much as I loved my baby and staying home with her, I had to do something more.

So I went back to school. I decided to continue my education through an online university (Capella University) so that I could still be with Veronica as much as possible. I studied while she slept and a year later I received a Graduate Certificate in Teaching and Training Online.

That same year I traveled to Las Vegas to attend a workshop on Accelerated Learning Techniques and became a certified trainer. Four months later I flew to Thailand to attend a Transformational

Thinking Certificate Program. By then Veronica was three and a half years old and I was "working" on having another baby.

When I got back from Thailand I was so full of ideas and desires to start a career in training that I decided to postpone having the second child. Yet, just two weeks later I discovered that I was pregnant!

"Well," I said to myself, "why should a pregnancy and a baby stop me from doing what I really want?!" So I proceeded to design my first workshop and delivered it when I was seven months pregnant. I have to mention that I had a terrible fear of public speaking and it took all my courage and determination not to give up on my idea.

After the success of my first workshop I was "too pregnant" to deliver any more but I still felt I had to do something, so I converted my workshop into an e-book, designed a website and six weeks later started selling it online. I knew absolutely nothing about e-books or selling them online when I had that idea.

My second baby, Julia, was born a week after Veronica's fourth birthday. Three months later we sold our house and moved to Bulgaria! My husband and I wanted to do corporate training for emerging markets and decided to be closer to the action. Not knowing anyone there and with two young children, we dived right in to finding clients and developing our first workshop.

I put my desk in the living room so that I would not miss "any action" while I was writing workbooks and doing my research. I also hired someone else to do the house chores so that when I did not work I could just be with my girls.

I still wrote songs and letters to my kids, as well as took lots of photos and videos. My career, though demanding, provided a perfect balance for me.

When Veronica turned seven and Julia turned three I felt like my life was getting a little easier. The girls were in school and more and more independent; I was in the middle of writing my second book and there was a big demand for my coaching services. Though I really wanted to have a boy, I decided my family was perfect as it was and that I should not have any more children and give more focus to my career.

Ha! As I said that to my gynecologist, he informed me (after the routine check-up) that I was pregnant! Completely shocked and realizing that with the third child I might have to let go or postpone quite a few of my dreams, I did not know what to do!

Since I am still not sure "how it happened" I thought to myself that this was really meant to be and it was not for me to decide whether this was the right time or not. So I just decided, as with everything else in my life, to take it one step at a time.

I did not give up on any of my dreams. Two weeks after my baby boy David was born, my book was published. I felt like I gave birth to two children that year. The joy and fulfillment was indescribable.

I chose to breastfeed all of my kids, which meant frequent wakings at night and not much power to think or do. Yet, I had to get back to work—my clients were waiting and the book needed attention.

When I had only Veronica and no career, I used to think that it would be impossible for me to take care of more children. I just could not image how some women did it. Now, with three children ages nine, five, and one, as well as a rapidly growing career, I realize that we greatly underestimate our power and our strength!

My new book, *The One Minute Coach: Change Your Life One Minute at a Time,* came out in October 2008. I am busy doing what I love and I have created a perfect balance between my career and my family.

My children are growing up understanding that taking care of personal needs is just as important, if not more, as taking care of other people's needs. I still work from home and I am a very involved mom—attending all of the recitals, teacher meetings, doing projects with my kids, and taking them on "dates with Mommy."

When we let go of our fears, do what we love, and just take it one step at a time—we can have it all!

~Masha Malka

56

How My Daughter's Simple Request Inspired Me

Children reinvent your world for you.
~Susan Sarandon

Before I had my first child in 1999, I truly enjoyed my professional career. But when I first held my son's hand, I knew that my life's journey was to be a full-time mom! I could not imagine leaving this adorably sweet little boy with anyone other than myself. My whole life was about being a mom.

Then, in 2002, my daughter was born. To be a stay-at-home mom was an even stronger passion now. Until October 2005. On Halloween, we were decorating the house, making costumes, and preparing for parties. My daughter, just two and a half, asked, "Mommy, can you draw me as a ballerina?" I said, "Of course, princess."

I believe everything happens for a reason. We might not know the reason right away, but during our lifetime, the reason will become clear. There was a reason for my daughter's request and why I decided to paint it on canvas. But the reason was not clear.

My daughter loved the painting, as did friends and family. I painted more characters, and started making some grocery money using a talent that was hidden inside me. Then, in January 2006, while I was recovering from an operation, I brought some paintings to a local retailer. I only had about fifteen minutes, as I needed to pick up my daughter from preschool, but thought I could make it. Remember, things happen for a reason.

The retailer agreed to display my paintings, and wanted to buy the rights to the characters for children's T-shirts. Was my painting hobby turning into a licensing opportunity?

My husband and I decided that instead of working out deals with lawyers, I should become an entrepreneur, or as we moms say, a mompreneur. That same moment, we started to brainstorm a name for the company. At my desk (aka the kitchen table), my husband and I remembered we used to call our son "little stinker." Not to describe his smell, but to appreciate his innocent curiosity. That memory led us to a name... StinkyKids. Things happen for a reason; there was a reason I chose StinkyKids, though it was not clear yet. But the reason for my daughter's request finally was.

Establishing my new company, I appreciated my own mom's entrepreneurial spirit. When her sister died from uterine cancer, my mom decided to leave the corporate world and form a non-profit in her honor which delivers gift boxes to children and adults battling cancer. I decided that StinkyKids would donate a percentage of its profits to her charity.

Juggling a full-time job as mom while my husband traveled, somehow I managed to create a T-shirt business. Late nights, early mornings, forgetting play dates, not sending birthday cards on time, leaving dishes in the sink, relying on the electronic babysitter was my new life. I asked my family for a "Free Pass" from all of the things I used to do in order to accomplish my goals.

In the beginning there were six characters (now there are ten) and I named each character after real people for inventory tracking. I also decided early on, as I was donating towards the fight against cancer, these characters could represent the importance of giving back and helping the community.

My brain cells were on overdrive and memories helped my business plan get better every day. The memory of my son playing with a friend, who was not nice, teaching him to "Always Be A Leader Of Good" made me think. What if these StinkyKids characters were "little stinkers," making right choices and spreading their motto "Always Be A Leader Of Good?" Things happen for a reason and these reasons were becoming clearer every day.

I began to work at art shows, drive to retailers to create business, and establish a website for online sales (www.stinkykids.com). I put together press kits, and much more. While doing this, my kids were either in the back of the car, under a table, or helping. It was hectic, but exciting. Looking back at the first year, I didn't realize how much I was teaching my kids about real life, hard work and the passion to succeed; lessons I might not have been able to give as just a stay-home mom. Reasons are clearer!

Sales began to take off, and from grass roots, StinkyKids was becoming a household name and the media was calling (*The Today Show, FOXNews, ABCNews*). Clients loved the characters so much, they demanded to learn more about them. Remember, things happen for a reason? Now I knew the reason I gave them names and called them StinkyKids. People were becoming emotionally attached to the characters; whether they remembered being called a little stinker themselves, or used the expression with their kids. The StinkyKids were taking on lives of their own and a brand was forming around these ten diverse characters.

With my business partners, my son, daughter and husband, we gave life to the StinkyKids. Each character is a "Leader Of Good" of some of life's important lessons. They have favorite hobbies, colors, foods, what they want to be when they grow up, and their special talents. All of this was written by my own kids; which makes the characters that much more significant.

In three years from that famous request, thousands of StinkyKids T-shirts have been sold. We have donated to help many other causes including finding cures for autism and sickle cell disease. We have donated products to orphans in the Congo, Ronald McDonald House, and created a T-shirt for Girls On The Run. A doodle is now on its way to becoming an animated series and a brand with endless opportunities. The reasons are clear!

I do not know how I accomplish it all in a twenty-four hour day. But every night, when I finally put my head on my pillow, I know my hard work and passion have made my life the most rewarding it has been in my forty years. Would I have ever thought I could be so passionate about anything other than my kids? Never. But the reasons are clear, the mission is strong, and my kids are better because of my decisions. My husband and I talk about more than our kids and we have a respected partnership. My daughter pretends to be an entrepreneur instead of playing with dolls and has set up her own "office." I discuss new ideas with my son and he is a big part of many of my business decisions.

My daughter's simple request inspired me to be more than just her mommy and is the greatest gift our family ever received. My kids inspire me to be who I was meant to be and to follow the path my life is meant to be on.

Things happen for a reason.

~Britt Menzies

57

A Golden Glow

We make a living by what we get, we make a life by what we give.
~Winston Churchill

It's 5:00 A.M. on a typical school day. I rise from bed to do my daily yoga regimen. The house is enveloped in darkness until I turn on my television to hear my instructor tell me in her calming voice to open up my heart to the energy of the morning. I feel my soul breathe in the peacefulness of a new day. As I finish the invigorating workout, the room begins to brighten with a glow of early light. A new day has started and I feel blessed.

As I walk up the stairs to my sons' room, I feel the same rush of emotion I did when I checked on them as babies sleeping in their cribs. Except now my older son's six-foot three-inch body dangles off his bed and my younger son's mop of long brown hair hides his face. As I gently kiss them good morning, they roll over and sigh contently, knowing they have a few more minutes of peace before their school day begins. As I open up their window blinds, their room becomes illuminated with a golden glow that warms and energizes my soul.

The morning soon becomes chaotic as these big lumbering bodies rush around the house trying to make the school bus stop on time. As they run out the door, the soft colors of early morning are gone and replaced by the clear light of day. They are off to school and I settle down at my home office to run my business.

Gracing my desk are three sentimental objects—an American Eagle Award given to me as a United States Small Business

Administration Women in Business Champion, a photograph of me holding a lacrosse stick with my older son and his teenage lacrosse friends, and a photograph of me with my two sons. All three items remind me every day how powerful my choice was to become a woman entrepreneur.

They say women are more likely to become entrepreneurs if they had female role models. I fit that statistic perfectly. My mother owned a clothing boutique as well as a ski shop with my father. My aunt owned restaurants and a real estate company. I remember how happy they were running their businesses while finding time to spend with their families. For the late 1960s, they were pioneering women, balancing work and family for the first time in generations. Their independence and zest for a more modern life than women before them must have sparked an entrepreneurial spirit in my soul that lay dormant until I became a mother.

One early morning, I started to awaken my sons with my morning kiss, when something deep inside me awakened too. I realized I didn't want to rush my sons out of bed anymore to bring them to a day care center just to rush to my events management job, where I would wish my day away because I wanted to be with them. I also knew I loved my profession. In that moment, I flashed back to my mother and aunt working in their businesses. In that golden glow of morning, the dormant entrepreneurial spirit awoke in me. I looked at the rising sun and knew I was going to start my own event management company. It was the dawning of a new day in my career and in my life.

Starting a business can be exhilarating and terrifying at the same time. I knew I could count on my eight years of event planning experience, education, female role models, and passion for my profession to provide a solid foundation to launch my company. My first clients were individuals who had worked with me before and trusted my abilities. Their confidence, combined with a strong purpose and determination, gave me all I needed to begin. I knew I couldn't let this golden opportunity pass me by. I knew I could create the life I desired.

Shortly after becoming a woman entrepreneur, I realized I needed to surround myself with women who were taking the same risks. I discovered an organization of women who met monthly to discuss the pros and cons of being business owners. Open communication, exchange of ideas, and unshakable support from these women ignited my early business success. One year later I had developed a deep passion for aiding and inspiring other women entrepreneurs and became the organization's leader.

One of my favorite members in the group was a boisterous, older female who once said, "To be a smart woman entrepreneur, you must set a course for your business, but if the road starts to naturally bend in another direction, you must follow the curve and see where it leads you." After ten years of running my company and nine years as the leader of this growing organization for women business owners, I remembered her words and created my second company, this one dedicated to promoting women entrepreneurship all over New York State. I announced the news at a gathering of 500 women at an event that celebrates and applauds women for taking chances. This was my chance—my chance to help even more women make the same choice I made looking out my sons' window one golden morning.

The eagle statue on my desk reminds me every day that I work on behalf of women entrepreneurs everywhere, helping them to move toward their own bright entrepreneurial future. It also represents a strong belief by the business community that I have made, and will continue to make, a positive impact on women entrepreneurship in the future.

The photograph of me holding the lacrosse stick with my sixteen-year-old son and his West Genesee friends was taken after they challenged me to a lacrosse contest with their junior varsity goalie. I was wearing my favorite pink shirt that stated, "Well behaved women rarely make history." The photo is a token of the challenge I took on with these young men, hoping they would see that girls and women can do anything boys and men can do. I wore it proudly and won their respect even though I lost the contest.

The photograph of my two sons reminds me that I will never

regret the personal and professional decisions I have made to be the best mother I can be while being the best woman I can be. When my life is over, I hope a sun is rising on the eastern horizon, more women are achieving business success because of my dedication to them and their companies, and my two wonderful sons appreciate the power of women to make the right choices for their lives — important choices that create a ripple effect that change the world.

As another day ends and the glow of the setting sun now shines on my desk, I look out the window and feel peaceful knowing tomorrow brings another golden opportunity for me to awaken my sons to a glorious new day and to shine more rays of inspiration and hope to women entrepreneurs everywhere. Life is golden.

Another day has ended and I feel blessed.

~Tracy Higginbotham

For Better or for Worse, and Yes, for Lunch

The most successful people are those who are good at plan B.
~James Yorke

W hy would I ever want to go to the trouble of starting my own business selling skin care?" I asked my
friend Cathy. I was "retired" from my career in New
York City and had settled comfortably into my cushy life as a stay-at-
home wife and mother of two young children in Connecticut.

Cathy had called me, all excited, to tell me about a health and
wellness company specializing in botanically based skincare. She
knew that healthy living was a priority for me and my family. Politely,
I told her that I had no interest in undertaking any kind of business
venture, but was definitely interested in learning more about what
types of products the company had to offer. I had been looking for
pure and safe products that actually did what they claimed to do for
about twenty years and had tried everything! Since Cathy was married to Al, my lifelong friend, I trusted her belief in the integrity of
this company and its products. Upon ordering a slew of products for
my entire family, I was blown away by how much we loved them. I
was sold on these products and the company, but not on the idea of
a business, at least not yet.

I felt so completely blessed that I had the luxury of being able to stay at home to raise my children without any financial pressures pulling me back into the workforce. Maybe on the outside my life looked about as good as it could get: a loving husband, two adorable children, two dogs, a beautiful home. The reality was, I felt restless. Being creative and working with people was always a great joy for me. I also liked change and was a bit of a gypsy. The life of a house-wife and mother was not conducive to satisfying this part of my soul. My friend Jenny teased me, saying, "You should start some type of a business, you like helping people and could be doing something profitable for your family as well as others." I wasn't interested. The risks verses the rewards just didn't seem worth my time and effort! Plus, I knew that I loved my flexibility and freedom.

My husband, Greg, travels a lot for his job. This often leaves me feeling angry, frustrated, alone and isolated. I had waited my entire life to meet someone like Greg. He is tall, handsome, kind and generous and has a great career. We love being together and with our children. We are both passionate about modeling for our kids the importance of being helpful and generous to others, especially with the sharing of our time. But again, Greg travels a lot (hmm, did I already say this?) He works in the investment business and travels all over the world, sometimes for weeks at a time. The kids and I spray his cologne on our T-shirts and sleep with them while he is away. He also has a whole lot of stress in his life. We watched his darling dad die from a stroke at age sixty-five, just a few checks into his social security, he used to joke. He was still working as a stockbroker at his own firm. I wonder what he would think of the financial industry today. It makes me shudder.

What I want more than anything in the world is to have my hus-band at home with me more, and for him to have less stress. During the lecture section of my women's Bible study one day, the speaker talked about her husband having been laid off from work. "Honey, what's for lunch?" he asked one day. She replied, "Dear, I took you for better, or for worse, but not for lunch!" Of course, we howled. And as I howled, all I could think of was how wonderful it would be to have Greg home "for lunch" more often!

Cathy asked me, "Elizabeth, If you could change anything in your life, what would it be?"

I immediately answered, "I would have Greg home with us more."

"What would you need to do to make this happen?" she asked.

Then it truly dawned on me. I had been clunking along in life, just trying to stay afloat after surviving the toddler years with my children. I had been thinking of my feelings, my fatigue, my day-to-day, my resentment with my husband being away so much! Wow, was I humbled! I had found an opportunity that could encompass all my passions: validation of my intelligence, travel, helping others and creating a stream of income large enough to give my husband the option to retire young and healthy. And all having the flexibility of working from home!

So I started my journey with Arbonne in March of 2006. This business hasn't always been easy. I have had to endure nights out, whining children wanting me off the phone, criticism from friends and family and a variety of other people from whom I least expected it. But I have refused to take my eye off my ultimate goal of giving my family a back-up should we have an unexpected shift in our livelihood. And I also am thrilled to have the ability to share this opportunity with others who are looking for the same.

I feel especially blessed that I am building a business that provides passive residual income, especially at this very unstable time in our country's economy. Saloons and salons are recession-proof businesses. This is the Ultimate Plan B in my book! My parents were depression-era folks, born in Mississippi in 1916 and 1923. They instilled in me the core values of honest work and never living beyond my means. They also taught me that "for whom much has been given, much is expected." I truly believe that being a servant to others is the only way to truly thrive. I am happy that I have the freedom to serve my family by relieving potential stress for the person I cherish so dearly! And I am particularly grateful for the guidance of my friends

Cathy, Karla and Rachelle, who have all helped me to develop my skills for success. Mostly, I look forward to many days of "What's for lunch honey?"

~Elizabeth Garrett

The Life with Lisa Show

The art of living lies less in eliminating our troubles than in growing with them.
~Bernard M. Birch

I could not have known when I was starting my Internet company, in order to supplement my husband's income and to stay at home with our four-year-old son, that a year later I would be a thirty-two-year-old widow and a single mom finding my way through an abyss of grief and recovery that seemed impossible to bridge much of the time.

After a year-long illness, my husband of nearly eleven years died and I was left with the agonizing reality that the two-person team that once brought this family through all things good and bad, had been reduced to just me. I'd met my husband, Wesley, when I was only eight years old and I couldn't remember my life without him in it. Wesley trusted that I would take care of our son and myself after he died, but facing life without him was arduous and lonely. Our son was counting on me to pull us both through.

Over the next several months, I learned to delegate responsibilities and concentrated on my son and rebuilding our life. There was nothing to juggle in the first two years after my husband died because I didn't allow chaos in our lives. I worked when I could and when I couldn't—I didn't. There was no negotiating what was needed of me. My son needed me and I needed him. Sales decreased in those early years of rebuilding my personal life but never to a level where the business wasn't profitable. Somehow, everything managed with and without me, with the care and extraordinary help of the quality people I had in place.

Within five years of starting my Internet company, I had been a guest on *The Rachel Ray Show* and the *Oprah & Friends* radio show. Numerous placements in national magazines sang the praises of our children's decorative products and our story, and our products were placed as set decoration on hit national television shows. It was then that I decided to make a change in my life and close my business, but not without a plan to better our lives and continue our ever evolving story.

When my son was nearing ten years old, I started to feel like I needed to show him more of the world outside of my home office and teach him that some people actually go to work to earn a living. I spent the first ten years of my son's life being there for him at every turn, every hour of every day. I loved this about our life and so did he. Now it was time to refresh my goals, achieve new dreams and bring him along as I did it.

I had been wanting to do a radio show for several months. I had developed an interest after being interviewed when my first book was released, and I was encouraged by a radio producer to move forward with my efforts. I told myself I would have a show by December 2007, within six months of setting the goal. By January of the following year I had done nothing to work toward that goal, so in February I finally got with it, produced a demo CD, and got a meeting with the general manager of seven radio stations in my area. After an hour-long meeting, I was given the opportunity to produce *The Life with Lisa Show* and was offered an additional job that I would be creating as the Community Service Coordinator for all seven stations.

I committed to part-time and made sure it was known that I would only work twenty hours a week on the community service aspect of my job and that my son was my first priority. I would still pick him up every day after school and be at every school and athletic event. And when summer came, we would need to create a new schedule that would accommodate my son's schedule. My new boss understood that I'd made promises to my son's dad to take care of him for both of us, and being the mom and the dad and doing it well was a full-time experience that I wouldn't trade for any job or opportunity. It is my life and I am grateful for all that it brings me every day.

One of the greatest benefits of my new venture is that it belongs to both of us. My son is involved in the community aspect of my work, learning to reach out to those in need who can benefit from our help. He enjoys coming to my office and often sits in the studio quietly listening as I interview guests and conduct my show live.

He recently asked me, "Mom, how did you get your radio show?"

"I paid attention," I told him.

"To what?" he asked.

"To life," I answered.

He smiled big. I love it when he smiles big.

I always tell my son that we can ask any question. We have the right to ask for anything, and it's best to have earned the right to ask the question. When I asked for my radio show, I knew I had lived enough life and worked through enough adversity and triumph to have earned a show I wanted to produce and call *The Life with Lisa Show*. The station I asked to air my show also had the right to say no, but they didn't. They said yes. And had they said no, I would've asked someone else, because I knew what I had to say was worth asking for.

In the past decade of my life I have been a wife and mother, a cancer survivor, an author, an entrepreneur and a widow. I have met countless survivors like myself, both in illness and in life, and my message has remained the same and is borrowed from Henry Ford: "Whether you believe you can do a thing or not, you are right."

This holds true in all areas of life and I consider this statement and its possibilities every day. Whether facing a life threatening illness, changing careers at middle age, going on a first date after fifteen years of thinking I'd never have to, or being enlightened by my child who I hope to inspire each day, there is possibility at every turn. I've always believed in finding the balance between what I have lost and what I can gain from the experience of life. And if I help others along my own journey, then it's the right life.

~Lisa Bradshaw

Fear No More

Wherever you go, go with all your heart.

~Confucius

I've been a work-at-home mom since 2001, and would consider myself successful now, although it certainly has been a long road to get here.

How did I get where I am? When the Twin Towers fell, I was expecting my second child. She was born a few days later, into a world full of fear. A week after that, my husband's department was closed and his job was gone. So our one-income family became a no-income family overnight, while I was adjusting to a brand new baby and caring for our four-year-old very active son. Of course, the bills keep right on coming whether you have a job or not. That was obviously not a happy time in our lives.

I never wanted my husband to feel that pressure again. And, I never wanted to feel that fear again.

As my husband was looking for a new job, I was searching online for work-at-home opportunities. The sites I found made me feel like I needed to take a shower to clean off after reading them. I also tried a few businesses that weren't right for me, and then, over a few years of networking and researching, I realized that I enjoyed writing and publishing my work on websites.

I created my first website, www.ShowMomtheMoney.com, in 2004. It was the site I wished I'd had when I started looking for online businesses—a warm, lighthearted place to learn, without feeling intimidated or pressured into business opportunities. I provide the knowledge that I gained from my successes and my failures online, and I have made it my mission to help other moms to work from home as well. Some of the ideas you'd find on my site are face painting at parties, tutoring, ghostwriting, and even administrative work.

Because of my income, my husband was able to quit his job as a software engineer to become a high school teacher and coach, which was always his dream. Now he is home at night, on weekends, during holidays, and all summer long. Our kids love it and I'm extremely proud that my income has allowed him to live a better life, and for the kids to have more memories of special time with their dad.

Of course, I am now able to go on field trips with my kids and attend special events at school without fail. When the kids are sick, I keep them home without worrying about what a boss might think if I miss another day. It used to be that my husband and I would have to "discuss" who would stay home when my son was ill. Now, I spend the day snuggling and caring for my sick child without a care in the world other than making him feel better.

Not only has working from home enabled me to be a better wife and mother, but it has also given me the opportunity to be a better daughter and granddaughter. Earlier this year, my mother had a health scare. I was terrified. She was terrified. And, due to working from home, I was able to go with her to each of her doctor's appointments. I could focus solely on her, not looking at the clock even once. That meant the world to me. Also, recently, my grandma had triple bypass surgery. I was able to spend three weeks with her and the rest of my extended family. Name one job that would give me three weeks off to cook for my grandma and sit with her to look through photos, and just look at her and enjoy the amazing woman that she is? I am very blessed, indeed.

One of my main goals as my business has grown was to hire other work-at-home moms and help them to stay home. As of today, I have twelve helpers who I pay each month. I think that is one thing that has meant the most to me.

Now, don't get me wrong, the road has been very bumpy. I'm the one at home, so it's assumed that I'll do everything. In fact, a few years ago, I wrote about the topic.

As work-at-home moms, we talk about our "Why" as a positive thing. Our "Why" is our purpose, our reason, our muse. We refer to our "Why" when we need inspiration or motivation to reach outside our comfort zone, to try a little harder, to keep going even when it's hard. Our "Why" helps us to succeed.

Today I was asking, "Why work from home?" in a slightly different tone. Today, I am home with a sick puppy and am up to my eyeballs in puppy puke.

I'm new to this puppy thing. I was warned up and down about how much work a puppy is, and I thought—I have two children. How hard can a puppy possibly be? Well, one difference is that newborn babies aren't born with fangs—at least mine weren't. So, in between changing the gauze patches on my shredded arms (those teeth are sharp!), and hours of puppy school, I fell in love with this furry beast. He was added to my list of "Why's."

So, today, while I was composing my newsletter, in the background I heard my fur-ball start to vomit—again. The thought that ran through my mind initially was not a happy "Why?" It was more like WHY in the world am I home to deal with this while my husband gets to run off to work, leaving me behind with a quick kiss and a "have a nice day, sweetie"?

WHY isn't HE dealing with cleaning up the eighth pile of yucky stuff?

WHY don't I get any peace and quiet while I work?

After I cleaned up the puppy, rubbed his head and got him clean blankets, threw in another load of laundry, and climbed into bed with my sick seven-year-old and my three-year-old to read stories, I had time to collect my thoughts. A little bit (okay, a LOT) of puppy puke was sure worth it.

And later, when I made my phone call to my husband to tell him about our day, it wasn't the puppy-puke I was telling him about.

I told him how our daughter said that she wanted to plant some jellybeans to grow a jellybean tree. And how the kids were playing the game of Life and I overheard their rules. They decided that the person who got the most parents into the little car won.

That's Why I stay at home.

And, if a furry little tail starts wagging when I walk into the room? Well, that's sure an added bonus.

So, the next time my warm and loving "Why" turns into a plea for help, I will take a deep breath and think of all the memories I would be missing—both good and not-so-good, if I weren't a work-at-home mom.

~Nicole Dean

61

Discovering and Living My Best Life

We shall draw from the heart of suffering itself the means of inspiration and survival.

~Winston Churchill

My father passed away suddenly in 2005. It was a life-altering experience. He and I had been tremendously close. I spoke with him every day. Everything I knew about business I had learned from him. Suddenly he was gone and I had a big hole in my life. It's not something that gets filled. But the edges smooth over as time goes by. He is still a big part of my life and all of the decisions I've made since then.

Up to that point I had worked my whole life, full-time, either in management or in sales. While sales offered me some flexibility, I was still the victim of other people's decisions. I had never before considered working less, or differently, though I had always wondered what it would be like to run my own business. Raising kids was challenging.

At the time, my son was nine years old and my daughter was six. My son was getting to the age where after-school care and summer camp would soon not be options. In addition, I really wanted to be in a position where my kids could come home right after school. At the time, we picked the kids up around five or six, rushed through dinner, homework and baths. Then off to bed. There was no real time for fun or playing or just enjoying each other's company. Imagine, I wondered, what it would be like for them to be able to do homework and then play BEFORE dinner!

I am blessed with a husband who is a true partner. We have always divided the family chores easily. We play to our strengths, so he cooks dinner ninety-nine percent of the time, and I handle the finances, groceries, school forms, scheduling and doctors. We share the laundry, parenting, and cleaning. I have never felt the burden of having to "do it all." I have, however, felt that things weren't quite as I would like them to be—in an ideal world. I just told myself that there really wasn't such a thing as an ideal world.

During the month of deconstructing my father's life, my sister and I had some conversations about our lives. We both felt a desire to have more of an impact on the world. Although I was selling a recycled product, it just didn't feel like I was giving enough back to the universe. I was also at a crossroads realizing that I wanted more flexibility to be able to do the things with my kids that they'd remember in the future.

Through a lot of soul searching and investigation I landed on my ideal career—coaching. It was a natural fit. As someone who was always the "go to" person, a natural problem solver, trainer, motivator, and enthusiast, I realized I'd spent my whole life preparing for this role.

After several conversations with my husband and a great deal of planning, I launched my own business in early 2006. Since it is a home-based business, it has afforded me the opportunity to be more flexible with my time. I no longer feel guilty about working when I want to be where my family is, or vice versa. My son now comes home directly from school and although my daughter is still in after-school care, I can pick her up earlier than in the past.

As I build my business, I am happier than I've ever been. I am doing work I truly love. Even though my best friend suggested I choose life coaching, I opted for business development coaching. I quickly realized that it is what I know best. And, it is completely rewarding. I now have the opportunity to help other people achieve success. To believe in others and help them believe in themselves, to see them do things they never thought possible, to see the "aha" moment — those are life-affirming experiences for me.

And the life lessons my children are learning are invaluable. They see my husband and me working together as a team. They see me helping other people succeed. They see me venturing into uncharted territory and excelling. My father used to tell me that I could do anything I wanted to as long as I was willing to do the work. He was so right. I am a living example of that belief. So not only do I tell it to my children, they see me doing it. They are learning that they, too, can be anything they want to be.

We have all grown from this experience. I am spending real quality time with my family and giving them a more balanced me. Our home is less stressful as well. We are all better communicators and listeners. And, by following my heart and creating my own path, I am as close to my father as I was when he was living. And I am closer to my children and my husband that I ever could have hoped for.

~Diane Helbig

62

Can Business and Baby Mix?

Call it a clan, call it a network, call it a tribe, call it a family. Whatever you call it, whoever you are, you need one.

~Jane Howard

When I gave birth to my first child, I wanted to be a stay-at-home mom. I gladly tossed off my pumps and suits and donned those bulky nursing sweaters. I'd been running a non-profit organization, possibly one of the most stressful jobs I can think of, and the idea of leaving that all behind relieved me. I joined a local mom's group and became inseparable from my son, Will.

I loved being with Will for every "first," spending days at the playground, exploring the five different libraries in neighboring towns, and finding the best story hour around. We took "Music Together" classes and both learned to sing on key. I also experienced some challenges typical to stay-at-home moms—feeling lonely, exhausted after a sleep-challenged night in the family bed, and trying to scrape together the money for things I wanted, from organic foods to children's books to a new pair of shoes.

When Will turned three, he began morning preschool and I started my career as an author, then a book coach, helping people write and publish their books. I loved the work and, over time, I became good at it and my business flourished. I also enjoyed the flexible hours that allowed me to shift into mommy mode when Will came home from school.

When I became pregnant with Luke, almost five years after Will's birth, I couldn't imagine not working. We relied on two paychecks and I enjoyed the personal growth.

When Luke was born, I took off a few sleepless, yet blissful, months and then slowly took on book coaching clients while a babysitter helped out. I worried that baby interruptions would make work impossible, so I tentatively asked my clients if they were open to a possible interruption. Lucky for me, I attracted flexible clients in those first six months, including several who'd nursed their babies. It worked. I occasionally even nursed Luke for a few minutes on a call.

The annual highlight of my business career is my stint on the faculty of Dr. Julie Silver's publishing course through Harvard Medical School. Many of my clients come from the course and they are always a pleasure to work with—intelligent, interesting, on the cutting edge of medicine, psychology, and even alternative healing. This year, I would be more than facilitating writing workshops. I would be a presenter and I wondered how on earth I'd pull that off.

Going to Boston for two days without my four-month-old nursing seemed impossible. I'd weathered too many breast infections with my first to take the chance, and besides, I couldn't imagine how hard it would be for him, since he slept in my bed and drank exclusively breast milk. Lucky me: I have possibly the best mother-in-law in the world. Mimi agreed to join me and watch Luke. Still, I worried how it would work having my baby in a professional setting.

We left Rhode Island during an April snowstorm, grateful for Mimi's four-wheel-drive. We sang our way to Boston and stopped to nurse when Luke cried. When we arrived, the clerk upgraded us to a spacious room on the top floor of Boston's Fairmont Hotel, overlooking a snow-covered Copley Square. I marveled at the view and credited Mimi's magical presence that is always sure to attract pleasant surprises.

As the day wore on, my nervousness about having Luke along began to ease. I met with physicians, therapists, and other aspiring authors to talk about their book projects, took a nursing break, returned for more meetings, then went back to nurse and join Mimi for dinner.

During my meetings, Mimi, a painter and sculptor and host of the PBS series, *Love to Paint with Mimi*, worked on sculpting Luke's head. She put Luke down for a nap and sculpted his head in wax so he could join his cousins and brother in a sculptural grouping in her garden. Later, she walked Luke in the lobby as people admired her smiling, blue-eyed, and almost bald grandson.

I'd planned to pump milk so Mimi wouldn't get stuck during my talk. Unfortunately, my irrational phobia from near-psychotic experiences in pumping for my first son had me put off the pumping test to the eleventh hour. When I finally tried, I eked out about a teaspoon and a half of breast milk. For a minute, I panicked. Why had I waited so long to test it? We came up with a new plan and Mimi and I remained in communication via cell phone: I'd time my breaks with Luke's hunger.

All seemed to be running like clockwork when I stepped into the room to facilitate my first workshop. There were four round tables each with a facilitator and eight or so writers eager for feedback on their work. I arrived early and, within minutes, Mimi and Luke appeared, Luke just beginning to cry. How could I get him to stop crying without becoming a public spectacle?

During the next two seconds my mind raced as Luke's volume rose. I could look for a place to nurse, but would risk being late for my group facilitation. That wouldn't be professional. I could stay and try to nurse in a quick seven minutes before the workshop began. But I wasn't even wearing a nursing top. Fear gripped my gut as Mimi handed me the sling and I threw it over my shoulder.

I slid Luke into the sling, lifted my shirt, and unclasped my nursing bra. Fortunately, between my suit jacket and the sling, my activity remained somewhat discreet—no Janet Jackson here. Still, how discreet could it be to nurse a baby in the midst of a business setting full of strangers?

Julie, the course founder and director, arrived and smiled at me.

What must she think of this? She never fired me, so I guess it couldn't have been too much of a gaffe. The people at my table graciously sat down and waited. I nervously watched the clock, hoping Luke wasn't in a twenty-minute nursing mood. On the dot, he stopped nursing. I slung off the sling and whisked him into Mimi's hands but not before a few people at my table admired my now-contented baby.

The next day, I gave my presentation in the Grand Ballroom *sans* baby, and met Mimi and Luke an hour later. I met several wonderful clients that year who now have agents and publishers for their books.

I'd wondered whether I could truly reconcile work and children. My trip to Boston taught me that the world is an accommodating place; most people are pretty darn flexible, especially where babies are concerned. I didn't have to hide my being a mom from the world. While I couldn't control when my baby needed me, I could do my best, go with the flow, and it would be fine. I learned that everything goes more smoothly with the help of family, especially Mimi. And I learned that I can be a mom and a book coach, sometimes even in the same moment.

~Lisa Tener

Happiness Is

When what we are is what we want to be, that's happiness.
~Malcolm S. Forbes

I n 1997, the year I founded my business, Liz Lange Maternity, I had been married exactly one year, but had not yet had my children. Looking back, it was a very different time. I never concerned myself with concepts like multi-tasking or balance. Today, I am always amused when people ask me how I manage to balance my professional life with the demands of parenthood. To me, the word "balance" connotes delicacy and grace: me with a smile on my face after a hard day of work, greeted by two smiling children who are thrilled to see me. "Juggling" better describes my reality; the idea of too many balls in the air is a much more apt description of the manner in which I navigate my life.

Many assume that my business grew out of my own need for maternity clothing when, ten years ago, I became pregnant with my son, Gus. The fact is that I started Liz Lange Maternity before I ever had my children! Never in my wildest dreams did I think that I would run my own business and be a mom at the same time: rushed, forgetful, dressed for a meeting at school drop-off. I always imagined my life would be similar to that of my mother and her friends who didn't work outside the home. Then and now, I think of myself as an accidental entrepreneur—and perhaps at this point, an accidental feminist as well.

In 1996, when I first got the idea for Liz Lange Maternity, I was newly married. I had bounced around different jobs after graduating from Brown with a degree in comparative literature. Many of my positions focused on fashion, but I also worked for a book publisher, and even put in a semester towards a Ph.D. in Psychology at NYU. The idea for my own business dawned on me when my friends started to get pregnant. They had always come to the showroom of the designer for whom I worked to buy our dresses wholesale—but I didn't think this would continue when they were pregnant.

But it did. And when I would ask them why they didn't just go shop at maternity stores, they all had the same negative reaction, telling me that maternity clothing was ugly and that they couldn't find anything cute to wear. *Aha* moment number one: there was something wrong with maternity clothing. *Aha* moment number two: my friends actually looked smaller and more fashionable when they squeezed themselves into some of our stretchy non-maternity dresses than they did when they came in wearing big, oversized pieces (which, believe it or not, were all the rage back then). It hit me that what pregnant women actually needed was cute, stretchy non-maternity looking and fitting clothing that could grow with them. I begged the designer I was working with to launch a special line of maternity dresses for this cohort, but he thought I was nuts.

I realized that if I didn't pursue this idea and someone else did, I wouldn't be able to live with myself. And that's how it all happened. I quit and I designed an eight-piece collection with crude sketches and the help of an amazing factory I found (they held my hand through most of it). I called the few pregnant friends I had, and decided that I would see clients by appointment and sell my clothing made to order, so that I wouldn't have to make anything in advance that might not end up selling. My concept was that women would spread the word to other women, since I didn't have any money for marketing or advertising.

Armed with this, and the then-novel concept of reaching out to pregnant celebrities, word spread even faster than I could have anticipated. Before long, my office answering machine was overflowing, magazines started writing about me, and I was working around the clock seeing customers, at the factory, packing boxes, setting up phone appointments. I was a one-woman band, but it was fun and I didn't have any children yet. And really, the business had become my baby.

But before long actually, just three months after I opened, I became pregnant with my son Gus. I worked up until the last minute and hired my first employee to fill in for me when I was out on my own "maternity leave."

To be honest, the first few years felt easy. I worked hard, but I loved it—and with a wonderful nanny to help out, it all seemed to be working. Two years later, pregnant with my daughter Alice, I opened our first real store, a dream come true: 2,500 square feet on Madison Avenue. The business had become crazy busy; I signed licensing deals with Nike and Target, did fashion shows in Bryant Park during NY Fashion Week, opened three real flagship boutiques, grew to fifty employees and developed an online business as well. But once the children hit school age, things became far more challenging. Here, for example, is a typical day:

6:00 A.M.: wake up before the children do, so that I can get dressed, have coffee, possibly walk our dog, prepare their breakfast;

7:00 A.M.: wake the children, feed them, help them get dressed (yes at ten and eight, they still like me in their rooms when they get dressed);

8:00 A.M.: take the children to school;

9:00 A.M.: work out;

10:00 A.M.: shower, hair, make-up, out the door;

11:00 A.M.-1:00 P.M.: meetings, deliver speeches, design meetings, TV appearances, (it all depends on the day!);

1:00 P.M.: lunch date, usually business, but every so often with a friend. (Ahh, what happened to time for friends?);

2:30 P.M.: back to work;

4:00 P.M.: pick the children up at school;

4:30-6:00 P.M.: desperately try to work from home while kids also need me;

6:00 P.M.: sit with the kids while they eat;

7:00 P.M.-8:30 P.M.: out at press appearances, movie openings, cocktail parties (I run around and hit many events quickly);

8:45 P.M.: back home to put the kids to bed;

9:00 P.M.-1:00 A.M.: more work, watch favorite TV shows to unwind;

1:00 A.M.-6:00 A.M.: sleep with BlackBerry by my pillow for last minute work e-mails all night.

As you can see, this kind of schedule is hardly a balancing act. Like I said before, it's more of a juggling act. But for our family, it feels normal and it mostly works. The weekends are entirely for my family, and I think that's what really makes it all okay.

I never dreamed that I would love a life that is this busy—or that I would be a mom who also runs her own business. But here's the funny thing: my life, as I said before, is a juggling act. Sometimes it's overwhelming, and sometimes it's frustrating. But it's the life I built. And I wouldn't have it any other way.

~Liz Lange

Chapter
7

Power MOMS

Gender Benders

Men Have Their Say

My Freaky Friday Is Going to Last for Six Days

The guys who fear becoming fathers don't understand that fathering is not something perfect men do, but something that perfects the man.
~Frank Pittman

Last Wednesday, I woke up in my wife's body—sort of. My three-year-old daughter, Melissa, jolted me out of sleep by tugging on my foot—*my* foot and not my wife's, as is her custom. The sound of running water informed me that Debbie, my wife, was awake and that she was skipping the three or four steps in her morning routine that included feeding and watering our two daughters.

Things were seriously out of whack at the Dickson house.

Somewhere between "Daddy, I'm thirsty" and "Daddy, I want cereal," I remembered that it was getaway day for Deb. She was escaping to Orlando to see a friend get married and I was skipping the next six days of work to play Mr. Mom. I promised myself and my kids an adventurous week of park trips and bike rides. But the fact that it's already Saturday and I'm writing this story while the girls watch *Jumanji* in the other room is pretty clear evidence that I haven't exactly followed my master plan.

I should have known from the start that planning every detail would be impossible. My first clue came when I attempted to get my second-grader, Darragh, to school on time. The Interstate was a parking lot. A mile or so into my crawl, I limped off in search of swifter passage, which I never found.

The week has played out like a tug-of-war ever since, with myriad occurrences—planned and unplanned—anchoring one end, and me on the other, pulling desperately to hold it all together. I've torched a frozen pizza, spilled juice all over the car and, with Melissa, visited what seemed like half the public bathrooms in Southern California. I've discovered the point of drive-through coffee shops and marveled at the predatory nature of mothers jockeying for position when it's time to pick up their kids from school. Most of all, I've gained an even greater appreciation for the "soccer mom."

I never cared for the term to begin with because it reeks of a professional elitism I've always found distasteful, as if the woman who makes it her life's work to manage her own home and raise her own children sits lower on the totem pole than the woman who packs a briefcase instead of a diaper bag.

Even before my head hit the pillow Wednesday night, I was convinced that Debbie's job is much more demanding than mine. I work in a world of deadlines, but they are nothing compared to the pressure I've faced since my wife flew east.

Cook, clean, feed. Drive, drop, prepare. Sort, stack, fold. Shop for dinner, but cut the coupons first. Bathe the kids, but not too close to bedtime or they'll go to sleep with wet hair. Check the homework, help with the school project and pick out tomorrow's outfits. Just be sure to check the weather first or you'll be adding a trip to the pediatrician to next week's list of errands.

The to-do list is endless and the stakes are so high. If I miss a deadline at work, I may hear some grumbling from my boss. But missing a deadline this week meant Melissa would go hungry or Darragh would miss a test.

The clock is indeed the oppressor of the stay-at-home mom, but it is a necessary evil. Now I understand why every room in my house holds at least two clocks and why Debbie often wears her watch to bed. And the demands go beyond the obvious. Exactly where in your day timer should you make room for imperatives like "play with the baby" and "make sure your toddler knows you love him as much as the new arrival?" What happens to your precious schedule when your three-year-old asks you to teach her the alphabet?

"Soccer moms" do it all day. They do it every day. My saving grace is knowing my shift ends Monday night. I'm fighting exhaustion—that and a nagging sense that I ought to be doing better. But it all ends soon. Debbie and her fellow full-timers enjoy no such respite. I'm looking at the untouched stack of books I brought home for my "vacation" and I can only laugh—almost as loudly as I now laugh when I remember the Saturday mornings I've magnanimously agreed to "watch" the kids while Debbie rushes off to coffee with friends.

I don't mean to paint too bleak a picture of what a stay-at-home parent faces. This week has been full of wonderful little moments too trivial to put into print, yet monumental enough to remember forever. It's been fun to hang out with my baby and discover that she actually does play with all the toys and games I'm always stepping over and insisting we should give away. It's been great to ask my older daughter for help and truly need it—and even better when she gives it so proudly.

On Friday we were all stuck in traffic. The delay was putting a crimp in my plans for dinner and forcing me to push back the kids' bath until Saturday morning. As I was contemplating what to cook while wondering if I should take a different road, Melissa flashed me a flower she'd drawn on her Magna Doodle sketchpad.

"I drew something just for you, Dad," she said.

Then Darragh spoke up. "You know, Dad, this week hasn't turned into such a catastrophe after all."

I smiled in response to both of them and sat a few inches higher in my seat. The work's been much harder than I ever imagined, but the pay is tough to beat.

~Bob Dickson

Reprinted by permission of Tom Swick
© 2008

My Mother, My Hero

There is nothing like a dream to create the future.
~Victor Hugo

From a traditional perspective, when a man mentions the hero in his family, he tends to be referring to his father. Although I love and respect my father, I must admit I do not fall in line with this classic stereotype.

Ever since I was a young man, the hero in my family has been my mom. Beyond being a loving and present mother, Wendy Lavitt created an inspiring career as an American folk art dealer and antiques writer. But she did not enter this brave new world of writing and antique dealing by leaving the children and the home behind. Instead, she brought us right along with her. Throughout the latter part of my childhood when her work adventure began, I always felt part of the journey. In my memory, as my mother's career grew to such an extent that she eventually was included in *Who's Who in America*, I was right by her side, sharing in her boundless enthusiasm for antiques and American folk art.

So how did a Manhattan housewife go from painting T-shirts at school bake sales to opening stores on Madison Avenue, authoring coffee table books, curating museum shows and lecturing on American folk art across the country? All passions must ignite, so here is the spark. In 1978, the American Folk Art Museum sponsored an antique show at the famous Armory in New York City. The museum hired a relatively unknown caterer named Martha Stewart who transformed the Armory into a barnyard setting, with live chickens in coops, and bales of hay. Describing the scene as "a feast to behold," my mom was entranced by the display booths overflowing with Americana from weathervanes to folk dolls. On the spot, she decided this was the world she wanted to be a part of for the rest of her life. She has never looked back.

Do not think the road, however, was easy and smooth because it took a lot of hard work and some wrong turns to transform the initial spark into a fire. Wendy began her journey with a combination of collecting as a neophyte antiques dealer and writing for trade publications. Although her first article, for which she was paid seventy-five dollars, was accepted by a little magazine in Iowa called *Antiques Journal*, the collecting did not always go so well. All families have classic stories, and we have the legend of the pipe stand. An early purchase, the pipe stand remained for several years in Wendy's collection. I would lug it back and forth to the antique shows where it never was close to being purchased. Upon its return to our house, my father would shake his head and laugh, believing my mother's new passion was headed for oblivion.

My mother always paid me what seemed like a lot to a young teenager to be the official lugger. Although I initially came along because of my desire to buy more comic books, I soon grew to share her passion for collecting.

Although the antiques collected were hit and miss in the beginning, the shows she chose to attend could be even more vexing. I remember tagging along for a show in the parking lot of Shea Stadium. As my mother set up her booth, things seemed a bit off to me. Nobody else really had antiques, and most of the vendors were selling junk. I will never forget when a woman picked up an antique tea set and looked at the price on the bottom label. She snorted, "Fifty cents is too much, but I will give you a quarter for it." My mom snatched it out of her hands with the exclamation, "This piece costs fifty dollars and is from New England in the early nineteenth century. It's almost two hundred years old!" By the end of that day, not a single piece had been sold. Heads bowed, we packed up the pipe stand and headed home.

I began to appreciate her perseverance even if I had to carry all the heavy furniture on each trip. This trail of early rising, many miles, and small profits eventually led to her Holy Grail when my mother opened up a store called Made In America in 1981. It contained a vibrant display of the best of Americana, overflowing with folk art and antique quilts. For four years, it did excellent business and helped my mother reach the next pinnacle of her career. Since her first publication, Wendy had continued writing articles on folk art for various magazines. Using her formidable networking skills, she translated this early success into a book deal with Alfred A. Knopf.

In 1982, Wendy's first coffee table picture book, *American Folk Dolls*, was published to excellent reviews, including in *Time Magazine* and *New York Magazine*. At last, she felt she had arrived in mainstream America. The publication led directly to her curating a museum show, "Children's Children: American Folk Dolls," at the American Folk Art Museum in New York City in 1983.

Never resting on her laurels, this initial success led my mom to a long career of publishing and lecturing. Wendy has published five other books, including *Animals in American Folk Art* and *Contemporary Pictorial Quilts*. As my mother researched her books, she often needed to visit various museums in New England. On the pretext of taking me to camp in Maine, we headed up the coast, stopping at antique fairs and historical societies. To bolster my lagging enthusiasm, she promised to stop at any amusement park we passed on the way and even go on the dreaded roller coaster with me. She recalls that one in Rhode Island almost did her in.

Wendy has gone on to publish countless magazine articles and curate a number of museum shows. Her courage is reflected in the choice she made when she decided to have cosmetic surgery in 1987. She wrote an article about her face-lift for *Salt Lake Magazine* that included a thirty-day diary of her recovery. She believed she could help other women make the right choice in regards to cosmetic surgery by being open. Arguably, she had one of the most public face-lifts at a time when most women preferred to keep them veiled in secrecy.

Wendy was a stay-at-home mom throughout her early career. She always was present for her husband and children, and in fact just celebrated her forty-ninth wedding anniversary. As her son, I do not recall a single time when I ever resented her choice to go for her passion. Rather, I am so proud of what she has accomplished. By finding a precise balance between her career and her family, my mother enriched my life by making me part of the journey she has taken since that fateful day in 1978. Yes, my mother is my hero, and I hope to be able to emulate her success, her passion and her determination in my ventures. Wendy's success reveals a wonderful truth—it is possible to have it all.

~John Lavitt

66

Balloons for Grandma Josie

No one in the world can take the place of your mother.
~Harry Truman

When the other moms chose careers, my mom chose to stay home because she didn't want us raised by babysitters or day care centers. When Dad was away on business, she donned a catcher's mitt and squatted in the backyard so I could practice for Little League pitching tryouts. Every year, she'd spend hours crafting sheets of cake into the shape of our favorite animal or TV character, so we'd have the perfect cake for our birthday parties. She truly loved being a mom, and by any standard, she was great at it.

Over the years, I developed a unique and special relationship with Mom. We had this strange, unexplainable ability to communicate, often without ever speaking. Even when I tried to hide it, she seemed to instinctively know when I'd had a bad day and always managed to cheer me up. Sometimes it was just a reassuring nod or a comforting smile, but it always managed to do the trick.

When I grew up and moved away, our relationship seemed to grow stronger. Mom would make quick calls to my office once or twice a week just to let me know she missed me. Her calls always brightened my day.

One night, Mom called. I could tell that something was wrong.

Through her tears, Mom told me her doctor had discovered a cancerous tumor in her right breast. They didn't know the extent to which the cancer had spread, but she was scheduled for a mastectomy later that week. The impact of her message didn't really hit me until after I hung up the phone. I couldn't understand why her God, who was so important in her life, would allow this to happen to such a wonderful person. I walked around the neighborhood for several hours that night and cried like a baby. I had never considered the idea that Mom might be gone one day—and now I was forced to deal with that possibility. I went to be with her for the surgery.

Mom had been lucky. Her surgery revealed the cancer had been confined to the tumor—it had not spread to any other part of her body.

My close relationship with Mom continued to grow stronger throughout the years that followed. When my wife, Tammie, and I called my mom to tell her that we would be having a child, I really think she was more excited than Tammie and I. From that moment forward, all conversations were about the baby, her first grandchild. We'd get several cards a week; some stuffed with dollar bills to "buy something for the baby." Her excitement was genuine.

I called Mom on the day Tammie went into labor. She was there within a few hours. She walked through the halls of the hospital, announcing, "I have a new grandbaby," to anyone who was polite enough to listen. When things finally calmed down, she sat us down to ask a pressing question—"Should Jessica call me Granny, or Grammy, or Grandma?" We found a sense of contentment in the joy Mom was experiencing at being Grandma Josie.

Not a single event ever happened in Jessica's life that wasn't recognized by Grandma Josie. Although Jessica wasn't walking or talking, my mom and my daughter were already developing a bond. I was comforted by knowing that Jessica would experience the same deep relationship with Grandma Josie as I had.

Seven years after her first diagnosis, I received another of those terrifying calls. A lump had been discovered in Mom's other breast, and preliminary tests indicated her lymphatic system was most likely infected with the cancer. Again, I went to her side. She didn't look like the mom I knew. She had lost a great deal of weight. Her body was bruised from the intravenous lines transporting the drugs to provide relief from her pain. I was told things were bad. Children were not allowed on the floor, but the nurse had been so impressed by Mom's insistence on seeing her grandbaby that she "bent the rules."

A few days later, the cancer had spread to her throat and paralyzed Mom's vocal chords. She was forced to use an electronic device that made her sound like a robot. This didn't really bother Mom, until she realized Jessica was afraid of her new electronic voice. So she communicated only with smiles and hugs. Still, as with me when I was growing up, there was an unspoken bond between my mom and my daughter.

After a couple of years battling the second cancer, Mom called. She seemed to be calm and peaceful. Mom had called to ask my permission to die. She told me that she was ready to leave this earth and asked me not to be mad at God. Her final words didn't need to be said, but she told me how much she loved me. Later that night, Mom joined the angels.

Mom's death left a huge void in my life. Even though I had a chance to prepare for her passing, I never realized the pain I'd feel when she was actually gone. For the longest time, I couldn't talk about Mom. I couldn't stand to watch videos that Mom was in or look at old family pictures. I'd be mowing the grass, or driving down the highway, or just relaxing around the house when something would remind me of Mom—and I'd get a huge, painful knot in my stomach.

Everyone knew that Mom was an issue not to be discussed with me. Everyone, that is, except Jessica. One day, seemingly out of nowhere, she asked, "Where's Grandma Josie right now?" After biting my lip and fighting back the tears, I explained that Grandma Josie had gone to heaven. She gladly accepted this as an answer and was occasionally overheard telling friends that her Grandma Josie was up in heaven.

After dinner in a local restaurant, Jessica was given a balloon, tied with a pretty pink ribbon. As I unlocked the car, I caught sight of Jessica's balloon escaping into the sky. I expected her cry. But instead, she looked up at her balloon and waved. "Here's a balloon for you, Grandma Josie," she said, smiling. Then, my young daughter told me that I didn't need to be sad for Grandma Josie anymore, because now she had something to play with in heaven.

Over the last few years, Jessica has sent many balloons to Grandma Josie, some with little handwritten notes attached. Ashley, our other daughter, who never knew my mom, now follows Jessica's instructions about how to send balloons to her Grandma Josie. As each balloon ascends into the clouds, I feel a little sad. But then, I find comfort in the fact that Jessica's bond with her grandmother seems to grow stronger, even though Grandma Josie is gone. In a strange way, my daughter has helped me cope with my loss. Balloons for Grandma Josie has become a ritual at our house—a ritual of remembrance for Jessica, and a ritual of healing for me.

~Gene Scriven, Jr.

67

My Stay-at-Home Lifesaver

My mother had a great deal of trouble with me, but I think she enjoyed it.
~Mark Twain

I grew up the youngest of seven children, six boys and one girl, and I am convinced that if my mother had to go off to work every day I would not be alive today. My brothers would have killed me about nine seconds after she left for work. Probably because I had ratted them out about something the night before, or maybe just for sport, but I'm positive her presence was the one thing standing between growing happily into old age and almost certain painful premature death.

Don't get me wrong, my mother went to work every day — she just never left the house to do it. Among the jobs she held daily were cook, dishwasher, diaper changer (in a time when there was no such thing as disposable diapers), referee, teacher, janitor, nurse, and when necessary, judge, jury, and (after my father got home) announcer of the execution.

Once, my brother, T.J., was diagnosed with a rare allergic skin reaction called Stephens-Johnson syndrome that caused painful blisters to form all over his body. My brother Doug, however, saw it as a potential moneymaker. He placed T.J., who was five at the time, in a chair in our garage and charged the neighborhood kids a nickel to come see his freak of a brother. He was very dramatic, even covering him with a blanket for each unveiling.

When my mother found out, she could have justifiably choked him to death but, instead, she calmly made him return all proceeds from the exhibit and kindly asked Doug to refrain from further child exploitation shows. Then she went inside and proceeded to laugh until she cried. What I remember most about my childhood was that constant stabilizing presence floating between the rooms of our house trying desperately to create some form of order from seemingly insurmountable chaos.

When my wife, Suzanne, and I had our first son we faced the same decision that a lot of new parents face these days: stay at home or go back to work. Because I was making about three times what she was, we agreed it might be better that I be the one to go back to work. Since we had sort of sworn off polygamy during our wedding vows, that left only one other person to stay home with the baby. However, we wanted to be thorough in our examination, so we added up her salary and subtracted out taxes and the cost of day care and came to the conclusion she could work full-time and still bring home minus two thousand dollars. The decision was surprisingly easy after that.

After two more sons and ten years, we look back on it as the best decision we ever made. I stand in awe of her ability to make everything in our house run so smoothly. She can switch from helping with homework one minute to getting someone to baseball practice the next, then home to make dinner and put everyone to bed. Her role as a stay-at-home mom has increased her capacity for love and patience with both our boys and myself. She makes me a better dad because of it. The result is three happy, healthy, confident, polite boys. Four, if you include me. Please and thank you.

A few years ago, Suzanne and I were building a house when my mother called and asked if we would consider building an in-law apartment for her. My father had passed away a few years earlier and her house was too big, too hard to maintain, and had too many memories for her. We readily agreed to have her in our household. This was the second best decision we ever made. When she moved in,

I told my mother that we would never burden her with babysitting or child rearing. She had raised her kids (unbelievably successfully) and we wanted her to know that she was in our house because we loved her and not because we wanted a full-time babysitter. It didn't matter. My children now have the combined benefit of sixty years of child-raising. They get from their parents the essential basics of childhood—love, stability, routine, more love, and a healthy dose of how to treat and be kind to people. From their Nana they get a healthy dose of love, chocolate and Nana bread.

In the end, my mother turned out six men who were able to let their wives be stay-at-home moms while the kids were young. Some wives still are. My sister was a stay-at-home mom for eight years until she chose to go back to work. While my mother was at it, she established an incredible bond amongst my siblings. To this day, we get together every year, without spouses, and just enjoy each other's company for a weekend. It is the end result of a great stay-at-home mom.

One added benefit of my mother living with me full time again—none of my siblings has tried to kill me in several years.

~David White

Dream Job

Until you have a child, you've never been certain you'd give your life for someone, you've never been so proud, you've never been so tired.
~Elizabeth Vargas

The transition from working a traditional job to becoming a stay-at-home mom is tough on anyone. But for my wife who worked as a nanny before having kids, it was particularly difficult. For over twelve years, she mothered other people's children. She changed diapers and cleaned up toys full-time. These may have been long days but at least she had a paycheck and the end of the day to look forward to.

Her first job after college was working full-time for a wealthy family of lawyers. This was before we had met and here's how she has described the experience: "The husband was horrible. He turned me into a housekeeper. Every day I had to run the dishwasher even if there were only a couple of things to clean and then empty it before they came home from work. I had to fold all the clothes and towels a specific way and position them in the closet facing the same direction on wood hangers. In the winter, I had to vacuum the ashes out of the fireplace every day. He would yell at me if I didn't do things exactly the way he wanted. It was the worst job I ever had." Despite being offered a raise to stay, she quit after working for this family for a year.

My wife has a family of her own now—a toddler son, an infant daughter, a fifty-pound Australian Shepherd, and a little Pomeranian/

Chihuahua puppy. She's been trying to cope with the fact that cleaning the house is a losing battle. I came home from work the other day and all the children ran to greet me, including the furry ones. My wife was sprawled on the couch and was the least enthused to see me. "Sorry about the house," she groaned. I surveyed what was left of the living room. It looked like the cave of a pack of wild animals. The floor was littered with toys, granola bar wrappers, and clumps of black dog hair. The coffee table was strewn with the day's mail, multiple board books, and overturned sippy cups. Sitting next to my wife on the couch was an unopened package of diapers. I put my keys on the kitchen table and noticed several used diapers next to the laptop.

I headed to the bedroom to take my shoes off and get comfortable. I saw a layer of toys on the floor and another layer in our bed, along with some folded laundry and a few snack wrappers. I made enough room on the bed to sit down and took off my socks and, as I threw them in the hamper, I saw the dirty clothes piled up to my waist.

My wife walked into the bedroom. "Honey, I know the house looks bad and I don't want to hear it," she said.

"I didn't say anything." But I couldn't help but think back to the obsessive lawyer and his dishwasher and wonder what he did right that maybe I was doing wrong. I decided to say, "I'm sure you've had a rough day," which I thought would be a neutral statement. However, she received a different message — you are not doing your job — and felt the need to defend herself.

"I have had a rough day. The baby's been crying since she woke up this morning at 6:00 A.M. She cried anytime I wasn't holding her. When I picked her up, she either thrashed around or hit me. The dogs got into the trash again. All your son ever says is, 'Can I watch a show?'" She paused for a moment. I thought she might be done but she was only considering how to go on.

"I know I should straighten up when they take their nap but I'm so tired I just need a break. You get to leave your job and come home. I never get a break. Even when you're here, they're still constantly all over me. They start before the sun comes up and don't stop until bedtime." She took a breath and put her arm over her forehead and lay on the bed quietly.

I waited a few moments to make sure she was done. When I thought it was safe, I said, "I'm sorry you've had a hard day. What can I do to help?"

"I don't know. Just keep everyone out of the kitchen so I can make dinner."

She got up and headed to the kitchen. I sat on the edge of the bed for a few moments. I thought about what she said and tried to sympathize. I'd worked a long, hard day but I had something to show for it, I had a boss and coworkers to tell me 'good job'. I felt bad for her because the house was in such bad shape that I couldn't even notice what she had done.

I realized the difference between the lawyer's home and our home was that she was being paid for her work. Keeping their home clean was her job. Mothering my children is not just her job, it is her whole life. It's futile to think that I could pay her an adequate salary for the tireless work that she does or the endless hours she puts in.

I remember a story my wife told me about another family she nannied for. She had been taking care of a boy who was around three years old. The two of them had a perfect day together. They played games and read books all day. He took a decent nap and ate his lunch well. He had no tantrums and she hadn't lost her temper once. They were watching a show together when his mom came home from work. The boy went into the next room as his mom and my wife discussed the day. After a minute or so, my wife looked over and saw that the boy was naked from the waist down and lion-taming the family dog with his step stool. "So we just looked at each other and laughed. Then I grabbed my keys and said, 'See you later.'"

I would think incidents like this one, as well as things like diapers and the countless hours without adult engagement as a nanny, would have worn her out before she even became a mother. But they haven't. She's so glad to have kids that she rarely complains about that stuff. It's the clutter that stresses her out. And it's not because she doesn't notice or care. That's what I love about her. She does notice the pile of laundry and the dishes. But she's just one person, who is drastically outnumbered.

I may be home only a few hours every day, but even I see the children pull toys out of their toy bins just to pull them out. They don't even play with the toys, they just move on to emptying the next bin. I think about the lion-taming incident and consider how my wife took for granted her job as a nanny, when at least she could look forward to going home at the end of the day. And I realize, as a grateful husband, that the workday of a stay-at-home mother never ends.

~Billy Cuchens

All Dressed Up

People tend to think of [full-time parenting] as babysitting, and that's only because they have never done it.
~Ann Crittenden

N o one noticed my Halloween costume, even though I had worn it all day. Not that I can blame anyone. The costume consisted of a gray sweatshirt, blue jeans, and black sneakers. I was in disguise as a stay-at-home parent. The biggest twist of my masquerade? I'm a dad.

Halloween or not, I've been wearing pretty much the same costume every day since I quit my job two and a half years ago to care for my son, Nicholas. Among the skeletons, witches and superheroes at the local Halloween parade, I was as much a freak as anyone.

I'm used to it. I'm regularly the only dad at the playground and at parent-child classes. Statistics, although all over the map, bear out this abnormality. Depending on the source of the numbers, I'm one of anywhere from a few hundred thousand to a couple of million men in the U.S. who stay at home to care for their children—a small minority.

Other than it being Halloween, the day was much like any other, pretty routine and unexciting, filled with errands and chores. I had worn my camouflage to the grocery store to shop with Nicholas. He sat in the shopping cart, wearing a glow-in-the-dark skeleton shirt, while I made my weekly rounds up and down the aisles among the moms and seniors. I collected enough food to last the week and supply a couple of dinners I would prepare.

We came home and I made lunch for the two of us. My wife, Beth, was at the office. During Nicholas's afternoon nap, I mowed the lawn. After that, I worked on a wooden toy garage I was making Nicholas as a Christmas gift. For a couple of hours, I almost felt like a regular dad.

When he woke up, it was really time to show off my costume. The Halloween parade is a big deal. Hundreds of kids and parents blanket the main street, many in elaborate outfits. Nicholas looked good in the skeleton shirt Beth had picked out.

I observed the parents as much as the costumes. There were plenty of dads who had taken time off from the office to be with their kids. But the parents I really related to were the stay-at-home moms. I had been working in their limbo since Nicholas was two months old. As I looked around at the moms, I knew that much of their virtuous work was probably unappreciated. Their day had likely already been filled with shopping, making meals, getting decorations ready, doing laundry, washing dishes, all with at least one very excited and unpredictable child in tow. None of this work was paraded.

I knew that at the end of another physically exhausting, mentally numbing and sometimes hellishly confining day, all that the husband saw was an exhausted wife. But before he got home, she had already worn many masks: teacher, cook, dishwasher, chauffeur, wrestler, musician, tour guide, psychologist, doctor.

I worked in offices for eighteen years before my role reversal allowed me to glimpse this other world. Sometimes that reversal took a funny twist. When Nicholas was just three months old, and I had only been home a month, we scheduled a boiler checkup. The "gas guy" showed up, wearing a Harley-Davidson T-shirt, and explained to me what a solid old boiler we have and how they don't make 'em like they used to.

"You've got a '59 Mustang here."

The gas guy's name? Mary. She worked and spoke while I sat

on the couch cradling Nicholas and feeding him his bottle. It was a shock to the system, but I became used to being the odd man out.

When Nicholas and I got home from the parade, I lit our jack o' lantern and displayed it in our window. Few trick-or-treaters came by, so Nicholas made his own plans for the rest of the evening.

"First we have food, then we see *Airplane and Moon* (a video he likes), then we go paint," he said. So we did. Then it was time for a bath, bedtime reading with Mom and lights out.

Does this sound like a rough day? Not necessarily, but that's the point. Staying at home is a marathon, not a sprint. Stay-at-home moms need to string together months and years of such days. Their strength lies in their ability to store vast reserves of the energy, patience, resilience and affection required to raise a child. Marathoners need a healthy heart, and so do stay-at-home moms.

Two nights after Halloween, Nicholas had a cold and his asthma kicked in. But we didn't let that get in the way of Halloween-season festivities. Nicholas ate his first pumpkin pie, which he helped me bake. Then we made another. I'd like to say we baked them from scratch, but I confess I used frozen crusts and canned mix. It was another of my disguises.

~Christopher Harder

The Pivotal Role of the Stay-at-Home Mum

There's no such thing as calling in sick on mommyhood.
~Cokie Roberts

Wednesday

"Only a disaster can stop the funding package from coming through," I said to my wife (whom I will call Harriet) as I left the family home in Gloucestershire. I kissed her, then climbed into the car for a two-hour drive to London, where I spent most of the working week. The all-important meeting with our Swedish investor was set for the afternoon at the Lanesborough Hotel. Together with our Chairman, we were in for tough final negotiations on a rescue financing. I was Chief Executive and would be relied upon heavily for my detailed knowledge of the company's current state, and also for my negotiating experience.

At noon, I arrived at the Knightsbridge apartment, tense but positive. Knowing that our investor liked to work well into the night, I had a quick bite to eat and laid down to rest for forty-five minutes, mobile phone switched to silent mode.

The alarm went and I looked at the phone. There were seventeen missed calls and four messages. The first started my head spinning.

It was from our family friend, George. "Everything is under control, nothing to gravely worry about, Harriet is sedated now and I'm in the ambulance with her on our way to the hospital...." The earlier messages from various other friends were more frantic and gave the basic picture. Harriet had missed a step holding our three-year-old, and in falling pushed her ankle through the two lower bones in her right leg—messy and excruciatingly painful. Our daughter was fine, but the central theme for the messages was to get to the hospital *now*.

I like to be in control; this wasn't happening. If I was tense before, I was really tense now. First call to our friend, "I'll be in the car in ten and on my way." I was moving within five minutes. Second call to our Chairman, "I cannot make the meeting—notes and memory stick are on my desk." Third call to top sports injury physiotherapist, "I need to find the best ankle specialist in Gloucestershire." Fourth call to hospital, "My wife is on her way... we need a private room." Physiotherapist calls, "Best surgeon is Mr. Ball and he will meet you at the hospital." Up-date call to friend. Very short exchange with Harriet. And so it went for two hours back to Gloucestershire. No call from Chairman.

Frazzled, I arrived at the hospital. Harriet was in the private room, the surgeon was on his way. Harriet was not in a great state. X-rays showed a complicated break. Morphine-sedated, she was worried about the children.

I was distressed when I saw her pain, which was clearly visible. Yet somehow she managed to dictate a list of all the things she needed at the hospital and remembered who had our daughters and what they had with them to take home. I duly noted it all, got in the car and drove an hour back to the house to pack her things and then an hour back to the hospital again just in time to meet the surgeon.

I was nervous and immediately attempted to micro-manage things. But this was his field, not mine, and he quickly put me in my place and focussed his attentions on Harriet. The operation was set for mid-morning the following day. Harriet was totally worn out when I left to fetch the girls. It was late and they were fractious when we finally got home at around 10:30 P.M. After a quick bath, and lots of reassuring about Mummy, they finally fell asleep. I followed soon after, with still no word from our Chairman.

Thursday

Up very early. Checked e-mails. Showered. Got dressed. Made breakfast. Woke the girls. Got them dressed. Breakfast. Packed school bags. Drove to school. Didn't know sports bag was needed. Drove back home. Found empty sports bag. Started searching for contents. Completed search. Drove back to school and dropped bag. I was exhausted and it was only 8:20 A.M. I had never realised the amount of work Harriet did just to get the day started. I felt I had only just managed. An hour back to the hospital and I found Harriet most apprehensive about the operation. I moaned about the amount of driving I had done; very churlish. As Harriet was wheeled out, she asked if I had organised pick-ups for the girls. "Yes," I lied convincingly. Thankfully, the same two mothers obliged immediately when I called.

Back in her room, with two six-inch plates in her leg, and a plaster cast from toe to hip, Harriet was shattered and frustrated at the prospect of a long convalescence. Thankfully, the operation had been a success and I apologetically thanked our surgeon. As I left to collect the girls, Harriet asked if I had bought dinner for them. "Of course," I lied again. "What — dinner? Surely there was some food in the house; must go shopping after drop-off tomorrow," I thought.

Two hours later the girls were happily eating Daddy's special baked beans on toast as I told them all about how well Mummy's operation had gone. Then homework. Bath time. Washed hair. Dried hair. Stories. Warm milk. More stories, because Daddy never reads them. "Go to sleep now." Cleared away gourmet dinner. Prepared school bags. Checked timetable, no sports. Found pile of washing. Worked washing machine. "No, really, really, please go to sleep now." Actually, the beans on toast looked quite good. Exhausted I fell asleep in admiration of Harriet's ability to manage all of this seemingly so easily and mostly on her own. I, however, knew I needed help urgently.

Friday

Things went much smoother the next day. Harriet was in much better mental shape but hurting badly as the various painkillers were wearing off. The cast was heavy and came with two cumbersome crutches. I described how well things were going at home but asked whether perhaps my mother could come to help out whilst she was recovering. It's always hard to ask the Chief Executive of an organisation to accept the services of an interim manager so some persuasion was needed, but in the end I think Harriet realised that it was really I who needed the help. My mother was on a plane that afternoon.

Saturday

Harriet was released and I felt a huge sense of relief as I picked her up. The girls were at home with Granny and overjoyed when Mummy hobbled through the door on her crutches. Harriet finally made herself comfortable as best she could in the kitchen and surveyed the scene. She soon asked for pen and paper and started making lists and issuing instructions to my mother and me. "Things were going to be fine now that Harriet is home," I thought. "Someone who knows what's going on is finally back in charge."

A little later I caught up with our Chairman. Negotiations with our investor had continued and had not gone well. The investor had left. The following Wednesday the company filed for bankruptcy.

~Matthias Hauger

71

Baby-Talk Mom

No matter how calmly you try to referee, parenting will eventually produce
bizarre behavior, and I'm not talking about the kids.
~Bill Cosby

Before our sweet blond baby girl arrived, my wife — a nurse — decided to be a stay-at-home mother. That decision worked great for all three of us, Jeanne, me, and our little Dawn. Each evening Jeanne excitedly shared with me Dawn's latest accomplishment — when she first rolled over, her first tooth sawing through, her first word and first step.

When Dawn was not quite two years old, our little David arrived. Jeanne and the babies were very happy and now Jeanne was sharing with me each new antic of both. But, by David's first birthday, my normally intelligent wife's sharing shocked and alarmed me. Jeanne now used mostly one-syllable words! "Baby sits up!" and "Dawn goes bye-bye with Grandma." She was talking baby talk to me! And here's the one that I couldn't ignore, "Dada want more birthday cake?" Not unusual, I tried to assure myself, since she talked only to a baby and toddler all day and seldom spoke to adults. But...

It was my turn to share. So I revealed "my" problem to Jeanne. She couldn't believe me at first. Then we had a good laugh and I finally got the courage to make a remedy suggestion.

"How about using a babysitter for two days a week while you do part-time nursing?"

"Wouldn't work," she said. "Remember I tried part-time before

Dawn was born, but the hospital kept pressing me for more and more days and, feeling guilty, I was soon working four days weekly. I don't want to leave Dawn and David to sitters that long."

"Then what? Think about it and let's come up with something that gets you out with adults and stimulates your thinking."

At dinner the next evening, after I'd heard all about the kids' latest antics delivered in their Mom's baby-talk, Jeanne said, "I've been thinking about something I might like to do that gets me away from the kids for a few hours." I looked up, more than a little excited. "Years ago, another student and I started a weekly newspaper at our nursing school," she said. "I really enjoyed writing feature articles for it, but I didn't care for the straight reporting. So maybe I would enjoy a class or two in creative writing."

The next day I rushed to check on creative writing courses offered at the nearby University of Tulsa's downtown division. Offered at night, those courses were taught by LaVere Anderson, then the editor of the *Tulsa World* Sunday book pages. Before she moved to Tulsa, Ms. Anderson had written hundreds of short stories and articles that were published in magazines across the country and she was still selling. When I told Jeanne, she was excited and especially happy the courses were offered at night because I could stay with the kids while she was gone.

Though Jeanne went to class only two nights a week, her class was filled with bright people and her teacher was superb. Not only did Jeanne's baby talk disappear, but I soon had my interesting conversationalist back across the breakfast table. If that were all that those writing classes accomplished, that would have been enough.

It wasn't. Two years after her first class, Jeanne sold her first article. Three weeks after that, she sold her first short story. The years of writing that followed never encroached upon her mothering because she wrote while the children napped in the afternoon (or later were at school). In fact, the mothering helped her writing because her first article sales were to mother and baby magazines. In time she developed her niche — writing narrative style articles, each building to a gem of truth at the end. Some of those, called "Art of Living" articles, sold and were published by *Reader's Digest*.

Shortly after our third child was born, she started writing a monthly column called "TLC" (Tender Loving Care) for the newsstand magazine *Children's Playmate*. By the time that child, Dixon, started kindergarten, Jeanne's published stories were being chosen for anthologies, she had just published her first book, and she was writing a second.

An inspirational writer and speaker, my wife is now a Contributing Editor to *Guideposts* magazine. She always enjoyed being a "room mother" at our children's schools and teaching Sunday school classes as well. But what she considers her greatest accomplishment is being a happy stay-at-home mom for our three children. And I am happy to have had a small part of pointing a Baby-Talk Mom toward a career as a successful, professional writer who has been my wonderful wife and best friend for fifty-seven years now.

~Louis A. Hill, Jr.

72

A Mom's Promise

Never forget that the most powerful force on earth is love.
~Nelson Rockefeller

The day my mom decided to stay at home is one of the happiest I can remember. My mom had raised the four of us single-handedly, and through thick and thin, good times and bad, she had managed to be there for us whenever we needed her. I missed her during the time each day she was at work, but we had school to keep us busy, and my baby brother really seemed to like his babysitter. During the summer, Sandy, my older sister, watched over us and did a good job of taking care of us. But she wasn't my mom, whom I missed terribly each day when she got on the bus and rode away.

Then came the summer day when my mom announced she was quitting her job. She told us her employer wanted her to work more hours, which meant she'd be gone even more. Instead, she'd decided she was going to stay home with us. We were all surprised at the news. But it didn't take long before smiles appeared on our faces and we jumped and shouted for joy. I must have shouted louder than anyone, because my mom was going to be home! I was happier than I had ever been before.

"But how are we going to buy food and pay the rent?" my sister asked.

"I was offered a job by the people who own these apartments," my mom explained. "They're going to let me work cleaning the empty apartments."

I tugged at my mom's skirt. "But I thought you weren't going to have a job. You promised to stay home with us."

"I am staying home with you," she told me as she touched my face. "And the job is something that I can do with all of you around me. And when school starts, I'll be done with work before you come home each day."

"Can we stay with you while you work?" Larry, my younger brother, asked.

My mom smiled. "Of course you can."

My sister put a finger to her chin. "Will we have Carl there with us, too?"

"Yes," Mom answered. "Your baby brother will be with us. I'll need you to watch over him while I work."

"And we'll all be together again," Larry said, smiling.

I wanted to smile, too, but I wondered how long it would be before my mom's work at home took her away from us again. I held back tears as my mom gathered me up in her arms and hugged me tight.

"Don't worry," she whispered softly to me. "I promise we'll be together."

And she was able to keep her promise, in the beginning. The apartment owners didn't mind us tagging along with my mom as she cleaned the empty rooms, made beds, and made sure everything looked clean and bright. My mom did all that work and still had time for us, taking lunch breaks where we shared sandwiches and funny stories, singing to us while she cleaned and we played with our baby brother, and dancing around with us in a shiny, sparkling apartment she had just cleaned.

But it didn't last. After a while my mom found herself pulled in different directions trying to clean the apartments and be with us. She began to fall behind in her work, and the apartment owners wondered if having her kids around was a good idea. Soon we were alone back in our apartment while my mom went off to work only a few feet from us. But as close as she was to us, it might as well have been halfway across the world for as much as I missed her.

Then one day while my sister was fixing lunch for my mom and the rest of us, we played clean-up with our baby brother. We took out dry cloths and brushes and pretended to clean pie pans and pots. I took a cloth and polished the kitchen table. Carl laughed and picked up a brush and started cleaning his baby shoe.

"There!" I said after I had finished polishing the table. "That's almost as good a job as Mom does."

My sister looked up from spreading peanut butter on a slice of bread. She smiled. "That's a great idea!"

"What's a great idea?" I asked.

Sandy finished the sandwiches and sat and ate with us. She practically swallowed her own sandwich whole. When we were through she quickly packed our mom's lunch and said, "I'm going to keep Mom company for a while. Watch the baby."

"But what about the owners?" Larry asked. "We could get Mom in trouble."

My sister smiled. "It'll be all right."

She was gone for about an hour when I began to get worried. I picked up the baby and my brothers and I walked over to the row of apartments I knew my mom was working in. When we climbed the stairs and looked into the apartment she was cleaning, I got a huge surprise. My mom was hard at work as always, cleaning the living room windows. But right beside her was my sister, pushing a vacuum across the carpet. Sandy was helping my mom clean!

We went inside the apartment. I smiled at my mom. Carl made baby noises, and Larry asked, "Can we help, too?"

After that, we all went to work. We took turns watching our baby brother while my mom showed us how to sweep and vacuum and dust. She never had us do much, just enough to quiet any objections from the owners.

My mom had found a way to keep her promise, to be home with us and work, and we'd found a way to help her. When the time came for us to begin school in the fall, I knew my mom would be all right, and that from now on she'd be waiting for us when we got home. The memory of seeing her smile each day as I came through the front door is something I'll always cherish.

~John Buentello

Power MOMS

The Dividends

Taking Stock of Special Moments

Top Ten Most Blush-Inducing Moments of Motherhood (So Far!)

I've concluded that motherhood, for most of us,
is like one long out-of-control roller coaster ride.
~Joan Leonard

10. Ivy asking someone at the supermarket checkout if they were having a baby. It was a dude.

9. Fletch, at eight months, getting a baby doll in music class and proceeding to breastfeed it, causing one mom to suggest I film and submit to *America's Funniest Home Videos*.

8. On a crowded airplane, baby Ivy having a very bad Code Brown, the up-the-back kind. (The Latin term might be *'rhea explosiva*.) It was so bad that when I walked her down the aisle passengers gasped as if in need of military-caliber gas masks.

7. Having Sadie ask a girl's father in her class if he was her Grandpa.

6. A toddler-aged Ivy hitting a little tiny baby so hard, we started calling her Cassius Kargman.

5. Sadie refusing to walk down the aisle as flower girl at a friend's 300-person wedding rehearsal.

4. Ivy announcing in a quiet restaurant that she has a BIG BIG POO.

3. Fletch projectile vomiting Similac onto the mommy's friend's silk dress.

2. Sadie telling an older heavy-set man with a long white beard that he looks "exactly like Santa."

... and the number one most blush-inducing moment....

1. On a packed JetBlue flight, having Sadie say (loudly) "Mommy, when the plane goes up, up, up in the sky, the wheels go up into the plane's vagina!"

Ahhh, the humbling job of motherhood. You can try and be prim and perfect with matchy-matchy sibling outfits, the hair bows, the table manners, the polished smiles for the holiday card. And just when you think you can exhale in a crowded birthday party because your kids are fabulous, one smashes a chocolate-frosted cupcake on another's white dress. Or pushes a tot in a bouncy castle. Or dances *Hannah Montana*-style... to organ music at a friend's christening.

We can be the most preened and controlled adults, and even the most anal of us are simply forced to let go and surrender to the Fisher-Price explosion. In the pre-parent years, when a kid spazzed in a crowded theater, threw peas in a restaurant, or smacked his mommy, I just told myself what people have been telling themselves for millennia in order to propagate our fine species of homo sapiens: when I have kids one day, they will never do that!

Oh, what a difference a broken water makes.

When the stork arrived with my oldest Sadie, I couldn't help but think she was the most perfect creature ever spawned. And of course all mommies shine their rose-colored lenses upon each of their babies as they innocently babble and roll and coo. And then... you get to know them. First of all, let the record reflect that I adore my kids. They are a spunky, quirky, colorful bunch and I relish our time together. They are a wacky crew full of incredible observations, big hearts, and electric smiles. And when I'm bummed or tired or stressed, their little arms around me in delicious hugs are the Hello Kitty Band-Aid on all that ails me.

And yet, of course, no kid is perfect. And by the way if they were, they'd probably be boring! Our edges make us what we are. Who doesn't love a little sass and spice? But what about when that spice gets racheted up to the level of, say, a glob of wasabi?

Take, for example the list above. Allow me to mention that, if need be, I could probably do a Top 100 list. Maybe David Letterman should hire me. This was easy! But when I think about some of the moments that made me blush, I realized that, sure they can be cringe-inducingly embarrassing, but they can also be... lovely. Here is one example.

When Sadie "graduated" nursery school, they literally had a whole rooftop ceremony complete with "Pomp and Circumstance" playing from an iPod dock. The children lined up at the base of the stairs leading to the super tall jungle gym. The parents were all in rows opposite the looming playground apparatus, cameras ready, grins wide. The head teacher then read each child's name. The child was to climb the stairs, walk to the tippy top of the long slide, and slide down. At the base of the slide was the assistant teacher who gave them their little diploma to fête the milestone. Applause ensued.

Kid after kid slid down to spirited clapping. It truly was the cutest thing ever, a brilliant idea to cap off their little careers as toddler students. Then came Sadie's turn. She walked up the stairs, and my husband Harry and I were poised, clutching digicam with pride. I

drew breath excitedly as my little munchkin got to the top. But then...
she didn't slide down. She just stood there.

"Come on, Sadie, sweetheart!" encouraged the teacher, after a
few seconds.

Nada.

"Honey, come on down!" she coaxed again.

I could feel the stares of the parents starting to look at us. While
they all loved Sadie, they knew she could be a total spitfire, prone to
clowning around.

"Geez, she's a handful!" a mom in a shoe store once said to me,
shaking her head after a little whiney outburst over M&Ms.

Harumph. I hate that expression. Yeah, a handful of flowers, of
Barbie shoes, of blond curls, of M&Ms. There's nothing more vulnerable than the suspicion that your kid is being judged.

"Slide on down, kiddo!" the teacher said, a tad agitated.

Probably only thirty or forty seconds passed but it seemed like
forever. My heart was beating, my husband was sweating, and just as
I was about to draw breath to call to her, she casually strolled across
the top of the jungle gym deck to the fireman's pole, and shot down.

That's my girl.

So, sure, I was nervous and even maybe a tad blushy at first that
she didn't follow directions. Kids are taught to do what they are told,
obviously. Still, it was a weirdly great moment. The assets that are
wonderful for life are not the ones that are wonderful for grammar
school. When we're adults, aren't we supposed to go outside the box,
break the chain, and have guts? Why should I have been embarrassed? What she did was actually pretty cool.

So when I thought about it on a macro-level, I sort of turn a
little mental page in the Mommy Book. Sure, I feel terrible if my
kids are freaking on a packed flight, but really, will I ever see these
people again? Why sweat a liter and feel the stress hormones cours-
ing through my veins? Why add wrinkles to my already grooved
forehead over a bizarre comment, a thrown object à la Russell Crowe,
or some whiney behavior?

Deep in my gut, I know one day, when my little nuggets are

older and have their wits and manners hammered into them as parents and society demand, I will feel wistful about all those inappropriate comments, the unusual hues of an off-color observation, or the unpredictability of a chaotic life. I will long for the pulse pounding that accompanies their innocent social blunders, their lack of edit buttons, their blissful lack of awareness. I will miss blushing.

~Jill Kargman

It Happened in an Instant

That is what learning is. You suddenly understand something
you've understood all your life, but in a new way.
~Doris Lessing

I couldn't see much, just the ceiling lights in the emergency room as the E.R. doctors and nurses quickly and cautiously cut my fluffy gray cashmere sweater (now soaked in blood) right down the middle so they could carefully take it off me. I was in shock, babbling about running marathons, a to-do list and asking, "how did I get here?" After about thirty minutes, the doctors assessed that I didn't have a broken neck, but I had fractured a bone in my face and suffered several very deep cuts, including a completely severed lip. I realized that it was kind of hard to talk without a top lip!

While still lying flat on the gurney, I was wheeled into the E.R. hallway as I waited for the plastic surgeon on duty to put my face back together. In silence, a warm tear rolled down my face and landed into my ear as I glanced over at my husband who was holding my hand. He didn't have to say a word because it was written all over his face. Silently my heart intuitively heard, I love you... your face looks beautiful, regardless of the scars... our children are so lucky they didn't lose you in the car accident today—as am I... everything will be okay. Then, I felt his grip on my hand get tighter as he quickly removed a tear from the corner of his eye.

Later that night in my hospital room, after the plastic surgeon had stitched up my face and reattached my lip, my husband kissed me goodbye and promised to return to the hospital the next day in hopes of taking me home. Now I was alone with my thoughts, an occasional attending nurse and the rhythmic pulse of the circulation machine's pads, which were wrapped around my legs to ensure that I didn't get a blood clot. How did I get myself into this mess?

I had gotten into a cab to meet a film crew to work on a segment for the Cool Globes summer lakefront exhibit (in Chicago), and the next thing I knew, my cab smashed into another car and wham, I hit the glass divider in the back seat. Right when I got into the cab, I remember checking my busy schedule on my hand-held, thinking, "There's just not enough time in the day... I have so much to do... pick up my sons at the bus, make dinner, exercise, do the laundry, write an article for my online magazine, work on the production sheet for my PBS TV series, sit, breathe, relax... how can I do it all?" Oh, such is the life of a Super Mom; trying to do it all, be it all and still fit into the perfect size dress. All of these busy thoughts were streaming through my head like an old fashioned movie, while, in slow motion, I was flung forward, looking right into the eyes of the man driving the other car.

Three days later, when I came home from the hospital, I was still a little shaky in my step and could really feel the pain of each and every cut, bruise and "feeling sorry for myself" emotion. I entered the house and was greeted by my tail-wagging cocker spaniel, Barkley, who didn't seem to notice my face, but appeared a little curious. My four-year-old son, on the other hand, innocently told me, "I love you mommy but I can't look at you because your face is scary." My heart sunk, as he avoided my glances and turned away when I hugged him (for dear life). My two older sons were a bit braver, but I could see that they, much like people who drive by a car accident, were very curious about the details and wounds. They assured me that it looked "okay" and that it would heal, and then they were business as usual—reminiscent of what I had heard my husband say earlier that day.

As the days went by and my stitches were removed, I began the process of getting my life back to normal. It was difficult to look in the mirror and see the new landscape of my face, so I decided to wait a few weeks before I really examined the damage. Instead, I concentrated on my family and home life. I spent extra time putting my sons to bed at night and my dog enjoyed the extra brushing and petting. What I discovered in my tender family moments was that, amidst the busy schedules and running around, we were all very happy. There was a feeling of joy and teamwork as we spent time together working on projects and playing! I slipped back into the regular mom I used to be when my sons were toddlers, before I donned my cape and mask as Super Mom. It felt good. Good to be back in the center of it all.

How did all of these layers of my life start to pile up? When did pregnancy turn into boo-boo kisser, story reader, ride-a-bike teacher, room mother, cookie maker, homework queen and work-from-home media company owner? Then I realized—it's what I've dreamed about of all of my life. When I was a little girl, I would don the apron, carry my baby doll, make pretend cookies, sweep the floor and play teacher, all in the same day. A-Ha! I've been a Super Mom since I was four! I've been rehearsing for this role for most of my life. I've juggled, multi-tasked and nurtured "babies" for as long as I can remember. People would ask me when I was younger what I wanted to be when I grew up. I would confidently tell them, "I want to be a mommy and help people."

I've always known that being a mother has given me membership to the greatest club in the world. But what that accident on the snowy January day gave me was a sharp reminder that by simply loving and being with your kids, you ARE a Super Mom. Regardless of how many plates you keep spinning in the air, your children will love you for just being you, for BEING there, not somewhere else. Sure, they'll be proud of your accomplishments, but what REALLY matters to them is that you are at their side, as much as you can be and that you love them for being them, your Super Kids.

~Elizabeth Aldrich

Channing's Dollhouse

*There came a moment quite suddenly when a mother realized that
a child was no longer hers.... without bothering to ask or even give notice,
her daughter had just grown up.*

~Alice Hoffman

Today I started putting away Channing's dollhouse. The truth is, she hasn't played with it for ages. It is dusty and I needed to make room for possessions more suited to her "tween" years, marked by her rapidly approaching tenth birthday.

The dollhouse was filled with miniatures of all types. In the drawer of a wooden dresser, I found a lavender foam heart. I put it in a Ziploc bag along with some pieces of furniture. In another bag went a mismatched set of the dollhouse residents: everything from a fabric Goldilocks to a plastic dolphin. I smiled at a white comforter made from a folded tissue. I wondered if I should save it. When in doubt, throw it out, except where I'm concerned. I better keep it, dust mites and all, so that when she's a grown-up I can remember how cute and resourceful she was during her early years.

As I worked, I remembered the excited look on her face when she received the dollhouse at age three. We bought one that would hold up over time. One that her children could play with one day. I wondered what Channing's children would be like. Will she have a girl to enjoy her dollhouse? I wondered if I would be lucky enough to enjoy grandmotherhood.

In my youth, I had devised the perfect plan for my life. I would graduate from college at twenty-two, then travel in Europe and return home in time to get married by twenty-five. Next, I'd have two children before turning thirty. My actual graduation was delayed by a year and the domino effect of that pushed out every other date in my master plan, exponentially. That's okay, because I learned in time that there was a better path for my life.

In my twenties, I had a definite view of success and it was something that was achieved in one's career. My goal was to be self-sufficient. Yes, I wanted children, but I needed to have a job that would enable me to support them, come what may. To that end, I turned my back on my dream of being a writer and I took a boring but secure job at an aerospace company. Being a stay-at-home mom was out of the question. What would happen to us if I ever got divorced?

My first marriage did end in divorce. Then, almost concurrently, I got laid off from the job that I thought would carry me to retirement. A decade later than planned, I was beginning my life again from scratch.

Luckily, in spite of the predicted odds, I had another chance at marriage while in my late thirties. With the encouragement of my new husband, I even started taking writing classes. Then, after almost three years of trying and nearly losing hope, I got pregnant. Knowing I was going to be a mommy changed me to the core! Suddenly the idea of being away from my baby was not only unthinkable, it was unbearable.

I thank God every day for giving us Channing. I am thankful that my husband also felt she should have a parent at home to be her private assistant as she goes through the long process of growing up. My definition of success changed with the birth of my daughter. For me, success meant being able to stay at home with my child.

As it turned out, the better plan for my life was still unfolding. Two days before my daughter was born, I got an offer on my manuscript for a children's book. If a character in a movie became a mother and a published author in the same week, I would say it was too unbelievable, but there I was.

First and foremost, I find my fulfillment in my family. To think that I could have that and also do the job of my dreams in my "spare time" was not a plan I would have dared to imagine. I'm certain that I wouldn't be a writer today had I chosen the corporate world over being a stay-at-home mom. More importantly, I would have missed out on so much of the joy of my true calling—being Channing's mother.

I am grateful. Really grateful. I didn't miss a thing during the first ten years of my daughter's life. I got to witness every milestone and I savored every moment.

Even so, while reaching into the dollhouse to remove the little Canadian geese, I still ached at closing this chapter and packing away the tangible evidence of Channing's early childhood.

This evening, when I returned from a meeting at her school, I went back to the dollhouse to finish my task. I smiled when I saw Channing sitting there. On the floor next to her feet were three empty Ziploc bags. She hadn't noticed me walk in. She was too busy putting all the furniture and residents back into the dollhouse, where they belonged.

~Marie Torres Cimarusti

Catching Up to My Past

If you want to understand today, you have to search yesterday.
~Pearl S. Buck

They say your past eventually catches up to you, but in my case, I needed to catch up to my past.

I never thought I'd be a mother. I was adopted, and when I was thirty-four I found my entire birth family — a mother, a father and two full-birth sisters. My birth parents were very young and unmarried when I was conceived. It was the 1960s and unwed mothers were looked down upon. Three months after they put me up for adoption, my birth parents got married. It was New Year's Eve, 1966. They went on to have two more daughters. I met the entire family and instantly fell in love with them. I had closure. But I never thought about having a baby myself.

That all changed when I met my husband. We fell in love and got married after three months of dating. Three months after that, I was pregnant with Ruby. I loved being pregnant. I absolutely loved it!

But nothing prepared me for the emotional moment of giving birth. When the doctor put her on my chest, I literally sobbed. I sobbed while they weighed her, I sobbed while my husband held her. I was just overcome with feelings about my own birth mother. She was allowed to hold me for just five minutes before she gave me away, and wasn't to see me again for thirty-four years. And so I sobbed for my birth mother, I cried for myself, and my own daughter Ruby. I told her I would never let her go.

It's something I find myself saying to her on a daily basis now. When she calls out to me from another room, "Mommy, Mommy," I always tell her, "Mommy is right here, I will *never* leave you." Each time it comes out of my mouth I am shocked. I have never felt a love like this in my life!

~Jillian Barberie-Reynolds

A Trip to Healing

There is no friendship, no love, like that of the parent for the child.
~Henry Ward Beecher

M om, where's my white jean skirt!?"

My daughter's voice rose to a timbre more befitting a house fire than a lost piece of clothing.

"Mom, if I can't find that, I'm just not going to school!"

It was the beginning of her thirteenth spring, and it was at that moment that I realized I was no longer the mother of a preteen. I was officially the mother of a teenager.

"Mom, I hate this breakfast." (The same one she happily ate yesterday.) "You don't even know what I eat! Are you actually wearing, (eating, doing, saying) that?" And the worst one of all because I'd said the exact same thing to my mother: "Don't embarrass me!" (Finger pointing included.)

At times she was as clingy as a toddler, but most of the time she was pushing me away. Everything had become a struggle. Somehow, I thought teenagerdom would pass me by, that I was immune to it. My daughter and I have always been extraordinarily close. I was proud of the fact that I was known as the "cool mom." We could just look at each other and burst out laughing. We would sail along like sisters, secure in our sacred bond and secret language.

Complicating matters further was that I was a stay-at-home mom who suddenly developed a hobby that consumed more and more of my time. "You're always at the art supply store. Another art class—didn't you just take one!?"

I felt that we were both striking out on our own but in opposite directions.

Packing for camp that summer was a nightmare. More clothes lay crumpled on the floor than in her giant duffel. We stood facing each other in a tense standoff.

"It's like we're not even friends anymore. It's like we're enemies," she yelled.

Later that night I sat on the bathroom floor, admonishing myself to try and do some yogic breathing.

"She's just a teenager," I repeated to myself like a mantra, through tears of hurt and frustration. I remembered her as a baby afraid to let go of me; holding onto my long hair like a talisman. But, it didn't still the ache in my heart.

I dropped her off at the camp bus that summer. We hugged each other hard, and I watched as she boarded the bus. Every other summer she would pop her head out and cheekily salute me with a kiss. This year she took her seat without a glance back.

I spent my summer painting, writing, and missing my daughter. I missed her and I missed the idea of her. I hoped our time apart would be somehow a time of healing.

Our last phone call before camp ended was a week before she was due home.

"Mom, will you pick me up?"

"Now?" I asked.

"No, at the end of camp."

"Don't you want to take the bus with your friends?"

I was calculating the driving time; nine hours in one day. Time I could be painting or catching up on the endless list of things that I always seem to be behind on.

"We could spend some time together," she pleaded.

I knew that she was reaching out to me.

"Yes," I said, "of course."

She swung her long legs into the car. She was silent and slumped dejectedly in her seat. She twirled her friendship bracelet, took out her camera, and began scrolling through her pictures.

"I wish I were back in camp," she announced. "I'm camp sick."

We were driving along beautiful, winding, country roads in the mountains of Pennsylvania. I didn't know what to say, so I just drove, trying to puzzle out what was ineffable—a loss I could not name.

Instead of feeling hurt and angry, I looked inside myself for something that I could give her, a gift that would somehow transform us both.

That summer day, we ate ice cream for lunch, sitting on the roof of the car, our feet dangling in the sunroof, ice cream melting down our chins.

We photographed barns, cows, silos and improbably a pirate ship that we imagined some ambitious parent had built—sailing on the vast green sea of a cow pasture.

We traveled on dirt roads that did not have names and led to nowhere.

We held hands and walked by the banks of a sun-dappled stream.

We talked about all the art we would make and all the poetry we would write.

And we laughed again, a sound precious to my ears.

We pulled onto our moonlit, tree-lined road late. I drove slowly, reluctant for the magical day to end. My daughter was sleeping, her beautiful profile limned in moonlight.

There at the side of the road, I noticed a doe with a fawn trailing behind, lazily eating the overgrown summer grass. I pulled the car beside them slowly, sure that they would see us and bolt. They continued to eat and gaze at us unconcerned. I opened the car window, my daughter stirred and I heard her intake of breath as she opened her eyes.

We stared into the eyes of our own reflections and smiled knowingly.

I knew then that the greatest gift that I had to give my daughter was my full attention.

In the midst of our busy, crazy lives, to give someone we love our undivided attention says: "You are what matters to me in all the world. Right here, right now."

My daughter reached for my hand in that moment.

"I love you," she whispered.

"I love you, too," I whispered back.

And we continued on the road home.

~Jennifer Mallin

Anywhere But Here

I just want a one-way flight to anywhere but here;
My home's a wreck and the baby's sick, and I'm on the verge of tears.
Ten loads of laundry and all the dishes piled up high;
By the time we've said our bedtime prayers another day's gone by.

I curse the mirror 'cause I don't like what I see;
And it scares me half to death my little girl wants to be like me.
Too many times I cave and just let her have her way;
And I scold my son over words I'm pretty sure he's heard me say.

But I kiss each one goodnight and pray that they'll be safe;
And then I crawl between the sheets and dream that I could run away
To anywhere but here.

'Cause life just isn't turning out quite the way I'd planned;
See I thought that I could handle things a lot better than I am.
Or maybe it's just fear that's calling me
To anywhere but here.

I watch the movies and I read the magazines;
They say to do what makes me happy 'cause it's all about me.
That I was meant to be more than just a mother and a wife and

I start to believe that I should lead a different life.

'Cause I'm torn between the here and now and this elusive fantasy;
That I deserve the fairytale and to be swept off my feet
To anywhere but here.

But where would I go?
And what would I do?
And would I tell myself that underneath all the lies I found the truth?

Oh, what would life be like to just leave all of this behind?
Would it come back to haunt me every single time
I thought of laughing with my daughter at pink curlers in her hair?
Or singing to my baby late nights in her rocking chair?

Who'd hug that little brown-eyed boy and kiss his banged-up knee?
Who's gonna turn the TV off when Daddy falls asleep?
It's gonna be me.

A lot of selfish reasons to just up and disappear;
But I can't imagine all the love I'd miss if I were
Anywhere but here;
Anywhere but here.

~Karen Fisher

79

Mom's Tip Money

Gratitude is the memory of the heart.
~Jean Baptiste Massieu, translated from French

I t was a sweltering day in Michigan and I was trying to escape the heat and yet continue to be productive. Our boys were both in high school and our daughter was in college. They all had jobs and were working, so there were many loads of clothes to wash and some ironing to do.

It was wonderful to have a basement to work in. There were two rooms in addition to a recreation room and office. In the laundry room was a washer/dryer, washtub, a place for folding and ironing clothes, walls lined with jars of homemade jams, fruits, vegetables, as well as other storage. The sun came in through a couple of small windows, but the concrete floors and older foundation allowed for a cool, comfortable place to work.

As the day progressed, however, I was ironing clothes and began to feel a bit overheated. I grabbed a nearby cloth to remove the perspiration from my brow and face. When our older son came in from work, he saw me ironing and seemed concerned.

"Mom, your face is red and you look hot," he said.

"It happens. I'm ironing, after all." I smiled.

"Don't you want a fan or something, Mom?" he asked.

"No, it has been fairly cool. I'll be done soon," I said, taking a drink of water from a nearby glass, removing some ice and cooling off my skin a bit.

He looked around at the clean, crisp clothes and, with a smile, left the room. An hour later when I had completed my task and was checking the freezer for something I could whip up for dinner, my son came back into the room.

"Mom, leave this right here on top of the dryer. I made this for you."

I saw an old shoe box which had paper glued to it and a picture of someone ironing. Inside the box were a dollar bill and a couple of quarters, and next to the picture, it read "Mom's Tip Money." I looked at the artwork and my son's face and realized how much he appreciated the little things I did—things that we often think go unnoticed or taken for granted. He had decided that my work was worthy of tip money and initiated a plan to make that happen. The box remained on the dryer until we moved a few years later.

During the days that followed, the kids gladly contributed dollars, quarters and spare change, and my hubby threw in some bills to round things off. It had always been a clear understanding that Mom had dibs on any money found in jeans, pants pockets or shirts, and anywhere else it tended to collect. But this box meant the world to me, not because of the change, but because it reminded me how much they all appreciated the small, everyday things I did.

Recently, when our son came to visit us in South Carolina, I did a few loads of laundry and washed his clothes. Our laundry room is very small now, and we no longer live in an area with large basements. After he left, I was striping the bedding and starting on some more laundry when my eyes caught sight of something on the dryer. It was a small piece of notepaper with a couple of dollars and some change on top. My eyes grew moist as I remembered a summer day over fifteen years before. His note was a reminder of that very special time. It read, simply, "Mom's Tip Money."

~Diane Dean White

80

Finding Sacred Moments in Silence

*If a child is to keep alive his inborn sense of wonder, he needs the companion-
ship of at least one adult who can share it, rediscovering with him the joy,
excitement and mystery of the world we live in.*

~Rachel Carson

Being a mother of five children and working from home has brought me many challenges; while at the same time some amazing gifts that have a timeless value. Sometimes when doing an interview, I am wiping a dirty face at the same time. Those are the times I am reminded how blessed I am to be able to get a goofy smile or a hug that most working mothers wouldn't be able to get. These are the extra perks that make it all worthwhile.

We have a camper in order to bring the kids with us when I have a lecture and mix vacation and business. While on a recent business trip with three of my five children, Matthew, fourteen, Hannah, six, and Asha, five, I was preparing for a workshop that my husband and I were doing together. My son Matthew asked me to go on a hike with him. I told him I had a lot to do and didn't think I would have time at that moment. I told him I just needed to have silence for a while.

"Come on Mom, this trip will add to your message. It's a true spiritual journey," Matthew coaxed.

"Okay, I can't pass up the opportunity to take a spiritual journey," I answered.

I put on my hiking shorts and set out on a walk with him. We came to the mouth of a river where rapids were flowing over a small waterfall.

"Are we going to climb down that waterfall?" I asked, hoping he would want to turn back.

He smiled at me and said, "Come on, Mom. It's about the silence you find at the end."

I stood there looking at the rushing water thinking, "Either I am crazy or lazy. How am I going to do this?"

Matthew's smile made me see that this was important to him, so we hung on to the side of some rock and climbed down the small waterfall. My body became drenched with water, and I wondered if we were going to get back in time for me to get my writing done for the lecture. Finally, we arrived at the bottom of the waterfall, and then followed the river to a crossing.

"Come on, Mom. You can do this. It's peaceful once you get there," Matthew urged.

At that point, I stepped on a large tree trunk that had fallen over the deep part of the river. It felt like we were in a movie, and I was nervous and excited at the same time. Once we crossed the water, we walked along the bank and into the shallow part of the stream. It was beautiful. The petrified wood embedded in the landscape was amazing. Its timeless wonder spoke to me, reminding me that nature does not worry about getting things done. It allows being in the moment.

"Mom, we are here. Look ahead." Matthew brought me out of my reverie. I looked ahead and saw a beautiful opening through the trees. He held out his hand and helped me climb upon a rock to get a better look. It was beautiful. Miles away, I could see a placid lake glistening in the sunlight. Matthew looked at me and said, "Here, Mom. Here is your silence."

I looked at him and replied, "Thank you for this." At that moment, I realized that the silence we often seek is not something that says, "Please leave me alone so I can concentrate and work." It is the moments we take with our children to observe real silence and reconnect with why we are here.

We returned to the camper, and I finished my work. I was amazed at how easily it flowed through my fingertips into my laptop.

Being a "power mom" can be crazy. Some say that it's easier to work away from home. But I believe that the most precious opportunities I have as a mother and career woman are these sacred moments that remind me of what really matters.

~Kimmie Rose Zapf

My Reality TV

In every conceivable manner,
the family is link to our past, bridge to our future.
~Alex Haley

I t was "dumpster day." The amount of clutter in our house had increased proportionately with the number of people and pets who live here. New items come into our house daily but very little goes out. The dumpster beckoned me as I considered the scope of the job ahead.

My husband and I trudged from room to room to purge our home of unused and unnecessary items. In my manic search to throw out anything that hadn't been touched by human hands in recent history, I went into the family room. Everything was fair game and the old Disney videos were no exception.

I dug through the videos and gleefully tossed aside those meant for preschoolers, not teenagers. My daughter, Katie, and her friend, Kim, entered the room. "What are you doing?" Katie questioned.

"Cleaning. If you see something you can't live without, speak up now or forever hold your peace." As the girls looked through the outcasts, I stumbled upon containers of family videos.

"Katie, look... videos of you and your sister when you were younger!" The descriptions on the sides of the tapes showed a journey through time, with birthdays, vacations, births and recitals.

"Can we watch the day you taped me and Kim while we played in the snow?" Katie asked.

"Sure, why not? I could use a break," I replied. The three of us plopped down on the couch.

"Remember how you yelled at Kim to get off the sled?" asked Katie.

"I did not!"

Kim laughed, "Yes, you did."

Confidently, I replied, "The proof is on this tape!" The next few minutes were filled with laughter from both the video, and the three of us, as we watched it.

Nicole, my older daughter, entered the room. "What are you watching?"

Katie replied, "A video of the day Mom yelled at Kim."

I looked at her and rolled my eyes. The proof came moments later. Evidently, my idea of speaking firmly is perceived as "yelling" by my kids. So much for instant replay.

The movie marathon continued and even the dogs joined in. Teddy, our over-sized Wheaton Terrier, barked at his own voice when he heard it on the tape and Mollie, our Miniature Schnauzer, joined in the chorus.

Over the next two and a half hours, the four of us sat in a row on the sofa munching on Goldfish crackers and watching the past seventeen years of our lives unfold before our eyes.

Precious moments, long forgotten, were acted out as if on a stage. My older daughter is now a mature young lady who talks about politics, life and college. But that afternoon I had the pleasure of seeing her filled with the joy of a six-year-old while she rode her bike and acted silly. She seemed much louder than I had remembered.

And we'd all forgotten Katie's use of the word "mudder," most commonly heard in the phase "You're not the mudder, Cole" directed at her sister Nicole's bossiness. I'd always wished that we had caught her "muddering" that word on tape... and much to my delight, we had!

Just like an *America's Funniest Home Videos* production, we watched a two-and-a-half-year-old Katie glide on her stomach down our new slide. Halfway down, she stopped herself with her hands.

Suddenly, Katie was no longer visible through the video camera lens. I panned the camera to the right and saw she had fallen off. We could hear her cries of, "Bug, it's a bug!" in the background. I walked closer to the slide and the camera eventually exposed a tiny, transparent bug barely visible to the naked eye in the center of the slide. Katie bawled in the background, "Go home to your mudder, bug!" I heard my own laughter in the video, which reminded me how enjoyable my time with them at that age had been.

My husband walked by with his arms filled with old board games. He stopped and turned his head in my direction and gave me a, "Hello... wanna help me?" look.

Instead, I smiled and said, "You should come watch with us. These videos are great!" He shook his head and continued out the garage door.

We watched a little while longer, but I realized my husband's recent trip past me was a sign to continue with my real mission for that day. I resumed my chores, but something inside me felt different.

Katie spent the rest of the day calling me "Mudder." Nicole, who was working in a summer kindergarten program at that time, kept making comparisons to herself at the age of six and some of her students. The antics she found so endearing in her students were some of the very things she used to do.

As my girls have reached their teenage years, I have often wondered where I am headed. I have wallowed in a mid-life quandary, which sometimes plagues me and makes me want more for myself.

When I watched those home videos, I was able to momentarily cast aside what I had previously felt. Maybe it's not only about where I am heading in the future, but also what I have done in the past.

It's easy to see what others have, but easier to miss what is right in front of you. That afternoon was one of the best moments of my life — an afternoon of television I will never forget.

Now, that's reality TV!

~Sharon Struth

Reprinted by permission of Tom Swick.
©2008

82

Crossing the Bridge

*In the final analysis, it is not what you do for your children
but what you have taught them to do for themselves that will make them
successful human beings.*

~Ann Landers

I t was a gloomy Saturday, drizzling and foggy but warm in Vancouver, Canada where I was filming a movie, and I was spending the day with my two young daughters, Rory, then six, and Piper, then three. We were told by some of the cast and crew that we must see the Capilano Suspension Bridge. Capilano has been around since the 1800s, when it was made out of rope and planks. It's now made of reinforced steel and is safely anchored in thirteen tons of concrete on either side of the canyon, with high, fully enclosed railings, which is a good thing, since it's 450 feet long and 230 feet high above a rushing river. I was balancing an umbrella in one hand and holding tightly to Piper with the other as we stepped onto the bridge. Rory was just a bit ahead, excited to be first across.

It was quite extraordinary and I was thinking this was going to be great fun, but when we got about a quarter of the way along the bridge, Rory looked down and suddenly got very upset. She clung to me and started chanting, "I'm scared Mommy, I want to go back, this is NOT fun, I'm so, so scared." I picked Rory up and kept walking, telling her that she was safe and that I would never put her in harm's way. She was crying and practically choking me as I tried to calm her. Meanwhile, Piper was bopping along, thoroughly unaware of how high up we were. She felt completely safe whereas Rory was panicking. This was very unlike Rory, as she's usually up for anything. I put Rory down, knelt to her level, looked determinedly into her eyes and said, "Honey, we are okay. I promise we will make it across this bridge and we'll be all right."

I closed my umbrella, realizing that I could not balance a fifty-pound child in one arm, an umbrella in the other and guide my three-year-old close to the rails so she wouldn't topple over. We were now getting wet but Rory was trying to calm down. We took a few more steps and she burst into tears again, telling me again she wanted to go back. We were more then halfway across the bridge by this point and turning back wasn't an option. I held her tightly and promised it would be all right.

Suddenly, out of the fog, an older woman appeared walking in the other direction. She smiled at Rory and said, "Are you scared?" Rory screamed, "Yes, this is not fun at all." The woman, like a little angel dropped down from heaven, leaned in a bit closer to Rory and said, "Just you wait. You're almost to the other side. And it's really worth it!" She patted my daughter warmly on the shoulder and continued on her way. Rory was somehow less hysterical after that, still clinging to me as hard as she could, but anticipating that the end was near and there might be something special on the other side. We pushed on and when we finally neared the end, Rory got a sudden burst of courage and jumped out of my arms and ran the last five planks and up the stairs to solid ground. Then she turned to me and said, "That wasn't so hard." I thought, "Well, for you maybe, but Mommy is exhausted!"

The girls ran around looking at everything, and I read to them about the plant life, as we passed plaques under towering trees with massive trunks. This was beautiful, lush, Vancouver forest. Following the path, we came to some stairs that led to what looked like the beginning of a huge tree house. Enthusiastically, both girls ran up the stairs, hoping to find something fun at the top. What was waiting for us were seven small suspension bridges connecting a bunch of evergreen trees which took us one hundred feet above the forest floor.

I thought, "Oh boy, this could be bad!" But Rory tentatively started across the first one on her own. I let her go. Luckily, these suspension bridges were only about ten feet long, connected by wooden observation decks built around each tree. The girls ran in circles around the decks before venturing onto the next bridge. Piper was so happy to have her big sister back and they were having a wonderful time. We talked about how we were like squirrels up so high in the trees and Rory got braver crossing each bridge and was able to skip across the last one.

At the end of the last one, she turned to me with a huge smile on her face and said, "Mommy I'm not even scared anymore. How did I do that?" After trying hard to love her through her terror and observing her joy and pride at overcoming it, I said, "Well honey, you just kept on going even though you were afraid and you pushed right past your fear!" It was a memorable moment for me as a mother, because I felt I had done a good job navigating the situation. I was thankful that I hadn't turned around and gone back. I was happy that the swinging bridge kept me just enough off balance physically that I had to remain centered emotionally. I never discounted Rory's feelings, but instead held her in love through the discomfort of her screams, and helped her find her way to the other side of the bridge — and her fear. The topper to it all was that when we got back to the giant bridge Rory went across the entire thing all by herself! Piper and I cheered.

As a woman who is also a mother and a passionate career person, I have faced what has sometimes felt like insurmountable fear. My business made it challenging to decide when the time was right to have children. I wasn't sure how it would affect my body or how being completely responsible for someone else's growth would affect my own. Ultimately, I did it when the time was right and it turned out that, not only did I love being pregnant and watching my body change, but I loved giving birth, experiencing someone coming through me into this world, and, of course, my children are the loves of my life. Like Rory, I got to the other side of that bridge. I, too, had guidance from my own angels who, with a warm touch on my shoulder, helped show me the way to those little bridges that I used to build my confidence. I found that by crossing them I was stronger, clearer, more focused and more energized to try traversing other bridges.

When Rory crossed the Capilano Bridge she found the joy of pushing through her fears. When I crossed the bridge into parenthood I found a plethora of gifts waiting for me on the other side. The voyage into the unknown, the ultimate challenge of being a successful parent, and allowing the depths of feeling that children bring infuse my work, has given me courage to always keep looking for the next bridge I might cross.

~Melora Hardin

Chapter
9

Power MOMS

Pink Slips

When the Greatest Success Means Getting Fired

83

Baby Cap to Army Hat

Children and mothers never truly part—
bound in the beating of each other's heart.
~Charlotte Gray

We loaded into the car to attend the family day at an army base in Washington. Our son would be going to war in Iraq. The day consisted of briefings about what to expect if something were to happen to our soldier.

I was very proud of my son. He looked so strong and handsome. There he stood in his fatigues and black hat. My mind drifted to the day he wore a baby cap and blanket instead. I was snapped to reality as the Sergeants talked of the sacrifice families were making so that freedom could be secured in Iraq.

As we hugged and said goodbye, tears flowed. I did not want to cry. He had a mission; he did not need a sloppy crying momma to deal with! It seemed I had no control. His brothers and sisters hugged him as they said their farewells. The young man clothed in green and gray was so brave, yet the tear in his eye showed him tender, too.

My job of raising him was done. Like when he was a baby, I wanted to scoop him up and rock him in my arms, but that was only a distant memory. Now, I would rock him in my heart and swaddle him in my prayers. I prayed that the seeds of love and sacrifice sown during his growing-up years would serve to comfort him in the distant lands.

I was reassured that day in a more profound way that my years as a stay-at-home mom were not in vain. I had poured my heart and soul into the heart and soul of my child. I knew the young soldier who stood before me was courageous, able, self-sacrificing; my son.

I encourage all mothers, everywhere, to embrace the moments with their children. We have all heard it said that they grow up so fast. I now enter the ranks of those who know this as fact.

~Sharon Hockenbury

Letting Go

It will be gone before you know it. The fingerprints on the wall appear higher and higher. Then suddenly they disappear.

~Dorothy Euslin

When my sons were younger, one of their favorite books was *Love You Forever* by Robert Munsch. It tells the story of a mother and her son. Each night she would rock him and sing a song about how she would love him forever and how he would always be her baby.

In the story, as her son grows, the mother continues to slip into his room and hold him and sing to him while he sleeps. The book takes a surprising turn when the son grows up and moves out. The mom gets into her car and drives across town. She sneaks into his bedroom and sings him the song.

That part of the story always disturbed me. For one thing, I couldn't imagine my sons growing up and moving out. However, my oldest turns eighteen in a few weeks, and what I once couldn't imagine may soon become quite real.

I don't know much about how boys turn into men. I understand the physiology of the process. Two of my soft, sweet cherubs are now scratchy-faced fellows who tower over me. However, I've found it difficult to move past the hands-on stage of parenting. I find myself asking, "what did you eat for lunch... is your homework finished... where's your coat?"

By contrast, my husband, Derek, has had some experience in

becoming a man. He's a retired military officer. He chides me for babying the boys and encourages me to let them do risky things—like fail.

"If you don't allow them to make mistakes, how are they going to learn?" he asks.

But I've spent years trying to keep my sons from sticking fingers into light sockets, from eating dirt, and from running into the street without looking. Watching these boys become men has been tougher than I thought possible. For Derek, it's more straightforward. We've taught them well, now let's watch them fly—or fall. He says if we make the nest too comfortable they'll never want to fly. He says this like it's a bad thing.

Last week, Derek and our second son exchanged heated words over a missed curfew. I bit my tongue and let them work it out, but late that night I couldn't sleep. I kept thinking about how little time we have left with this young man in our home. I've watched how quickly his older brother's high school years have flown.

So, I quietly opened the door to his room. Just like in the children's story, I crept to the foot of his bed.

"What?" his deep voice mumbled.

"It's just me," I said.

He grunted and rolled over. I scooted to the edge of his bed and wrapped my arms around him. When did his chest get so broad? How did his arms get so muscular?

I whispered the words from *Love You Forever*.

And suddenly, I remembered a scene I'd witnessed recently in the lobby of a nursing home. A woman sat slumped in a wheelchair near the entrance. She wasn't lovely to look at. Her white hair was thin and straggly and she didn't have many teeth. Her shoulders were bowed and bent. She didn't make eye contact with anyone.

The doors opened and a balding gentleman entered. He went right to the woman and knelt in front of her. "Hello, mother," he said. She lifted her head and placed a trembling hand on the side of his face. She didn't speak, but her eyes lit up and her smile transformed her.

Yes. I understand that little boys become men. I'm grateful my own have their dad to help them through the process. But we mothers know a secret.

At the end of that children's story, the mother has become too frail to hold her son. So he goes to her. He picks her up and rocks her, and he sings her the same song she used to sing to him.

So, I'll hold these boys while I can. I'll let them go when I should. And someday maybe they'll return and do the same for me.

~Cindy Hval

"Thanks, Mom, for eighteen years of hard work and devotion. Your services are no longer required."

Bittersweet

The mother-child relationship is paradoxical and, in a sense, tragic.
It requires the most intense love on the mother's side, yet this very love must
help the child grow away from the mother and to become fully independent.

~Erich Fromm

Maxine stood in front of the cake with thirteen unlit candles. She was confident and poised, her long reddish blond hair curled into ringlets falling down her back. She was wearing a full-length blue strapless gown. This was not the little girl who I had taken to the park and cheered as she yelled "higher" on the swings, or strolled through supermarkets saying, "Look, Maxine, those are peas, peas are green; that's pasta, yes, pasta begins with a p." Nor was she the obstinate child who refused to brush her hair, or only wore a backwards baseball cap and denim overalls.

It was the celebration of her Bat Mitzvah, and we had reached the point in the celebration called the "candle lighting." This was not one of the cakes that I had baked each year marking her growth. There were no *Sesame Street* characters, no *Rugrats* that I had painstakingly drawn the morning of her birthday party. This cake had a photo of her as a child at the beach and palm trees sprouting from it, and had been baked in someone else's oven. She had designed this cake herself and had given very careful instructions to the bakery as to how it was to be done.

I had felt the strings that tied us loosening as we planned her

Bat Mitzvah, a celebration of her "becoming a woman" in the Jewish faith. She had very definite ideas about how this event was to be. The guest list, the party plan, the theme, were all her choices. No longer did she rely on me to make all of the decisions for her. She was becoming an independent young woman. I was okay with this, I told myself. After all, I had raised her to think for herself and express her opinions. I held on to the illusion that I was the keeper of her secrets, the person she turned to for guidance as she navigated her growth into womanhood.

When we arrived at the temple I asked her if she was nervous about doing her Torah portion in front of everyone. She smiled at me and said, "No Mom, I know what I'm doing. I'll be fine." I reached out for her hand as I had done so many times in the past, and held it ever so briefly before she took her place next to the cantor. This was the hand of a woman, no longer that of the child that I held crossing the street, or let go as she walked into her classroom at nursery school.

She read her Torah portion and assisted in conducting the service with a strong, unwavering voice. Her lesson was "The Golden Rule;" a part of the Bible that crossed religions. It was the universal rule that enabled me to make the switch from Christianity to Judaism before I got married; the rule that I lived by and had taught my daughters to live by.

Following the service, we were off to the ballroom for the party. Again, I felt the strings loosening as she greeted her guests and went off to speak with her friends in hushed voices. I could hear their laughter, but was not privy to the jokes. She was off on her own, not looking for me to be her anchor.

As the candle lighting began, Maxine commanded the room. She read the short poems she had written about everyone being honored during the ceremony. Tears sprang to my eyes as I listened to her, and marveled at how she had accomplished this on her own. Each poem was thoughtful, and showed her depth of feeling for each individual. She affectionately remembered her grandparents, now deceased; a vacation with family friends; her aunts and uncles, bringing up special memories of each of them. She embraced her cousins, recounting special childhood moments they had shared. When the candle for her friends came up, there were secret giggles, and hugs and smiles among them.

At that moment, I realized the strings had unraveled; I was no longer the center of her world. She had moved from the nucleus of the extended family into a bigger world—a world that centered on her friends, with their in-jokes and secrets. I was on the outside of the window, looking in. "When did this happen?" I thought to myself through misted eyes filled with joy, or more likely a sense of loss. It was a bittersweet moment, which still puts a lump in my throat and brings tears to my eyes. I realized then that she had let go, probably years ago, and it was now time for me to let go of the little girl and embrace the wonderful young woman that she had become.

When she finished with her friends, she called upon her sister, with whom she has had a stormy relationship over the years. Their bond was strengthening as they joined together to face off against their parents, a natural rite of passage during puberty. Finally, she called up her parents, who had divorced several years earlier, and joined us together in celebration as she read this poem:

Without you I wouldn't be here today, so thank you for all you've done;
Adventures, parties and picnics, oh it was all so fun.

Playing darts, having parties and barbeques;
It was always so great spending time with you.

Mommy's yummy dinners, Daddy's red sauce was so good;
I tried to keep my clothes clean, but I never could.

Plays, parties, dressing up, you were always there;
Videotaping everything just because you care.

You were there for all my life, each and every day;

From my first word to my first step, you were always there.

Both of you mean so much to me that I can't tell;
I guess that's why in the past I have done so well.

Since you are the two best parents and you are never mean;
Will my parents please light candle number thirteen.

Maxine is off to college this fall. This will be the first time that we will be separated for a long time. Again, my heartstrings are pulled, and the lump of sadness rises in my chest. But, this time I know that the roots are strong and she is ready to soar into her own world. My role in her life will change, but that's the way it should be and I'm proud to call her my daughter.

~Karen Krugman

86

Radio Mom

I may not have gone where I intended to go,
but I think I have ended up where I intended to be.
~Douglas Adams

Perhaps I'm a throw back from past generations, as most of my contemporaries married and had children later than I did. Many went to grad school or worked after college. I got married. While my roommates were going off to dental school, med school or to complete an MBA, I was registering for china at Fortunoff's. (Lenox Somerset—luckily, still available!)

I have never regretted this choice, since I did things just the way they were done when I was growing up, with a mom who was there for us. I never thought about whether she wanted something else—she was just always there to take care of my sisters and me. I knew then that when I grew up I wanted the same. When I was older, she and I talked about her choices and I was happy to learn that it wasn't just a matter of the way things worked out—this was what she wanted. She was very proud of the family she raised and the women we became. There could be no better role model and so it was only natural that I'd want more of the same. I'm not sure she saw herself as creative, but she was. She just didn't have the opportunity to express it.

I am a full-time mother in a different way—with more time and opportunities to do things that interest me, as I'm not fully focused on the details of the day. The cleaning, food shopping and such.

Perhaps that's not entirely true, but our way of life, the conveniences, make it possible to manage things in a more efficient way, leaving us more leisure time. As the truth is often sometimes in the middle, I'll leave it at that.

The years when the kids are small seem to go so slowly when sitting around with a group of women (or men) that you could never otherwise imagine yourself hanging with. Your daughter likes Riley so you hang with Riley's mom. It seems that only a few years later you are hearing them whine that you are never ever ever ever going to let them drive like EVERYONE else is, or see an R-rated movie that every OTHER thirteen-year-old is able to see, and then one day they're driving to R-rated movies! The next big leap is the college process. Through it all you are looking back and thinking how quickly went the play dates with Riley, the endless boxes of mac and cheese, the events missed due to (luckily) harmless childhood illness—strep, croup, and the like. The applications are done—the agonizing over which schools to apply to—the possible rejections. Rejection? Who would reject my child! Your first goes off and even though you are told by those who have already traveled this path that it will be okay, you cannot imagine that it will be. And somehow it is.

But when the last one is gone, it's different somehow. It's not that you feel like you will no longer be needed, but the day-to-day of seeing how they manage for themselves is gone. If we've done a good job it will all be as it should be. If one more person asks me what I'll be doing now that the kids are no longer home full time I'll... well, I'll likely respond in the polite manner in which I was raised (all the while screaming inside). It's endless and predictable. But I didn't see this one coming. What am I going to do—a Robin with an empty nest?

Having had the opportunity to explore my creative side while raising my children, I feel fortunate to have kept my interests alive while being a fully involved stay-at-home mom. The best of both worlds. It's so important for kids to see that as moms we also have our own interests, jobs, and hobbies, whatever they are. We're there for them but are also so much more. I'm sure my children would remember the time I spent addicted to talk radio as less productive than I do, but for the sake of this piece we'll go with my adult memory rather than their nine- and twelve-year-old ones.

I hadn't had a paying job since before they were born so they had no reference for having a mom who earned an income. When that became necessary, I worked from a home office in order to work and still be home. I'd have the radio on while I worked and it was at this time that I discovered that Talk Radio was more than just static on the AM dial. It was funny, interactive and a chance to be creative! In a short time, I had a favorite show and after a few days of talking to the radio, I picked up the phone to speak with the host. We developed an immediate rapport and I found myself waking up earlier and earlier to study the top stories of the day and to prepare my pithy comments.

After a few months, I was invited into the studio (it was the first time a caller became an on-air personality on this particular show) and I was smitten. The radio station, the microphone, the wattage — the whole thing. The first time I sat in that production studio, filling in for the host and wondering how in the world I was being left in control of the show, is something I will never forget. I was excited, nervous and wondering why I hadn't brought in a co-host. Dead air is the loudest sound on the radio. The idea for hosting and producing my own radio show was born from this experience. I loved books and loved to talk about them so the obvious choice was to host a show about authors and books.

Reading With Robin launched in November of 2002. After six years of being involved with the show, I have become familiar with the many aspects of writing and publishing. Being able to combine the show with fundraising for favorite causes such as literacy and breast cancer awareness has taken this experience to an even higher level. Having my children see this show go from conception to fruition is one of the best parts of this project. Being able to connect them with some of their favorite authors has most definitely upped my "mom stock!" We've all heard the "having it all... having it all at same time" discussion and the jury still seems to be out on this one.

One person's "having it all" is another's "didn't get enough." It's all perception. What ultimately matters of course is how we as mothers decide it all went.

And as it all goes by too quickly, I am confident in my assertion that staying at home, raising my beautiful children and maintaining my interests and balancing the best I could stands me in good stead for the next chapter of my life as both mother and radio host. While I suppose some may view it as being "fired" from my full-time job, I feel more like on "furlough"—always ready at a moment's notice.

~Robin Kall

87

Memories and Tears

You never realize how much your mother loves you till you
explore the attic — and find every letter you ever sent her, every finger
painting, clay pot, bead necklace, Easter chicken, cardboard Santa Claus,
paperlace Mother's Day card, and school report since day one.

~Pam Brown

My closet is filled with photo albums. I think that I was a mere six years old when my parents gave me my very first camera and I've been snapping away ever since. Being the sentimental person that I am, pictures have always been extremely important to me.

I have a zillion snapshots of my children, starting from the minute they entered this world up through today. Poring over those pictures, I often relive the wonderful days when my daughters were so young. Now, at ages six and eight, they seem quite grown up at times. It's often difficult to remember what they were like when they were babies. Thankfully, photos help me recall those wonderful moments.

Recently, as I was looking through some of my albums, I discovered a few pictures of my daughters taken in their old nursery. Tucked away next to those pictures was a piece of paper with my handwriting on it. Opening the letter, I was suddenly face to face with something that I had written several years ago. The tears came, and I read on. This is what lay before me:

I just took down our crib. It was easy. All I had to do was take out eight screws. Eight screws and my crib was completely unassembled. Eight screws, and it was the end of an era.

I remember so vividly the day the guy came from Babies "R" Us to deliver that crib. I watched him so intently as he brought each piece of baby furniture up the stairs and into the room that soon would be a nursery, filled with smiles and cries and a precious little baby. My baby. My first-born. I was the most excited mother-to-be in the entire universe.

I will never forget the night we brought Hannah home from the hospital, the first of many nights that she slept in that crib. So many nights I went to that bed every hour to nurse her. So many nights my husband and I carried her carefully to that bed, trying not to wake her as we placed her gently on the mattress. She first rolled over in that crib. She pulled herself to a stand in that crib. So many memories.

And then, one day, it was time to move Hannah to a new room, to a big bed. Baby Jordyn was on the way.

Jordyn really enjoyed that crib. She loved to kiss us through the slats, and then she'd laugh and beg for more kisses. She also loved to throw things out of the crib and then scream for me to come get them. As she got older, she would jump up and down in the crib, just for fun. Thankfully she never got hurt.

Occasionally, Hannah would climb into the crib with Jordyn and I would find the two of them laughing together as they played with the millions of stuffed animals that lay between them. My girls bonded in there. So many magical times.

"It's just a crib," I kept telling myself as I took out each screw and it started to come apart. What was once a sturdy haven for my *babies was now in pieces in my hands. So, if it's just a crib, why are the tears streaming down my face?*

I slowly folded up the paper and put it back in the album, next to the pictures where it belonged. The tears were there, both in the words and on my cheeks. I know that those tears will come time and time again throughout my life. The first day of kindergarten, graduations, weddings, births. Yet, it's the wonderful moments, the love I feel for my children, and my beautiful daughters themselves, that inspire such emotion. I wouldn't trade any of this. Not ever.

~Sharon Dunski Vermont

The Other Side of SAHM

The act of putting pen to paper encourages pause for thought, this in turn makes us think more deeply about life, which helps us regain our equilibrium.
~Norbet Platt

There is life after full-time parenting. I'm living proof. I was blessed to be home for ten years. For six more after that, I dipped one toe in the employment waters, teaching drama a few hours a week. Then, through a series of circumstances brought on by a little witch we call Hurricane Katrina, I've found myself pretty much working full-time—at least as full-time as I care to be.

Let me be the first to tell you. It's great! I adored the years I was home with my kids and can never thank my husband enough for making it possible. The friendships I forged with other moms will last forever. The three happy, healthy, well-rounded kids who are a product of my undivided attention are a blessing to me every day—even on the days when I want to strangle them.

They were sixteen lean years. Dinners out and trips to the movies were replaced with picnics and excursions to the library. The latest fashions gave way to their not-too-out-of-date counterparts from the consignment shop. My furniture grew shabby and the odometer on our minivan rolled over, but the kids and I and my SAHM friends and their kids honestly did not miss a thing that money could buy.

We found ways to entertain ourselves and each other. We moms formed a Girl's Night Out group. With the kids we had a Mother/Daughter Book Club. We tapped into every free storytime in town. We took nature walks at state parks. We had "dates" for dinner at each other's homes. As a drama teacher, I'd take all the kids on occasional Saturdays, and spend the day putting together a show. The other parents would show up that night each with part of the meal and we'd enjoy our own dinner theater.

You can't put a price tag on never being in a hurry when your kids are young. If they wanted to sit and watch the ants carry crumbs across the sidewalk, there was nothing to stop us. If they asked to read *Where's My Teddy* three more times or take a bubble bath, even though they'd had two that day already, no problem. We read mountains of books, checked out movies from the library, went to the beach, recycled everything we could into art supplies, swapped toys back and forth with other families to keep them "new," and used our imaginations.

Now I'm on the other side of my SAHM adventure and, may I just be permitted to say, woo hoo! Don't get me wrong. My kids are still my priority and, at sixteen, fifteen, and eleven they need me more than ever. But their lives are full of activities now that don't include me. So I'm freed up to do the thing I missed most and—who knew—that turned out to be work. Okay, work and money. As a freelance writer I kept a few writing gigs going during the home years—enough to scratch my creative itch, pay for birthdays and Christmas for the kids, and pitch in on a few vacations.

Now, in addition to my freelance work, I have a full-time writing deal, but again, as full-time as I want it to be. I work "from kid to kid"—from the time they leave for school in the morning until they return again.

My employers probably think I'm a little nuts for being so gung ho, so excited about each and every assignment they give me, for turning stories in consistently ahead of deadline. Good thing they aren't around to see my victory dance each month when my paycheck arrives in the mail. Likely they're waiting for me to burn out but I don't think I will.

Just like my friends who deferred college until their adult years, then surprised themselves with how hungry they were to learn, I'm thrilled by every single assignment, starved for the approval of the editors, filled-up by the accolades from the readers, and greedy for more, more, more to write.

How do I love working again? Let me count the ways. I love waking up knowing I have a list of assignments to delve into. I love surprising the kids with extras we couldn't afford before. I love calling it quits when the school bus pulls up, without regrets about what I didn't get done. I did it all. Would I feel this way if I hadn't dropped out of the wage earner wars for a decade and a half? Would I spend Christmas break enjoying the kids but eager for the week to pass so I could get back to work? I don't think so.

I enjoyed the years I had at home. I didn't take anything for granted—not the ragweed bouquets offered with a Kool-Aid smile, not the snuggling and giggling and looking for shapes in the clouds. I didn't miss a single Play-Doh, finger paint, peanut butter and jelly, gummy bear, Knock Knock, Who's There?, bird's nest on the table, frogs in the bathtub minute of this chapter of my life. But now I know for certain that, yes, there is life after staying at home.

~Mimi Greenwood Knight

89

What Are You Going To Be When You Grow Up?

*I looked on child-rearing not only as a work of love and duty but as a
profession that was fully as interesting and challenging as any honorable
profession in the world and one that demanded the best that I could bring to it.*

~Rose Fitzgerald Kennedy

Sometimes life takes unexpected turns, and your future is determined without intention. This is a story about how being a stay-at-home mom prepared me for an unexpected destiny.

At ten years old, I remember meeting a friend of my mother. After the usual "hellos" were exchanged, the dreaded question came, "And what do you want to be when you grow up?"

I graciously answered, "The President."

The kind lady smiled, "Oh my! Such a bright little girl, so ambitious. Isn't she cute?" I knew she was really thinking to herself, "Good grief! What a dreamer!"

Of course, aspiring to be President wasn't a dream. I always wanted to be someone important and famous, so why not the President? Or, maybe I would be a doctor, a lawyer, or better yet, a movie star! I just believed that my future was destined to be important, glamorous, and most of all, exciting!

As I grew older, I seriously had to start thinking about what I wanted to be when I grew up. I became slightly more realistic, and I understood that being the President was no longer an option. Instead, I remember considering being a secret agent, a news commentator, or an airline pilot—career choices that had an element of importance, glamour, and excitement. But each one vanished as I realized my limitations.

Consequently, there I was, a senior in high school, and I still didn't know "what I wanted to be when I grew up." I decided to go to college and find my destiny there. I majored in English and went through my first two years clueless as to where my education would lead me. Then something happened that determined my future.

During this time, I had a serious boyfriend. We went to different colleges, so when we saw each other on vacations it was very special. During the summer of my second and third year of college, I got pregnant! I was in a panic! What about all my dreams of being someone important and famous? What about college? On the up side, I became responsible and finally discovered what I was going to be when I grew up. At twenty years old, I had an angelic daughter followed by another one the next year, and I became a full-time stay-at-home mom!

My new husband attended college at night and worked a day job to pay the bills. After the completion of his education, he began a career on Wall Street and was very successful. He became an important figure in his industry, and I became an executive wife. We had three more children and lived quite comfortably in a prestigious community. The life of a stay-at-home mom brought everything I would ever want. However, it all changed when my marriage ended, and my life took another turn.

All of a sudden, I was no longer a stay-at-home mom. I had to find a career at the age of fifty-two. I knew my role as a stay-at-home mom would end someday, but I was planning for a wonderful retirement in Florida. I had pictured myself being a stay-at-home grandma after my role as stay-at-home mom ended.

Yikes! "What do I want to be when I grow up?" The daunting

question was back in my lap. I could no longer dodge the question or the decision. I went to the want ads. There was an ad for a concierge position at a nearby resort, an ad for a local newspaper journalist, and one for a radio broadcaster. They all sounded important and exciting. However, after applying for each, I was told, "Sorry, you have no experience."

Finally, out of frustration, I revisited an ad I had bypassed. It was for an English teacher at a charter middle school. I never thought I would be applying for a "tedious" job like being a teacher, but I was desperate at this point.

I walked into the Principal's office for an interview and was shocked to see a very stern looking woman. As she reviewed my resume, I sat looking at her degrees on the wall: a BA, MA and Ph.D., all from distinguished universities. I squirmed in my seat as I knew she would be looking at my education and experience.

She said to me, "I see you have a degree in General Studies. What is that?"

I answered, "My university offered this degree for adult students who were not career-oriented."

"Ah," she replied. She eyed the paper again and asked, "So, you have never taken an education course?"

"No," I weakly replied. "However," I perked up, "in my first two years, I majored in English."

Leaving my education, she jumped to my work experience. "I see here that you worked part time at YMCAs when you were in college and for eight years after that. I don't see the rest of your work experience on your resume," she stated, with a puzzled inflection.

"Well, there isn't any," I explained with a tone of embarrassment. "In the beginning of my marriage, to help out with bills, I worked part time in the YMCA organization. After that, my husband was able to provide for the family. So, I was a stay-at-home mom for all those years."

"For twenty-five years, you were a stay-at-home mom?" she asked in astonishment.

"Yes."

"How many children do you have?"

"Five."

"You raised five children?" she asked with amazement.

"Yes."

She looked at me, put my resume down, and stood up. I guessed what was coming, "I'm sorry, but you have no experience. Thank you for applying. Good luck to you."

But instead, she looked at me and said, "You're hired! Anyone who has been a stay-at-home mom for more than twenty-five years has had plenty of experience in teaching children. Congratulations!"

Well, that was it. I finally knew what I was going to be when I grew up. I have been teaching for six years and love it! I went on to finish my Master's Degree in Education Leadership, and I am working toward the goal of becoming a principal and completing a Doctorate in Education.

I am so thankful that I was a stay-at-home mom. It led me to the opportunity of turning young minds on to learning and exposing them to knowledge and creative thinking. What could be more important and exciting? Being a stay-at-home mom is the basis of who I am today and my unexpected destiny.

~Terrilynne Walker

90

The Heart to Let Go

The successful mother sets her children free and becomes
more free herself in the process.
~Robert J. Havighurst

I t seems like just yesterday those little notes signed, "(heart), your only daughter," would pop up around the house for no special reason. I often wondered if she was feeling insecure. Was I giving more attention to her older brothers, or was she just being the loving little girl who blessed my life every day? Bottom line is this: I took so much for granted.

As the teen years approached, I looked upon my budding blossom, with her modest attire, her many academic achievements, and her compliant behavior; and I couldn't imagine that she and I would ever be "at odds" with one another. I attended every soccer game and special event. She and I teamed up to decorate for family birthdays, exchange pedicures, shop, or watch a movie. We baked goodies in the kitchen as I tried to instill in her the importance of serving others and extending hospitality. She was a "good girl" and I was a proud mama. She told me that many of her schoolmates were promiscuous, pregnant, drinking, or worse, adding, "You don't know how bad other parents have it, Mom." I assumed that she would never fall into those traps, because I was always there—the devoted stay-at-home mom with great kids to show for it.

Then everything began to fall apart right before my eyes.

One morning our car was missing. My husband and I checked

our daughter's room, only to find her missing as well. Frantic, we began making phone calls to her cell phone, her friend's homes, etc. No response. Then finally she answered, confessing that she was "on the freeway, coming back from a party." She had defied our rules, sneaked out of our home, took our car, and we were flabbergasted! As she entered the house that morning, the tears began to flow. "I'm sick of being a good girl!" she cried. I stared at her with my mouth open, speechless. After so many years, for the first time in her young life, she was grounded.

The little "heart" notes began to dwindle from sight. Our times together in the kitchen became few and far between. Her clothing choices became more revealing and our "talks" turned into "twenty questions," as the gap between me and my daughter grew wider.

It was Christmas Eve, and I was busy preparing the meal when I urged the kids to help out. Although our two sons were included, I always expected more from my daughter. In the midst of my complaining to her, she burst out with an emotional, "Mom, I'm not like you... I hate domestic duties... I'm going to be a career woman with a maid and a cook! I'm not going to be a stay-at-home mom; I am going to be more than that!" The lump in my throat was obvious as I responded, in self-defense, reminding her of the jobs I'd held during her childhood, working graveyard shifts so that I could be home for her and her brothers. Through uncontrolled tears, I pointed out the sacrifices I'd made to ensure that she'd have all the loving training I could give. How dare she make me feel like my life "was a waste" and not worth emulating? I was deeply hurt.

In the months that followed, it was made clear that my counsel was "old fashioned" and my morals were "outdated." My daughter no longer wanted me to shop with her, talk with her, or anything. I was losing her. My friends tried to console me by saying, "this too will pass." But my heart was heavy with worry.

When we moved to a new city, our teenage daughter, who was now in college informed us that she'd be moving out on her own with a friend. It was heartbreaking when our two sons left the nest, but it was devastating for me to see my baby go. There was so much more to teach her, to give her, to prepare her, I thought. I cried to her father, "Why doesn't she need us anymore?"

The day we packed up her belongings and set her up in her own apartment was extremely painful. I must have called her cell phone five times in the first fifteen minutes after heading for home. She never answered. I sat in the middle of her empty room, once filled with pink lace, trophies, and collector dolls, and cried my eyes out.

It wasn't long before her father and I learned that her "roommate" was her boyfriend. My husband was just as upset as I was, realizing that things would never be the same. Then, at age twenty, she became an egg donor. I balked at that, too. Family and friends reassured us, again, that our daughter was just trying to "find herself." I, however, continued to pressure her about her life decisions.

Two years have passed since that Christmas Eve when I lost connection with my daughter. During that time, she'd call and chat with her father about work or car maintenance. The call usually ended without even a "let me talk to Mom" comment. I realized that I had pushed her away with all my judgments over her choices.

This was a turning point for me. Having felt like a failure as a parent and a role model, a heavy cloud had formed over my head. I knew that God was in control, and I was angry with Him for allowing things to turn out this way. Finally, I decided that I would stop judging and just love my daughter no matter what she did, or how different she was from me. I began to let go, and entrust her to God.

Sometimes, we have to learn the hard way, don't we?

Our parental plight pales in comparison to others, but the answer is still the same: Accepting our children as they are, and loving them unconditionally. My daughter eventually found her way. She is engaged to a wonderful man, and has our blessing. She calls nearly every day now, with a need to "just talk," or a "quick question." She may ask me for a family recipe, or to go shopping together. I smile inside. It spreads to my face as I listen to her, and as I see her with new eyes.

We're enjoying womanhood together, and newfound treasures! I thought I had lost her, but when I learned to let go, I found her heart again. When I gave up trying to control her life, I found my own peace. I may not always agree with what she does, but I agree with who she is!

Recently, a card came in the mail from my daughter, thanking me "for always being there for her." She added, "You raised me into a woman, a reflection of you. I cherish the times when people say, 'you're so much like your mom,' yet I know I still have much to learn from you. Thank you for being so patient... I love you."

And it was signed, "(heart), your only daughter."

~Ginger Boda

91

Run the River

She never quite leaves her children at home,
even when she doesn't take them along.
~Margaret Culkin Banning

He is five, a hooded smudge of color trudging through the deep, vast white. I watch from the window, watch the golden Lab spring behind him, ahead of him, beside. Malakai turns sharp to the north, tromping out into the field's markerless sea of white snow. His hood turns to see: is our dog following? Then a sharp turn to the west, and a glance to see if the canine is tracking. Together the two zigzag across winter and I am happily mesmerized, warm inside, watching my boy with his dog out in the quiet wonder of it all.

When he slips back inside, life flushes his nose, flames his cheeks. He pulls off mittens and coat and words, fragments of stories, tumble out of him, and I nod, trying to etch him in my mind like this. (Do all mothers do this? Memorize moments?) For some reason, I don't trust ink and paper, sensors of cameras. I carve it down in synapses and neurons—in heart fibers—before he, who he is now, is gone, mellow voice turned deep, untried hands lined deep with days.

I wrap this flashing instant of boy up in an afghan, he and his little sister with her cloud of blond, and pull them close to read a Richard Scarry book before flickering hearth. On illustrated page, Huckle the Cat is dreaming of what he will be when he grows up: a pilot? A farmer? An apple-pie tester?

Malakai thumps my arm, words surging, "Mom, Mom, I'd like to be an apple-pie tester when I grow up. But I can't, because I am going to be a farmer. But I am not going to be a farmer, because know what? I am not going to get any bigger 'cause I just want to be your little kid, and you can be the big Mama. Shalom, will you stay the baby for Mama?"

The sweet pain of love wells. How did he know how time stings a mother's heart? How I keep reaching through its relentless current to pluck out a moment, to hold now, bringing it close to lips, to breathe life into it, to keep what is now, refusing to let it become but a memory, stiff and lifeless. But all is wet, slippery, elusive... gone and carried on. Malakai and Shalom slide off the couch and chatter away into imaginary places. I catch nothing. Ever. Foaming, roaring, racing, time's torrent sweeps all away, and I am left with river stones. Memorials worn smooth by all that once rushed by.

Come night, our embryonic man growing in little boy's body lays head on pillow, pulling quilts tight under chin. I press lips and heart to his forehead, and Malakai whispers, "Remember, I am not going to get much bigger? Just a bit, but I am staying little, so I can be your boy. And you can be my big Mama." He snuggles into dreams.

I sit in the dark watching him breathe. A whorl wisps at his temple, a remnant tendril from a long ago halo of baby curls. Out his window, the moon bulges like a luminous woman, full with child. I wonder if I can forever stay Big Mama, netting time.

In the gray blue of next dawn, we rouse boys for barn chores, turn on lights, gently calling their names. Like disoriented moths drawn to light, they stumble into the kitchen. I tousle a sleepyhead, teasing; "I think you grew an inch in the night, Levi. And your brother caught it too—look how long and lean he is." My husband playfully pokes Caleb and Joshua, handing them their coats for the run to the barn.

And I grab a river stone.

"Remember, Darryl?" I turn from my husband's face to look at these boys. "When they were babies and we'd wake and dress them and prop them beside the heat register, bundle them in snowsuits?

Then make that dash through the drifts and cold to the barn, to begin. And you'd set those two little boys in a feed cart to play while we chored?" The boys stretch in the doorway. "Just look at them now."

Caleb extends to his dad's shoulder, Joshua up to his chest. That once baby, long ago toddler are molting, emerging, growing into near men. My husband shakes his head, chuckling dismay. I feel his worn work hand rest on my shoulder, steadying me in the rushing current of years.

I ease down into the water. And let go. Malakai can grow up. Big Mama can become Old Mama. The river of life has plans, places, purposes that time's current will carry these young persons to—off to destinations, to new skin, to their own dreams. If I dammed up the river, froze time solid, wouldn't these becoming people become mortuary specimens—icy, petrified, set?

Malakai wanders sleepily from the dark hallway into the kitchen light. I embrace his slender frame; feeling ribs, warm skin, little chest pressed close. Am I dreaming or does he smell aquatic, like a newborn wrinkled from the waters?

And I whisper....

Run with the river, son. She's flowing us Home.

~Ann Voskamp

Chapter 10

Power MOMS

Looking Back

Tributes and Reflections

92

A Mother's Intuition

The intuitive mind is a sacred gift...
~Albert Einstein

W hen I look back on my life as a mother, I know that one of my biggest lessons learned (finally), was that I should always trust my instincts, because my gut consistently told the truth. Sometimes, I found this out in hindsight, after I had ignored the little red flags waving on my mama radar.

When Britney was about eight, we got talked into doing a "Little Miss Something" pageant, because this one supposedly stressed talent over beauty. Britney was begging me to do it, and part of me thought, well, what's the harm if this truly is a talent competition? The other part of me knew I was rationalizing because it just didn't feel right. The truth is, I never wanted her near one of those beauty pageants for little girls, because they were set up in a way that seemed so unfair to some children.

While a young girl could work hard to make her leap higher or her steps more precise, there was nothing much she could do to improve the countenance God gave her.

The pageant lived up to my fears, and then some. The mothers were appalling backstage, fussing over their daughters and backstabbing the other contestants. I was repulsed by the whole thing. Of course, since we were completely green about the pageant system, I put her in the wrong dress (it didn't even fit properly) and the wrong kind of socks. Britney ended up placing near the bottom, and the poor little thing was in tears.

I should have known better, and in fact, I did know better. I wanted Britney to feel good about herself because of who she was and how she treated people, not because some silly pageant told her she was or was not pretty enough. I had failed to trust my gut. It's our job as moms to act on that sixth sense we have, the one that tells us something is not as it seems; when I ignored it the result was tears and a very unpleasant day.

But on another occasion, when the stakes were much higher, I followed my instincts, and I thank God to this day that I did.

My oldest child, Bryan, had chronic asthma from the time he was a baby until he was nine years old. The members of the Spears family were regulars at the McComb, Mississippi hospital and children's clinic; we knew everyone in pediatrics on a first name basis and even spent one Christmas in the hospital with a sick little Bryan.

One incident will stick with me forever as an example of the power of a mother's inner knowledge when it comes to her children.

Britney was only two weeks old, and Bryan was having one of his asthma episodes; he was congested and his breath was a bit labored. I took my little boy, then just four, to the children's clinic, where a doctor diagnosed him with bronchitis and asthma once again and prescribed the usual medication.

Bryan was a very active boy, and usually, the asthma medicine would accelerate this in him, not the other way around. This time, though, he seemed very sluggish, and around bedtime I noticed him hanging his head off my bed, something he would do when he couldn't get enough breath.

I took one look at him and knew this episode was much more serious than the others that had preceded it. My antennae shot up. His breathing was loud and gasping, and his skin color had turned from a healthy pink to an alarming, mottled white with a bluish tinge. I called his daddy, Jamie, into the room and he was also very concerned about Bryan's lack of color. As I cradled him in my arms, I called the doctor in a panic. He was quite calm, instructing me to give him more of the inhalant and wait for the medicine to take effect, which we did three times in the next thirty minutes. Surely the doctor knew what he was talking about, right? Inwardly, I battled between trusting a seasoned physician and believing my own gut, which was telling me Bryan was in big trouble.

I called the doctor again, insisting Bryan needed to be brought in despite his assurances that the medicine would work soon. He finally agreed to meet us at the hospital, where Jamie, Bryan and I rushed as soon as Jamie's aunt had come over to care for baby Britney.

Throughout the night, the doctor worked on Bryan, trying to get him to breathe properly. At one point, he even thought he might have to do a tracheotomy to open his breathing passages. Finally, after many tortuous hours and various medicines and procedures, the doctor administered some kind of steroid, and it worked — Bryan began breathing regularly, much to our enormous relief. (Steroid use for treating pediatric asthma was relatively new at the time.)

The next morning, the doctor told me how dire the situation had been for Bryan. He was so glad I had insisted on bringing my son in to the hospital, because Bryan would not have made it through the night without medical assistance.

In that life or death situation, my mother's instinct kicked into high gear and a tragedy was averted. What I learned that night was to pay attention to those strong impulses (it was the more subtle clues that I sometimes failed to heed). My three children are grown now and out of the house, but I still try and listen to those gut feelings, big and small, when it comes to them. I know better than most the very real power of a mother's intuition.

~Lynne Spears

The Mother I Am

It was my mother who gave me my voice. She did this, I know now, by clearing a space where my words could fall, grow, then find their way to others.
~Paula Giddings

Dear Mom.

I looked up briefly, through my tears, to see you listening intently as I delivered part of the eulogy at my mother-in-law's memorial. I was speaking about the relationship that she and I developed once I became a mother—and how intimate and profound it is to walk in another's shoes. It was a privilege to share the motherhood experience with her, and thoughts of this consumed me as I said my goodbyes. I have wondered since if you felt any pangs while listening to me that day—whether you questioned my feelings about sharing motherhood with you and when you might have the opportunity to hear them.

The passage into motherhood brings so many opportunities for finding kindred others—friends who have made the same leap, women who you meet through your children, mothers from generations before. But none have been as special as you. The moment my first child was born, I came undone—my heart, fears, dreams all exposed for the world to see. And yet for so many, these pieces of me are not visible. You see them.

Every woman should be lucky enough to be able to pick up the phone and ask her mother how to cook Chinese mushrooms so they don't leave a pungent scent in the house for days, or how best to restrain herself from showing up on the doorstep of the child who breaks her daughter's heart on the playground.

When I flip through my portfolio of childhood memories, I can see those parts of you that were invisible to so many. I see now that it was a sacrifice for you to stay home with us—that although it was a choice you made, it wasn't always easy for you to tame your free spirit. I marvel at how you gave us a childhood that felt huge and worldly, without access to any transportation. I am humbled at how rich we felt, even when we weren't. I am amazed at how you trudged through the loneliness while Dad worked long hours to provide for us.

I've considered that I might have disappointed you when I found myself jumping off the career track I was so ferociously pursuing—the one that would have presented the perfect medal at the end of the education-marathon through which you and Dad relentlessly cheered.

You should know that you gave me the childhood that makes it impossible to imagine not being at the door when my kids walk through at the end of their day, that makes it impossible not to be sitting at the edge of the community pool shredding the ends of the sleeves on my sweaters as I watch my children jump into the deep end, impossible not to be sitting at the back of the school auditorium sick to my stomach as I listen to my child spell a word like "chrysan-themum" at the spelling bee.

Very recently I have felt the crushing swell of motherhood pain and heartache, when my son was diagnosed with the same medical condition that I've lived my life with. And in this time, new revelations have been unwrapped. How did you keep me so sheltered from the fear that I now carry for my child in every single beat of my heart? How did you excel at keeping me out of the "not normal" circles in life? The reason I threw myself head first into becoming a mother, even with the risks of passing on my genetics, is because I saw no reason not to. I wonder if you know what an indescribable gift that was.

In my greatest moments of self-blame, you have dug me out. Don't be afraid, you tell me. Fear will not protect him from what lies ahead but love will pick up the pieces. And I am listening, because I know you know best.

I remember standing graveside shortly after burying my grandmother—your mother. I was a young adult then, not yet a mother. It struck me to see you standing alone, weeping so wretchedly for your loss. I was caught by surprise to see you as her daughter. And now I clearly see it is the mother-child relationship that lays the foundation for a daughter to become a mother herself.

I mourned deeply when I lost my mother-in-law and I can only hope she knew how much it meant that she was in mine and my children's lives. But I want you to know what I feel for you—knowing what it was like for you to be the mother in my childhood. When I pick up the phone later today, I probably won't get around to sharing all of this with you. We'll be too busy talking about today's adventures and tomorrow's plans. But I want you to hear these things—now, when you have years to bask in knowing them. You are the mother who makes me the mother I am—and it's been a privilege to share this journey with you.

~Louise Gleeson

94

Necklace of Memories

Mother's love grows by giving.
~Charles Lamb

M y mother recently called me over to witness a discovery she'd made. Tucked into the very corner of the family attic, the discovery was an old cardboard oatmeal container wrapped in blue paper. On the lid was a childish crayon drawing of the eight-year-old-me-I-had-been, complete with glasses and long brown braids. And on the side was the legend: "Kerrie Barney Time Capsule, 1986." My mom's eyes twinkled quite a bit as she handed it over. "I thought you should be the one to open it," she said.

The strange thing was, until that moment I hadn't even remembered the time capsule, the product of a third-grade school project. Both excited and a little apprehensive, I carried it into the dining room and spilled out the contents on my mom's table. There was a photocopied worksheet full of questions like "How tall are you?" and "What's your favorite food?" painstakingly filled out in my awkward beginner's cursive. There was a handful of rocks I'd picked up on the playground, a tiny little doll I now remembered as having been very precious, my first pair of glasses, and a baggie full of twenty-year-old rabbit food that I'm sure I meant to be symbolic of our family pet. And there were handful after handful of beaded necklaces.

They spilled out of the time capsule like confetti, all conceivable shapes and colors, a veritable rainbow of history that instantly took me back in time. When I was six years old, my mother took the unprecedented step of starting her own business. It was an exciting, terrifying year in our family history, and since a fledgling entrepreneur like my mother couldn't afford either office rent or child care, I ended up spending a lot of time in the home office my mother made of our basement. Every day after school I'd walk down the steps to the basement, to spend my evenings reading or doing homework at a spare desk in the corner. More often than not, I'd fall asleep under the conference table before Mom was able to get away, and she'd have to carry me upstairs to bed when her workday finally ended.

I have to say that, despite being distracted by a thousand pressing worries, my mother never forgot just how hard spending so much time in an adult environment could be on a child. She always made sure that we spent the dinner hour eating together, even if that dinner was a frozen meal hurriedly heated in the office's microwave and eaten at her desk between phone calls. And at least once a week she visited the city's teaching supply company where she could get good deals on art supplies and craft kits to keep me occupied. I had crayons and poster paints and modeling clay galore, all tucked into my very own drawer at the bottom of her filing cabinet. And then one day she bought me The Beads.

The fact that I refer to The Beads with capital letters does not mean they were expensive by any means. Made of plastic and purchased by the pound—I think my mother paid seven dollars for a five pound bag—they were hardly the stuff award-winning jewelry is made of. But they were colorful, made of a bright, pure, translucent plastic that sparkled in the sunlight like a pirate's hoard. And to my eight-year-old eyes they were the most beautiful things in the world. Mom helped me transfer them into Grandma's old canning jars so they would be easier to transport without spilling, and for the next two years I was a girl possessed, spending hours sorting The Beads by color and shape, painstakingly searching for matches I could string into jewelry. My mom bought me a cone of weaver's carpet warp, a strong, thick, white thread just the right weight for childish fingers to manage, and I made necklace after necklace, fascinated by the way the different colors blended together to make works of art. Some of these creations I wore to school or for make believe, transforming myself into a princess or a fairy queen. Most I gave to my mother, who wore one to every business meeting and power lunch with pride.

Looking at these necklaces now, strung on their finger-soiled cotton warp and finished by the simple expedient of tying the thread in a knot and leaving the ends to dangle (it would be years before I learned about clasps or crimp beads), part of me has to wonder if the whole reason Mom let me have them for the time capsule in the first place was her subtle way of getting out of wearing them. Still, when I can banish my inner critic and look at the necklaces honestly, I can see that they really are beautiful. The colors and shapes are blended together in surprisingly sophisticated ways, proving that even at eight, I was already playing with design in an effort to realize my own visions. And the love they represent — the love of a mother taking time to nurture her daughter's creative spirit even under very trying circumstances, and the love of a daughter taking that nurturing and offering it back in beaded form — is a beautiful thing indeed.

I had opened that time capsule expecting to see how much I had changed in the last twenty years, how much time and growth had transformed me. Instead, I am overwhelmed by how much of me has stayed the same. My braids are long gone, but I still wear glasses. I still pick up rocks that catch my eye when I'm walking to and from work. I still love animals and seem to spend an inordinate amount of time and money on keeping them fed. And yes, I still love beads, supplementing my income by selling hand knotted gemstone jewelry at craft fairs, and I still make necklaces for my mother. And she still wears them with pride.

So the woman that I am, and the girl that I was, are not so different after all — instead we're inextricably connected. As connected as two beads glittering on the same strand.

~Kerrie Barney

95

A Mother and Her Daughters: Different Choices

The self is not something ready-made,
but something in continuous formation through choice of action.
~John Dewey

O ur daughter Amy is in California—or "the coast," as she now calls it. This is a business, not pleasure, trip for Amy, the TV producer.

It takes a little getting used to.

Amy is currently in one of the most cutthroat businesses in the entire world, and she is making it. Some might even say making it big. I'm not here to brag about Amy's accomplishments, though the temptation is mighty because I am, after all, her mom. I'm here to examine, instead, the working lives of young mothers like Amy who are doing things undreamt of by their own mothers—and yes, that includes me.

I've never been on a business trip in my life. I've never had a "real job." I chose the high-risk, freewheeling world of freelance writing because it allowed for my other—and in my view, far more important—job. Motherhood.

For me, the road not taken was a full-time, full-speed-ahead journalism career. I entered the fray sticking to the edges of the playing field, always aware that no matter how important the story to be covered, no matter how consuming the essay I yearned to finish, I wanted and needed to be where my three daughters were at least a majority of the time. Male editors looked astounded when I turned down a chance to cover a national political convention or an interview with this or that celebrity. And frankly, there were a few female editors who seemed to share that astonishment.

But I stuck to my guns and my self-imposed double life with the heavy emphasis on stay-at-home motherhood. As a freelance writer, I never got rich. And like other freelancers, I had the benefit of absolutely NO benefits. Still, the arrangement worked for me. I could have my fix, my passion for words and communicating, and have the deep pleasures and enormous perils of motherhood, too. I never got to the top of the heap, and our accountant shuddered at the cost-effective aspect of how I earned my living.

But I got "income" of a different sort. I was there on the front lines when Jill, Amy, or Nancy was nursing a bruised knee or a battered soul. I bore witness to the minor and major milestones of their lives, from listening as a proud first grader read her first book aloud, to watching a stage-struck child perform in a major production called "Melissa The Martian."

I had room-mother stamped on my forehead for a full decade before I stepped aside and let others experience the exhilaration of dragging cookies and juice to classroom parties, and helping bus-sick kids through grade school excursions to the zoo.

I could have gone on and on, but full-time motherhood is finite. I suppose that's what I sensed so many years ago, when I turned down my first full-time job offer, the one that might have led, ultimately, to an important title and maybe even a corner office in a newsroom.

And how did my example affect my daughters?

Jill, Amy and Nancy have all had "real" jobs, executed from offices that are not the leftover room in a rambling old house.

As I watched my daughters and their friends, listened to the exhaustion in their voices, and saw it etched on their faces when they managed to make it home, I felt mingled awe and worry.

I used to wonder what would happen when Jill, the married

lawyer, became Jill the mother. And I found out. The majesty of the law was put on hold, sidelined by the majesty of diapers, formula and the "Terrible Two's." Only in the last couple of years has Jill gone back to the workplace she left as a new mom now that her "babies" are in or approaching middle school.

And yes, she's lost professional ground, and of course, income. But it was the path she chose.

Nancy, too, was content to stop saving the world long enough to nurse a redheaded baby named Sam, and then his sweet brother Jonah. When Danny came along, she was already back out there doing work as a clinical psychologist, which brings her joy and meaning. And Danny, she suspects, is the most adjusted of her little men.

But is it tough? You bet it is. Nancy is walking that modern tightrope and managing, so far, to keep her balance. But if the babysitter is sick or one piece of the house of cards tumbles, down goes the whole structure.

And now that motherhood appears on Amy's resume, those trips to the coast are fraught with guilt, endless planning and always the rush to return. Amy talks wistfully about slowing down, but it's an oxymoron in her industry. She pushes on.

So yes, my daughters have chosen varied paths, different from one another, and surely different from mine.

Recently, Jill, the newly minted full-time worker, asked me whether I'd do it all again in the same way. Did I have regrets about the road not taken?

I'd be fudging if I said there were none.

But in late midlife, I have a memory bank bulging with images that are irreplaceable. I have the sweeping satisfaction of knowing that while the choice I made is hardly for everyone, it was the only one for me. I watch my daughters, all mothers now, from the sidelines. I cheer them on. And now I relieve their struggles with babysitting gigs whenever I can.

And as I worry and wonder about the paths they've chosen, I still wish them Godspeed.

At the very least, every mother, no matter what her path, deserves that.

~Sally Friedman

Reprinted by permission of Tom Swick
© 2008

96

Unseen Blessings

A mother's arms are more comforting than anyone else's.
~Diana, Princess of Wales

So much of life is spent pursuing life. So much of living is spent in preparation to live. The goal we prepare for is never wholly reached, and time passes, and the someday was yesterday.

As I held my new baby, kissed my other children, and held my husband's hand as he slept on this New Year's Eve, I realized I have mattered. Without me, these three children would not exist; without me, my husband's life would be completely different.

During my daily routine, I may touch or influence someone in a way that might guide or enrich them in some way. I will continue to matter just as my parents mattered to me, for my philosophy, self-expression, and beliefs stem from their roots.

In days to come, my children might enjoy beauty because I directed their eyes, might understand pain because I eased them into the knowledge of it, might love deeply because I gave them mine daily, and complete giving will be all they know.

I don't run from solitary moments or down moods. Bliss is a fleeting moment; life while it is lived, is not. In retrospect, truly living is a moment of many small moments one may never see.

As this year progresses, I must step back and occasionally observe that I am living now, and I must regard my work with the dignity it deserves. It is true anyone can change a diaper or wipe a runny nose, but the stroke of my hand or the gentleness of my voice someone else cannot give. The complete devotion to my loved ones, and the enjoyment of their pleasures or anguish at their pains, only I can give.

My new year will continue to mean my usefulness; my happy new year must come from within in accepting what I have and cherishing it for its pricelessness. The "Mommy I need you" and "Darling I love you" are not a someday away nor were they searched for.

They exist because I do. How blessed am I.

~Lois Stone

97

Labouring Love

Mother's love is peace. It need not be acquired, it need not be deserved.
~Erich Fromm

It was three short years ago that I first entered the unknown frontier known as Motherhood. I remember the moment like it was yesterday—the overwhelming feeling of relief once the birth of my daughter had come to an end. As my small, screaming baby was placed into my shaking arms, I was instantly transported into another world. I felt comfort as I quickly realized that the birthing pains that had helped bring my child onto this earth were finally finished. However, as I look back, I've begun to see that once a woman becomes a mother, the labour pains never truly end. They may lesson, they may change but they can never fully leave a mother's heart. It was my own mother who taught me this truth long before I knew it personally for myself.

Throughout my childhood and adolescence, I knew that as sure as the sun would rise the next morning, my mother would be found tucking me into bed that night and whispering prayers into my ear. And every weekday morning, mom read the Bible out loud to me, as I hurriedly scarfed down my bowl of soggy cornflakes while at the same time rushing throughout the house in frantic search of half-finished homework. And missing socks. No matter what mood each day found me in, I don't think I ever left the house without a hug, a kiss and a little love note tucked deep inside my tattered school bag.

As I grew older, I thought that once I entered adult life, I wouldn't need my mom in the same way that I had in my childhood or teen-age years. Those bedtime prayers were nice but surely their meaning would lessen as I matured. I was wrong. For it was at the grand "old" age of twenty-three that I discovered the truth. And the truth was that I didn't need my mother in the same way at all; I needed her much more than ever before.

I was twenty years old when I got married. I was naive and idealistic and so when my life started to crash, I completely fell apart. The evening began on a cold, Halloween night many years ago. This was when I was told by my husband of three and a half years, "I don't love you anymore, and I don't think that I ever really did." I think that if my heart had instead been stabbed that night by a pitchfork, the pain would have been easier to bear. Instead, as those words continually replayed in my mind, my heart was repeatedly destroyed. Again. And again. And again. Rejection wields many knives and their power to destroy goes far deeper then any surface wound.

After the dust settled, I moved back into my parents' home. At the time, I saw it as my only option, but in the end it turned out to be the best decision I could have made. My parents' home was the safest place in the world for me to lay my shattered heart. Mom and Dad provided a safe sanctuary where judgments and criticisms failed to find me.

And just like the good 'ole days, my bedtime ritual soon included a visit from my mom just before I went to sleep. She'd again tuck me into my bed and pray with me as I fought to forget the brokenness that had now become my existence.

One sleepless night, I lay in my bed, weeping. I thought I was alone in my room until I looked up into the dark and realized my mother was standing next to my bed. She was crying too. "Mom," I sobbed, my body shaking, "I want to die!" The mess that swirled around me had dealt such a harsh blow to my heart that I was left with out a clue as to how I could possibly recover from it.

I'll never forget my mom's response as she looked me squarely in the eye, as I lay curled on my bed. "No, Ruthie," was her firm answer. "You will live."

Living didn't start that night or even the next day, but eventually her words of faith took root deep inside my heart and truth began to grow. And watered by her persistent love, I slowly came to live once more.

I will never forget the darkness of that season, and how it nearly strangled me in its suffocating grip. But alongside that memory is a gift that is more precious to me than words will ever express. It is the memory of my mother's gift of life. A gift that she not only laboured to give to me at the start of my life on this earth, but has continued to give to me on many occasions ever since.

~Ruth Bergen

Coming Out of My Shell

A mother is not a person to lean on but a person to make leaning unnecessary.
~Dorothy Canfield Fisher

A few years ago, I encountered one of the most difficult challenges I have ever faced. I now know that it was my mother's influence that guided me.

Since that journey, I have learned about the life of the Hawksbill Turtle, and I have come to think of my experience as it relates to these incredible creatures. The home of the Hawksbill Turtle is its shell, and it carries this home with it wherever it travels. In many ways, my mother has been my home. She has been a stay-at-home mom all my life and has given me a special type of shell. This shell is the one that has grown from all of our time together; it protects me, comforts me, grows with me, and loves me, even when she can't be with me herself.

When a turtle is in its shell, its surroundings remain familiar, it is comfortable, and it has little doubt that it will be safe. Having my mom at home, I always knew my needs would be met. But when I turned ten years old, my parents felt it was time for me to go away for three weeks during the summer. My mother and I did our research, and we learned about a camp in Switzerland that offered cooking, tennis, and French classes. We decided that it was perfect for me and I was excited as we began to prepare for my departure.

My mother flew with me to Switzerland and when we reached the campus I gasped. The mountains, the valleys, the little town off in the distance—it really was beautiful. While I was examining the scenery, my mother was speaking to a counselor. We were directed into a tall building, up the stairs to the fifth floor, down a short hall, and into the room on the left. My mother helped me to unpack and make my bed. As we organized the room, she encouraged me in her usual way to "be nice, be good, be strong, work hard, make friends, and have fun." Then she handed me a small book and said, "Read a little each day to remind yourself how much I love you." That was when the realization hit me. I had been looking right past the fact that I was going to be on the other side of the world for three weeks, away from everything and everyone I knew. It was unfamiliar, it was uncomfortable, and that was when I began to cry.

Once a turtle hatches, it must make its way to the water without any help. Then it must travel around the world and learn to fend for itself without any guidance. The blurry image of my mother pulling out of the camp driveway still saddens me. But soon the fear of the unfamiliar surroundings wore off and I began to make new friends and enjoy many activities. I took a train to town each day, participated in a cooking class, went whitewater rafting, and even visited a cheese farm. I also got to go to the Swiss Open tennis tournament, twice!

But despite all the fun, there was no question that I was on my own and would have to fend for myself. I was prepared for the fact that the majority of the people didn't speak English, but this proved to be harder to deal with than I thought. *"Quest-ce qu'il y a? Quest-ce que c'est passé?"* The camp nurse only spoke French, and could not understand what I needed after I was hurt playing basketball. All around me, things were happening that I had never experienced before. Some of the girls were smoking, something I had not been exposed to at home. And then one of the girls was pushed off the high-dive during the swimming trip, landing on the pavement. She broke her leg, lost some teeth, and kept screaming that she couldn't breathe.

Finally, the bombings of Lebanon were being broadcast on the news and many people who went to my camp had friends or family living there. I didn't know where Lebanon was on the map, or if it was near my camp or near my family. The sound of people crying, yelling, and frantically dialing the telephones made me more scared than ever. I tried to be brave on the outside, but I was desperate to be back home, back in my shell and the comfort of my mother's protection.

After traveling around the world, the turtle must find its way back to the beach on which it hatched. Waking up at five o'clock in the morning on the day of my departure, I arrived at the airport and boarded my plane. It was the first time I had ever flown on an airplane by myself, and I was a bit frightened. The flight was about nine and a half hours long. When I finally arrived, I had butterflies in my stomach, I knew that when I stepped off that plane, my parents would be there, and they were. Their searching eyes stopped on me and they smiled. My mom began to cry and my dad looked so happy. I ran to them and hugged them both. The most wonderfully happy feeling came over me that night. I am not sure if it was comfort, familiarity, safety, or the combination of all of the above, but I had made it home, and that was enough. Though I didn't know it the day my mother left me at camp, the lessons she had taught me and the inner strength they created had seen me through.

Eventually, the turtle must leave again and head back out into the ocean. The journey it takes will be more familiar, it will be more comfortable being alone, and the turtle will feel safer. I went to a different camp the following year, and to be honest, I did not feel familiar, comfortable, or safe, but I knew I would be able to do it. The shell my mother built for me would protect me, comfort me, grow with me, and love me, even though my mother wouldn't be with me. I would take the lessons "Mama" gave me every day at home during my early childhood; if I am nice, good, strong, work hard, make friends, and have fun, I can succeed at anything. Then, when I reunite with my family and when we gather each night at the dinner table, I will have a story to tell, and I will be proud of what I accomplished.

~Chloe Polikoff, age 13

Gratitude

Children are the living messages we send to a time we will not see.
~John W. Whitehead

Extra-long twin sheets, comforter, pillow, laundry soap, boxes of granola bars and snacks loaded miraculously in the trunk of my small car. My son, Matt, celebrated his eighteenth birthday a few weeks ago and now we are driving him to college. I feel proud. He won a scholarship, participated in sports and did it all without succumbing to the many temptations facing teenagers today.

It happened somewhere between unloading the car in the college parking lot and the hug goodbye. The separation. My son, no longer mine solely, now another member of the human race. The job of watching over him now rested on the shoulders of the world.

It's a moment just like any other, but the silence marks this one as profound. Driving home in the car without his voice, his presence. That is when it hit me—gratitude, from the depth of my bones to my goose-bumped flesh. Gratitude for being a stay-at-home mom. This was the day it counted—the dirty diapers, the late nights when he was sick, his first days at school, homework, all of the inside-out grimy socks, the cold bleachers, his messy room, and the fender bender. It all led up to today. I am grateful for all the times I stopped and listened and all the moments in between. Especially those.

When I got pregnant I assumed I would be a working mom. I liked working and climbing the corporate banking ladder and I felt that I could continue with my plan even with a baby. But you know what they say, "The best laid plans often go astray." Three days before my due date, I began to have contractions. It took another day and a half before my water broke. Forty-two hours later, and after three hours of pushing, my son arrived right on schedule, forever changing my world.

The doctor placed my beautiful boy in my tired arms. The feel of him, warm and comfortably heavy, wrapped tightly in the soft pale-blue blanket caught me by surprise. Feelings of wonder and a tremendous love overwhelmed me. I wanted to protect this little piece of heaven forever. He looked at me with big brown eyes and said wordlessly, "Hi Mom, don't you want to spend every minute you can with me?"

My heart responded with an intensity that surprised me. "Absolutely!" A wave of motherly love flooded through my body, rearranging all of the plans I had made, in just a moment's time.

"And just how will we make this work?" my mind asked my heart. "We need to get Dave (my husband) through his last year of law school. How will we pay the bills and who will cover our medical and dental plans?"

The entire silent conversation took place in the time it took Dave to walk from the chair a few feet away to my side. "How am I going to tell him that I do not want to return to work?"

"Wait, there will be a right time," my heart offered. "Do not worry, it will all work out."

After eight weeks of mothering, walks in the woods, late nights of rocking and a surprising number of dirty diapers, I returned reluctantly to my job as a branch manager of a bank. I never found the time to broach the subject with my husband. Two more months went by, our bank went through a "buy-out" by a larger national bank and I began to hear rumors of cutbacks.

"Just be patient," my heart said on those days when I cried the entire way to work. My desire to be with my son and watch him grow became more urgent with each passing week. "Have faith! It will all work out since you desire it so," the twinkle in my baby's eyes seemed to say.

Three months later my boss stopped by my branch to meet with me. Butterflies in my stomach alerted me that something big was coming.

"We are going to close your branch. The new bank feels that this branch is not needed, with the larger one only a mile away. You have two options: walk away with a six-month severance package, insurance and pension, or apply for any other open position within the system."

"Wow, I'll have to think about it," I replied with my best poker face, knowing full well which option I would choose.

"Oh, and you have thirty days until we close," she added.

Around the same time, my husband got an early offer for a great opportunity in upstate New York. This meant my severance salary would take us right up until his new job started.

I watched my son's first steps, encouraged his first words, witnessed his first soccer goal, bandaged his cuts, dusted him off after he fell, and greeted him at the bus every day. After a few years we had another boy, Mitchell, and I renewed my resolve to stay home. Despite the fact that it was not always easy, I never wavered, never doubted the silent commitment I made to both children to be there.

This inspired me to think creatively and to build work around my children's schedules. I ran a small interior design business from my home for the first nine years. The birth of my second son also inspired me to begin teaching yoga and meditation classes. Eventually I opened a yoga studio, working mother's hours of course, with the goal of helping people release stress and live healthier, happier lives. A number of my teachers are stay-at-home moms, desiring to contribute something to the world while raising their children.

I have five more years of moments to savor before we reach this milestone for Mitchell, our youngest and I intend to make the most out of each and every one of them.

~Kaye Khalsa

Salad – An Amusing Musing of a Former SAHM

No party is any fun unless seasoned with folly.
~Desiderius Erasmus

For many years, I worked in my home raising my three girls and caring for my husband. I am ninety-three years old now, a grandmother of seven and great-grandmother of six. Many things have changed for women who stay home to raise their families. There are conveniences we did not imagine, hectic schedules that would have been impossible fifty years ago. And yet some things are exactly the same.

Being at home all day, I rarely had an opportunity to get dressed up. But one Christmas, my husband and I were invited to attend a gala. I wanted to look very elegant to impress the high society friends who had invited me out. I got a fancy hairdo, bought a fancy dress and shoes. It was a whole new me. I looked and felt gorgeous and was eager for a good time.

When I arrived at the club where the party was being held, the weather suddenly changed to a windy sleet storm. As I got out of the car, I immediately fell into a puddle. I got up and kept walking, but my fancy high heels would not support me and I kept falling with every step, giving in to the wind. I felt very undignified, grasping bushes to aid me as I crawled up the icy driveway. When I finally made it to the top, I entered, soaked and disheveled.

Giving up on the chance to be glamorous, I instead sat at a corner table to be inconspicuous. When dinner was served, an inexperienced waiter approached our table, and then tripped as he began to serve us. Two large platters of salad slid down my head into my strapless gown. The partygoers were overcome with laughter as I stood up, oil and vinegar dripping from my face while I extricated lettuce and tomatoes from my bosom. It was a rare night for me as a housewife. And while my impromptu performance wasn't elegant, I know I made quite an impression!

~Estel Kempf

Always Waiting

Human beings are the only creatures that allow their children to come back home.
~Bill Cosby

Everyone wants me to leave my home. Not forever, they say. Just for a long weekend. A very long one. They tell me I've been an at-home mom too long. That there are no children living at home anymore. They are grown with children of their own. That doesn't faze me at all. I know when they come home, I'll be waiting. There will be other things to do, places to go, errands to run, friendships to enjoy, but my children will know where to reach me if ever I am needed.

It all started when my first child came along. Motherhood gave me an opportunity to be at home. Some of my friends were working outside the home. It didn't tempt me. I was exactly where I wanted to be—at home with my daughter.

It wasn't that I liked housecleaning or housekeeping or cooking or any of the things one does at home. It was just the wonderful feeling that I was creating a place that everyone wanted to return to at the end of the day. I had found a partner to build it with and I knew from the beginning of our marriage that our refuge would stand strong against life's changing currents.

And when my son came along, I had another reason to be there. I found it a wonderful experience to greet everyone when they entered my home and to wave goodbye when they left. Standing in the doorway on the uninspiring days, I looked like a bag lady in need of a makeover. But on the good days, nothing could equal my contentment or my sense of accomplishment.

After all, I thought, what was more wonderful than opening the door to your home, especially when you are a child, and knowing someone you love is going to be there to love you back? I was there. Not always entertaining. Not always blissfully content. Certainly not always glad to be there. But wherever I had been, home was where I returned, where all things began and sometimes, where all things ended.

That is where I wanted to be. My children knew it while they sat in school and they knew it when they ran down the block toward home and they knew it when they knocked on the door or when they grew older and unlocked it with their own keys. They knew of all the doors they passed, the door to home would always welcome them.

Sometimes I would wonder about that outside world. It seemed very far away. My husband was part of it all day and often late into the night. He would return home and I would be there waiting most of the time. It did not seem to be a waste of time to me, this waiting. Waiting for my children. Waiting for my husband. It seemed to be more of a gift. One I was offering. One I did not mind giving. One that enabled me to develop the skills that would take me through the rest of my life. Waiting was one of them. Waiting to regain my health when it left. Waiting to recover from widowhood. Waiting to regain my sense of self when it lost its way.

During the later years, there was a letting go I had to do and it was not easy. Children who were once content to be at home sought their own dreams and celebrated their own adulthood. But I knew as far as they traveled, they would return and as long as possible, I would be there. To listen to those dreams. To cheer the victories. To be part of whatever they wished to share with me. No matter what else I accomplished in life, nothing gave me greater pleasure then seeing one of their faces approach me. No matter how many times, it was never enough.

Fifty years later, I am still at home. The children, though they coax me to do something else, travel, have fun, they know when they drive up to my house, I will be there.

Always waiting. If not here, then somewhere.

~Harriet May Savitz

Reader's Guide
Meet Our Contributors
About the Authors
Acknowledgments
About Chicken Soup

Reader's Guide

In **Chapter One (Decisions, Decisions)** women share the emotions and life circumstances that shaped their decisions about whether to leave their paying jobs and stay home with their children.

- *Are there any common themes present throughout all or most of the stories?*

- *What were some of the obstacles and internal struggles these women faced when making this decision?*

- *These stories contain some very different views and feelings about motherhood. What are the most striking contrasts you found?*

In **Chapter Two (The Daily Grind)** mothers come clean about what it's really like to be a home with their kids.

- *What aspects of this job seem to be universal?*

- *How would you describe this job to someone who has never done it?*

- *What role does friendship play in the life of a stay-at-home or work-from-home mom?*

In **Chapter Three (Outside the Box)** contributors discuss alternative styles of parenting and life-planning.

- *Which of these, if any, are appealing to you and why?*

- *Given the myriad ways to be a stay-at-home or work-from-home mom, how can women who choose this path ever measure their performance?*

- *Is it even possible to measure performance in this line of work? And if not, how can women maintain their self-esteem while staying home?*

In **Chapter Four (Becoming a Specialist)** we are given access to the very personal lives of women in difficult circumstances.

- *How did you feel about the struggles these women faced?*

- *Did reading their stories change the way you view your own life and the struggles you have faced?*

- *Which of these stories did you find the most inspirational?*

The stories in **Chapter Five (Working from Home)** let us glimpse inside the everyday lives of women who have found ways to work from home.

- *Did you feel that they had found a way to "have it all"?*

- *Do you think there is a real difference between the lives of women who work from home and those who go to an office?*

- *Is there a common thread among the different paying jobs these women are able to do from their homes?*

In **Chapter Six (Ladies Who Launch)** we meet women who have created their own careers while staying home with their children.

- *What were some of the forces that drove these women to start businesses from their homes?*

- *Do you think the traditional workplace has played a role in the growing number of women who choose alternative paths to making money? If so, how?*

- *Do you think the traditional workplace has become more or less "family friendly" over the past few decades?*

How did you feel about what the men had to say in **Chapter 7 (Gender Benders)**?

- *Do you feel that society today truly values the work that women do at home?*

- *If it is true that most stay-at-home parents are still women, why is this so?*

- *Do you think this reflects limitations on women's choices, or an expression of their power to make choices?*

The profound rewards of staying home with children are expressed in the stories of **Chapter 8 (The Dividends)**.

- *Did you notice that all of the women wrote about the benefits to themselves from staying home rather than to their children?*

- *Do you think this reshapes the ongoing debate about whether a parent should stay at home?*

- *How does this change the social conversation about the decisions women face throughout their lives?*

Chapter 9 (Pink Slips) looks at the bittersweet job of stay-home mothering, whose ultimate success results in "getting fired."

- *Do you think letting go is more difficult for parents who have stayed at home full time to raise their children?*

- *Do you think there is a recent trend towards extending childhood as* many young adults are moving back home after college? If so, do you think this trend has been aided by stay-home parents?

- Do the stories about finding new careers after children leave the nest affect your view of how women are shaping their lives over time?

In **Chapter 10 (Looking Back)** women reflect on their choices and children pay tribute to their stay-at-home moms.

- After reading about the choices, doubts, and daily struggles of stay-at-home and work-from-home moms, does this chapter provide any resolution?

- Do these stories make the decisions women face easier or more difficult?

- If most people, upon reflection, value time with their families above all else, how can we weigh the value of work outside the home when making this choice is financially possible?

Chicken Soup for the Soul: Power Moms takes us through a journey of life choices, self-discovery and even self-reinvention.

- Did any of the stories evoke new realizations about your own life?

- Did any of the stories inspire you to make changes in your life or affect how you look at your life and the choices you have made?

- What story would you tell about yourself?

Meet Our Contributors

Elizabeth Aldrich, mother of three, an Integrative Health and Nutrition Coach, writer, and public speaker, is the founder and publisher of ForHerInformation.com, an information source for conscious-minded women. She has produced and hosted her own PBS television series, *For Her Information*, and the Seattle radio show, *A Balanced Life*. Contact her at Beth@RestoringEssence.com.

Heather B. Armstrong, has won numerous awards for her widely read blog, dooce®, including a Lifetime Achievement award in 2008. Heather was named in *Forbes'* "The Web Celeb 25," and has been profiled in several national newspapers and business magazines. She has appeared on numerous national television news shows.

Carol Band is a mother of three and an award-winning humor writer. In her spare time, she raises champion dust bunnies and kills houseplants. Visit her website at www.carolband.com.

Jillian Barberie-Reynolds is co-host of the Fox morning show *Good Day LA*, and has also appeared on television shows and in films. She has a degree in Broadcast Journalism from Mohawk College of Applied Arts & Technology. Jillian and husband Grant Reynolds have a beautiful daughter, Ruby Raven. Visit her at www.askjillian.com.

Kerrie Barney still occasionally falls asleep in her mother's office... but now it's because she works long hours in the family business as a bookkeeper and licensed tax preparer. Her writing has been published in many craft and hobby publications, including Taunton's *Threads*, *Knit Simple*, *Crochet!* and *Rock & Gem*.

Kimberly Beauchamp, ND, earned her doctoral degree in naturopathic medicine from Bastyr University. She took time off from private practice to be at home with her two young daughters. Dr. Beauchamp is currently writing a book about simple ways to improve your children's nutrition. She can be contacted at Dr.KimBeauchamp@verizon.net.

Lisa Belkin is a reporter for *The New York Times Magazine* and author of the daily Motherlode blog on nytimes.com/parenting. She wrote the much discussed cover story, "The Opt Out Revolution," for *The New York Times* in 2003 and has been writing about parents and work ever since.

Ruth Bergen has been married to Brian for five years. She is a mom to two little princesses and spends her days baking cinnamon buns, shopping at thrift stores, and coloring on her driveway with sidewalk chalk.

Ginger Boda has contributed to various online publications. She's also been published in *Chicken Soup for the Bride's Soul, Chicken Soup for the Soul: Teens Talk Middle School*, and the *God's Way Series* : Christmas Edition. Ginger resides in California with her husband and has three grown children. E-mail her at Rhymerbabe@aol.com.

Pam Bostwick's many articles appear in magazines, newspapers and anthologies, including several editions of *Chicken Soup for the Soul*. She is legally blind and hearing impaired and enjoys her life, her country home, the beach, playing guitar, being a volunteer counselor, her seven children and ten grandchildren, and her new husband. E-mail her at pamloves7@verizon.net.

Farley Boyle received her Bachelor of Arts in Communications on a full athletic and academic scholarship from Jacksonville University in 1993. Upon graduating, she pursued a lucrative modeling career for fifteen years and is now a full-time mother and wife and Founding Director of C.H.A.S.E. for Life (CPR-Heimlich-Awareness-Safety-Education). Please visit chaseforlife.org.

Lisa Bradshaw is a mother, a cancer survivor, an entrepreneur and a widow. She hosts *The Life with Lisa Show*, a radio talk show. Lisa is writing her second book, *Just Earth*. Her mission is learning, enlightening and laughing through her writing and *The Life with Lisa Show*.

John P. Buentello is a writer who has published essays, short stories, and poetry. He is the co-author, with Lawrence Buentello, of the novel *Reproduction Rights*, and the short story collection *Binary Tales*. He's currently at work on a new novel. He can be reached at jakkhakk@yahoo.com.

Astacia Carter is a stay-at-home mom of two daughters. She has been married to her husband, Michael, for nine years. When she is not transporting her girls all over town she is likely on her laptop. She loves social media. She also enjoys reading and sewing.

Elise Chidley received her Master of Fine Arts from Pennsylvania State University in 1995. She has worked as a journalist, college lecturer, and public relations manager. Her first novel, *Your Roots Are Showing*, was published in October 2008. Please visit her website, www.elisechidley.com.

Marie Torres Cimarusti and husband, Don, live in Palos Verdes, CA, with their daughter, Channing. Marie, a graduate of UCLA, has always loved writing and her work has appeared in numerous publications. She is an award-winning author of children's books. Her favorites include *Peek-a-Moo!* and *Peek-a-Choo-Choo!* Please contact her at writemariehow@gmail.com.

Julie Cole L.L.B, M.A, B.A, is the co-founder of Mabel's Labels Inc. (www.mabel.ca) and the busy but proud mother of five small children. She can be reached at julie@mabel.ca and her blog can be found at www.blog.mabel.ca.

Victoria Colligan is the Founder and CEO of Ladies Who Launch and is co-author of *Ladies Who Launch: Embracing Entrepreneurship* *and Creativity as a Lifestyle.* She has been featured on *The Today Show* and in *The New York Times*, among other media outlets. She holds a JD/MBA from Case Western Reserve University and a BA from Brown University.

Billy Cuchens' wife became a stay-at-home mom in 2006 when they adopted their son. She was then promoted to a second child the following year when they adopted their daughter. To read more of his humorous essays about his life, please go to goggycoffee.blogspot.com or e-mail him at billycuchens@yahoo.com.

Barbara Curtis lives with her husband, Tripp, and the last five of their twelve children in Bluemont, Virginia. Barbara is also a prolific writer with nine books and 900 articles to her credit. She blogs daily at www.MommyLife.net.

Nicole Dean is the mostly-sane work-at-home mom behind ShowMomTheMoney.com. She also created ShowKidsTheMoney.com—an informative resource to inspire parents to teach their children business skills from a young age. Nicole lives in Florida with her much adored husband and two silly children.

Bob Dickson is a professional writer from Southern California, where he lives with his wife and two daughters. He's written for *The Signal* (Santa Clarita), *The L.A. Daily News, The L.A. Times Newspaper Group*, and several magazines. He also teaches writing at The Master's College. Bob can be reached at Bob@BobsWordFactory.com.

Though without physical sight, **Janet Perez Eckles** is an international speaker, writer and author of the inspirational book, *Trials of Today, Treasures for Tomorrow: Overcoming Adversities in Life.* Her stories, which appear in a dozen books and numerous magazines, relate how adversity turned to triumph, success, and contagious joy. www.janetperezeckles.com.

HJ Eggers recently returned from the Maui Writers Retreat. She's now happily laboring over her first book, *The Prodigal Wife*. After abandoning her husband and child, a contrite wife longs for reconciliation. But she stumbles into a horrific storm. Available in 2009. Please e-mail her at hjs01234@aol.com.

Karen Fisher is a singer/songwriter living with her husband and three children in Midland, TX. She is a stay-home mom who sings and speaks at women's events off and on throughout the year. She graduated from Sanford University with a BS in Education in 1990.

Sally Friedman's proudest work is as the mother of three daughters. Over her three decades of writing, those daughters are often her subject matter. Sally contributes frequently to *The New York Times, The Philadelphia Inquirer*, and other national newspapers and magazines. E-mail: pinegander@aol.com.

Danielle Ganek is an author, whose first novel, *Lulu Meets God And Doubts Him*, has been translated into several languages, including Romanian. *The New York Times* said she had a "savvy satirical eye," and she was selected for Barnes and Noble Discover Great New Writers program in 2007.

Elizabeth Garrett divides her time as Director of Domestic Affairs for her home in New Canaan, CT, and as Executive National Vice President in qualification with Arbonne International. Elizabeth's passions are her family and educating people about health and wellness and home-based businesses. Contact her at elizabethgarrett@myarbonne.com.

Pamela Gilsenan is the mother of five adult children whose names all begin with "J." She is a Rocky Mountain regional writer and graduate of Stephens College. She has written and published two children's books and several specialty cookbooks. Her upcoming cookbook is *Rhubarb! Rhubarb!*. Please e-mail her at p_Gilsenan@hotmail.com.

Jo Glading-DiLorenzo always dreamed of running away with the circus. Fortunately, motherhood brought the circus to her. She lives in Northampton, Massachusetts, where she writes, coaches and manages three thrilling rings of fun with her wife, Lise, and their three daughters. Incidentally, she was educated at Colgate and Columbia Universities.

Louise Gleeson received her Bachelor of Science, Master of Science and Master of Journalism degrees in Ontario, Canada. She currently juggles working as a freelance journalist and editor with raising three young children. She can be reached at louise@louisegleeson.com.

Erin Barrette Goodman is a law-of-attraction-inspired writer, workshop facilitator, yoga teacher and mother of two. She is the founder of the Rhode Island Birth Network, which promotes empowered decision-making during the childbearing years. Visit her blog (www.eringoodman.com/blog) to explore her joyful—and honest—daily musings.

Jane Green is the author of ten best-selling novels, including *Jemina J.*, *Second Chance*, and *The Beach House*. Jane is a recent winner of a Cosmopolitan Fun Fearless Fiction Award and a native Londoner. She lives in Connecticut with husband, Ian Warburg, and their five children. Visit her blog at www.janegreen.com.

Christopher Harder is a freelance writer who lives in New Jersey with his wife and son. He quit his job at *The Wall Street Journal* website in 2005 to stay at home with his son. Chris is the author of a children's book, illustrated by his father, entitled *It's Tough to Nap on a Turtle*. Chris has been a journalist for nineteen years.

Melora Hardin is an actress, wife and mother of two young daughters. She currently stars in *The Office*, and has appeared in numerous movies, including *Absolute Power* and *27 Dresses*. She also stars in *Hannah Montana: The Movie* and *17 Again*. She recently made her directorial debut with the independent feature *You* (www.youthefilm.com). Visit her at www.melora.com.

Matthias Hauger received a Bachelor of Arts degree from King's College, University of London. He was an investment banker for ten years before becoming an entrepreneur active across a variety of sectors. He loves skiing and tennis, gardening, reading and board games.

Robin D. Hayes received her Ph.D. from the University of North Carolina at Chapel Hill in 2002 and writes about education and adoption. Dr. Hayes is the author of *The Truth about Older Child Adoption: What Your Adoption Agency Won't Tell You*, and can be reached at www.adoptingtheolderchild.com.

Diane Helbig is a professional development coach in Ohio. She works with small business owners and salespeople on successful business development strategies. Diane is also the mother of two kids ages twelve and nine. Diane writes business-related articles and has a monthly newsletter. Please e-mail her at diane@seizethisdaycoaching.com.

Tracy Higginbotham has been promoting women entrepreneurship since 1996. Her passion for creating stronger economic connections between women entrepreneurs led to the creation of her company, Women TIES (Women Together Inspiring Entrepreneurial Success) in 2005. She is dedicated to her husband, two sons, and women entrepreneurs. Contact Tracy at www.womenties.com.

Miriam Hill is co-author of *Fabulous Florida* and a frequent contributor to *Chicken Soup for the Soul* books. She's been published in *The Christian Science Monitor, Grit, St. Petersburg Times, The Sacramento Bee* and *Poynter Online*. Miriam's manuscript received Honorable Mention for Inspirational Writing in a Writer's Digest Writing Competition.

Louis A. Hill, Jr. has authored three books and many articles. He earned a Ph.D. in structural engineering, designed bridges and buildings and joined the engineering faculty at Arizona State University. He retired an Emeritus Dean of Engineering from The University of Akron. He is listed in *Who's Who in America*.

Mary Scott Himes received her Bachelor of Arts from McGill University in 1988 and her Bachelor of Fine Arts from Parsons School of Design in 1993. She worked in restaurant design in New York City for a year and as a market editor and stylist for various design magazines until 2008. Mary enjoys travel, friends, nature, rowing and the arts.

Sharon Hockenbury has been married to Doug for twenty-eight years. She is the mother of nine children. She loves blogging and writing to encourage mothers and wives. She is an herbalist, folk singer and guitarist. Please e-mail her at hockenburychickensoup@gmail.com.

Amy Hudock, Ph.D., Founding Co-Editor of *LiteraryMama.com*, is a single mom who teaches English in South Carolina. She is the co-editor of *Literary Mama: Reading for the Maternally Inclined* and *American Women Prose Writers, 1820-1870*. Her work has appeared in *Mama Ph.D.*, *Cup of Comfort, Chicken Soup for the Soul*, and *Single State of the Union*.

Cindy Hval is a freelance writer whose work has appeared in five previous *Chicken Soup for the Soul* collections. She's a regular contributor to several regional magazines and is a columnist and correspondent for the *Spokesman Review* newspaper in Spokane, WA, where she and her husband are raising their four sons. E-mail her at dchval@juno.com.

Robin Kall received her Bachelor of Arts degree from SUNY Binghamton in 1985. Married that same year, she has been living in Rhode Island with her husband and two children and dog. Robin's radio show *Reading With Robin* (www.readingwithrobin.com) brings together her love of books and love of talk!

Jill Kargman is the author of *Momzillas* and *The Ex-Mrs. Hedgefund*. She lives in New York City with her husband and three children and can be cyber-visited at www.jillkargman.com.

Estel Kempf is ninety-three years old and was a stay-at-home mom until her three daughters were adults. She will relive the past only to reminisce of happy moments and spontaneous amusing incidents.

Kaye Khalsa received her Bachelor of Arts degree from St. Anselm College. She owns and operates a yoga and wellness business and writes inspirational books and articles for adults and children. Kaye is also co-founder of a rain forest preserve in Costa Rica. Please e-mail her at prempyar@mac.com.

Mimi Greenwood Knight is a "Luzianna" mother of four and freelance writer specializing in articles and humorous essays on motherhood. Her collection, *Mom, You're Not Going to WRITE About This, Are You?* is currently in search of a publisher. Visit her blog at blog.nola.com/faith/mimi_greenwood_knight.

Cheryl Kremer lives in Lancaster, PA, with her husband, Jack, sixteen-year-old Nikki, fourteen-year-old Cobi and three dogs and two cats. She enjoys writing about her life experiences and has been previously published in many other *Chicken Soup for the Soul* books. She can be reached at j_kremer@verizon.net.

Karen Krugman lives in New York City with her two daughters, Maxine and Jordan, who provide wonderful fodder for stories and the memoir she is currently working on.

Donna La Scala received her BA, *cum laude*, from Queens College in 1981. She currently resides on Long Island with her husband, Bob, and two children, Alexandra and Samantha. Donna is a financial professional with AXA Advisors LLC in Lake Success. She enjoys dancing, music and reading historical novels. Contact Donna at rmldel1@aol.com.

Liz Lange founded Liz Lange Maternity. Her secondary line, Liz Lange for Target, is Target's exclusive maternity line. Her book, *Liz Lange's Maternity Style: How to Look Fabulous During the Most Fashion-Challenged Time*, will be followed by *The Fourth Trimester*. Lange is a member of the Committee of 200 and a board member of Fertile Hope. She lives in New York with husband, Jeffrey Lange, and children, Gus and Alice.

John Lavitt lived on the Greek island of Patmos, studying with the poet Robert Lax. First published in a William Burroughs tribute collection, John barely survived his wild and crazy Hollywood years as the Lavinator to help start The 12 Angels, a nonprofit investment company. He can be reached at lavinatorproductions@yahoo.com.

Andrea Lehner graduated *summa cum laude* from the University of Colorado's English Writing program in 2008 while educating and entertaining her two vivacious children. In addition to being a wife, mother, and aspiring novelist, Andrea enjoys reading, raising horses, painting, studying history, and volunteering with youth programs. E-mail her at aclehner@gmail.com.

Heather Pemberton Levy loves raising her two young children in southeastern Connecticut but sometimes misses life in the corporate fast lane as a former vice president, magazine editor, and technology journalist. She captures the joys, frustrations and lessons of parenting in her blog, *Mommy Truths*, at www.mommytruths.blogspot.com.

Janeen Lewis, freelance writer, lives in Lawrenceburg, KY, with husband, Jesse, and son, Andrew. She has degrees in journalism and elementary education from Eastern Kentucky University. After the birth of her son in 2006, she left her teaching job to stay at home. Her favorite job is being CEO for the Lewis household.

Cristina T. Lopez is a communication consultant and author. She published her non-fiction book, *Finding Francis*, in 2003 and is currently working on a poetry chapbook as well as a full-length fiction novel entitled *Letters to Helen*. Cristina lives in Stewart Manor, NY, with her husband, Thomas, and two daughters.

Terri Major-Kincade received her B.S. in Biology from Prairie View A&M, and her M.D. and M.P.H. from UCLA. She is a neonatologist in Dallas, Texas. She enjoys time with her family, bible study, traveling, and writing. She is working on a book for NICU families. E-mail her at terrikincade@msn.com.

Masha Malka is an international speaker and author of *The One Minute Coach: Change your Life One Minute at a Time.* Successfully balancing the demands of her busy career with three children, she is passionate about showing others how they can do it, too. Please e-mail her at masga@mashamalka.com.

Jennifer Mallin received her bachelor of Fine Arts with honors from Brandeis University in 1983. She has published writing in art criticism as well as poetry. Her interests include travel and dressage. She is currently a painter specializing in portraits, and lives with her husband, daughter, and two stepsons in Greenwich, CT.

Victoria Hoffmann Marsh grew up in New York City, and received a B.S. from the University of New Hampshire in 1986. She resides in Connecticut with husband Patrick, son Ian, and daughter Delaney. To contribute to the Sean Robert Marsh Pediatric Heart Foundation: PO Box 4820, Stamford, CT 06907, pvmarsh@optonline.net.

Britt Menzies is the creator and spirit behind StinkyKids™ (www.stinkykids.com). Inspired by her own two beautiful "StinkyKids," Britt's passion is to make StinkyKids a trusted brand. Britt is also an active volunteer with Books, Bears and Bonnets, Inc. (www.booksbearsbonnets.org) to which StinkyKids donates a portion of its profits.

Amy S. Mercer is a freelance writer living in Charleston, SC, with her husband and two young sons. She has been a stay-at-home mom ever since her first son was born, and wouldn't change a thing. Amy is working on a book about growing up with diabetes. You can read her blog at www.alsmercer.wordpress.com.

Wendy Miller received her Bachelor of Arts (writing concentration) from Wittenberg University in 1997. Wendy is thrilled to have completed her first novel. She enjoys hiking, running, reading, writing short stories and spending time with her husband and three children. Please e-mail her at: millerct1@cox.net.

Stephanie Wolff Mirmina lives in Arlington, VA, with her two-year-old son and husband. Her previous work can be seen in *Chicken Soup for the New Mom's Soul*. She is a reading specialist who is currently enjoying being at home with her son.

Rebecca Khamneipur Morrison received her bachelor's and law degrees from Georgetown University and George Washington Law School respectively, both with honors. She practiced law for eleven years before starting her own consulting business so that she could stay at home with her children and write. Contact her at rebeccakhamneipur@hotmail.com.

For twenty years **Susan Morrow** has been photographing professionally, from distinctive corporate and literary headshots to her renowned family portraiture. She has published *Lovies* and *The Next Station to Heaven*. Susan contributes her gift to many groups including Figure Skating of Harlem and Now I Lay Me Down to Sleep. www.susanmorrow.com.

Kate Osborne Munno received her B.A. in Geology from Bates College, and her M.A. in Geology from Queens College, CUNY. After opting out of an environmental consulting career, she is currently an at-home mom. Kate lives in Connecticut with her husband, two children, two Border Collies, and a cat.

Sherrie Page Najarian is a freelance writer and registered nurse who lives with her family in Richmond, VA.

Amy Newmark is the publisher of *Chicken Soup for the Soul*, but she spent her child-raising years mostly as a stay-at-home, sometimes working-from-home mom. Her non-mom career has included stints as a Wall Street analyst, a hedge fund manager, and a corporate executive and board member.

Lori Odhner and her husband, John, have nine children, including an autistic son and identical twin girls, for comic relief. Their marriage ministry is their passion and Lori thinks about it before her eyes are open in the morning. In addition, they write Christian music. Visit them at www.caringformarriage.org.

Isla Penrose lives with her partner and three daughters. She writes and illustrates stories for children, and novels for young adults. She loves music, oil painting, reading, gardening and the color turquoise.

Jodi Picoult is the #1 *New York Times* bestselling author of sixteen novels. She lives in Hanover, NH, with her husband and three children. Visit her website at www.jodipicoult.com.

Chloe Polikoff is fourteen years old and is in the eighth grade. She has three younger brothers. In her free time she enjoys snorkeling, sailing, tennis, golf and squash as well as making desserts!

Diane Powis graduated with honors from Colgate University with a B.A. in Psychology. After various work and travel experiences, she subsequently returned to school and obtained her Ph.D. in Clinical Psychology from Fairleigh Dickinson University. She is married, has two children and is working part time at a local hospital.

Jennifer Quist is a writer, researcher, accomplished laundress, and mother of five young sons. Currently, she writes features on social issues for an oil industry magazine. She is also a published poet, columnist, essayist, and reporter with a Bachelor of Arts degree in Sociology from the University of Alberta.

Jennifer Reed is an award-winning children's author. She always knew she wanted to be a writer, but it wasn't until she became a stay-at-home mom that she pursued children's writing and articles for parents. She has published over twenty books and one hundred stories and articles. Jennifer also teaches writing. Her website is www.jennifer-reed.com.

Valerie Rosenberg's early career was on Wall Street in strategic planning. Currently, she lives in New Canaan, CT, with her loving husband, three kids, three cats, two dogs and a bookcase full of travel books. She's home schooling her three kids as they travel cross-country this year. Contact her via e-mail at ValerieMBR@hotmail.com.

Sally Rubenstone is Senior Advisor at CollegeConfidential.com and the co-author of *Panicked Parents' Guide to College Admissions* and two other college-admission guidebooks. She's cautiously optimistic that she won't panic when her own son applies to college but admits that—since he's only twelve—it's too early to guarantee.

Harriet May Savitz is the award-winning author of twenty-six books, including *Run Don't Walk*, adapted into an ABC Afterschool Special. Her essays appear in twenty *Chicken Soup for the Soul* books. Her books, including *The Gifts Animals Can Give*, can be found at www.iUniverse.com, www.harrietmaysavitz.com, or www.authorhouse.com. Contact her at greetingsfromasburypark@verizon.net.

Suzanne Schryver is a freelance writer of fiction and nonfiction, an educator, and a power mom. Her stories have appeared in various anthologies. She works in a college writing center and teaches writing online. She lives with her family in New Hampshire. Please e-mail her at suzanneschryver@gmail.com.

Gene Scriven, Jr. is a USAF Veteran, currently the Chief of Information Security for a Fortune-20 company. Gene enjoys photography, electronics, and spending time with his family. He is a Texan, transplanted to the metropolitan Atlanta area with his wife, Tammie, and daughters, Jessica and Ashley. Please e-mail him at genescriven@yahoo.com.

Renee Sklarew, mother of two girls, writes a monthly column on families for *Northern Virginia Magazine* and her blog, DCwritermom. com. A former PTA President, she teaches newspaper writing. Her twelve-year-old daughter received her heart transplant in August 2000, and remains healthy and active.

Lynne Spears is the proud mother of three and the blessed grandmother of three. A long-time resident of Kentwood, LA, she has a B.A. from Southeastern Louisiana University. She taught school for many years and owned and operated a preschool/daycare. Lynne is the author of three books including her latest, *Through the Storm*.

Marian Brown Sprague is a mom who also works as a freelance writer and consultant to nonprofit organizations. Following a peripatetic childhood as a "foreign service brat," she now enjoys traveling with her husband and daughter from her home base in California. She graduated with honors from Duke University.

Johnna Stein received her B.A. from the College of William & Mary. She's a stay-at-home mom who's volunteered as musical director, KidZchurch leader and School Council representative. She speaks Dutch and French and has been to five continents. She is currently writing children's books and short stories.

Lois Greene Stone, writer and poet, has been syndicated worldwide. Poetry and personal essays have been included in hardcover and paperback book anthologies. Collections of her personal items, photos, and memorabilia are in major museums including twelve different divisions of The Smithsonian.

Sharon Struth is a freelance writer who lives in Connecticut with her two teenage daughters and husband. She received a Bachelors

Degree from Marist College in 1981. Her work can also be seen in *Sasee Magazine* and *A Cup of Comfort for New Mothers*.

Tom Swick is a cartoonist and illustrator whose work has appeared in *The New York Times Book Review* and in *Playboy Magazine*, as well as on the cover of the CD *Rapture of the Deep* by Deep Purple, and in publications of the San Francisco Symphony and the John F. Kennedy Center for the Performing Arts. Contact Tom at tomswick@hotmail.com.

Lisa Tener is proud mother of two boys. As a book coach, she helps people to successfully write and publish their books. She serves on the faculty of Harvard Medical School's publishing course. She loves to dance and read with her sons. Her websites are www.LisaTener.com and www.writeabookuniversity.com.

Sharon Dunski Vermont is a part-time pediatrician, full-time mother, and freelance writer. In 1993, Sharon received her M.D. from the University of Missouri-Kansas City. In her spare time she enjoys reading, writing and spending time with her husband, Laird, and two daughters, Hannah and Jordyn. Please e-mail her at svermont1987@yahoo.com.

Mama to six exuberant children, **Ann Voskamp** home educates, farms 600 acres with her husband, and, on the fringe hours, writes a column for the *San Antonio Beacon*. She writes of the sacred in the common at her daily blog www.aholyexperience.com.

Terrilynne Walker was a stay-at-home mom for over twenty-five years and now is an educator, grant writer, fundraiser, world traveler, champion golfer, fisherwoman, and grandmother. Her mission is to help young minds focus on the future, enjoy learning and expand their potential.

Emily Weaver is a stay-at-home mom of three in Springfield, MO. Emily's work has appeared in several *Chicken Soup for the Soul* books. She and her husband enjoy traveling, gardening and golfing. She can be reached by e-mail at emily-weaver@sbcglobal.net.

David White received his English degree from the University of Connecticut. David enjoys spending time with his wife, Suzanne, and three great boys Hunter, Logan, and Kelsey. He also tries to squeeze in a little golf when he can. He can be e-mailed at DavidPWhite@Allstate.com.

Diane Dean White is a freelance writer who resides on the Carolina Coast with her husband of thirty-six years. She is the author of *Beach Walks* and *Carolina in the Morning*. Diane enjoys sharing memories about her own life and her children. Visit her website at www.dianedeanwhite.com or e-mail her at thelamb212@aol.com.

Kim Wierman has been freelance writing since 1994. She is a co-owner of Waves of Gratitude, an online inspirational jewelry website. Kim lives with her three sons, Joshua, Lucas and Casey. Her work is always dedicated to the love of her life, her late husband Don. E-mail her at kim@wavesofgratitude.com.

Sue Wilkey graduated from Cornell University with a B.S. in Communications. She is currently a freelance writer, mother of three and author of the blog *Happy Meals and Happy Hour*. (www.happymealsandhappyhour.blogspot.com).

Patti Woods is a freelance writer whose articles have appeared in numerous national consumer and trade magazines. Her clients have included *Health Magazine, Wine Spectator, Alternative Medicine Magazine, Men's Edge Magazine, Better Nutrition Magazine*, and *The Christian Science Monitor*. She lives in Trumbull, CT, with her husband and son.

Kimmie Rose Zapf is a wife and mother of five. She hosts CBS Radio's *InnerViews with Kimmie and Steve*, and is the author of several books including *Wake Up Your Intuition*. A recent N.D.E. inspired her to reach out to people through lectures to help them embrace the stillness within. For more information visit her website at www.kimmierose.com.

Who Is
Jack Canfield?

Jack Canfield is the co-creator and editor of the *Chicken Soup for the Soul* series, which *Time* magazine has called "the publishing phenomenon of the decade." Jack is also the co-author of eight other bestselling books including *The Success Principles™: How to Get from Where You Are to Where You Want to Be, Dare to Win, The Aladdin Factor, You've Got to Read This Book*, and *The Power of Focus: How to Hit Your Business and Personal and Financial Targets with Absolute Certainty*.

Jack is the CEO of the Canfield Training Group in Santa Barbara, California, and founder of the Foundation for Self-Esteem in Culver City, California. He has conducted intensive personal and professional development seminars on the principles of success for over a million people in twenty-three countries. Jack is a dynamic keynote speaker and he has spoken to hundreds of thousands of others at more than 1,000 corporations, universities, professional conferences and conventions, and has been seen by millions more on national television shows such as *The Today Show, Fox and Friends, Inside Edition, Hard Copy*, CNN's *Talk Back Live, 20/20, Eye to Eye*, and the *NBC Nightly News* and the *CBS Evening News*.

Jack is the recipient of many awards and honors, including three honorary doctorates and a Guinness World Records Certificate for having seven books from the *Chicken Soup for the Soul* series appearing on the New York Times bestseller list on May 24, 1998.

You can reach Jack at:

Jack Canfield
The Canfield Companies
P. O. Box 30880 • Santa Barbara, CA 93130
phone: 805-563-2935 • fax: 805-563-2945
www.jackcanfield.com

Who Is
Mark Victor Hansen?

Mark Victor Hansen is the co-founder of Chicken Soup for the Soul, along with Jack Canfield. He is also a sought-after keynote speaker, bestselling author, and marketing maven. For more than thirty years, Mark's powerful messages of possibility, opportunity, and action have created powerful change in thousands of organizations and millions of individuals worldwide.

Mark's credentials include a lifetime of entrepreneurial success. He is a prolific writer with many bestselling books, such as *The One Minute Millionaire*, *Cracking the Millionaire Code*, *How to Make the Rest of Your Life the Best of Your Life*, *The Power of Focus*, *The Aladdin Factor*, and *Dare to Win*, in addition to the *Chicken Soup for the Soul* series. Mark has had a profound influence in the field of human potential through his library of audios, videos, and articles in the areas of big thinking, sales achievement, wealth building, publishing success, and personal and professional development. Mark is also the founder of the MEGA Seminar Series.

He has appeared on *Oprah*, CNN, and *The Today Show*. He has been quoted in *Time*, *U.S. News & World Report*, *USA Today*, *The New York Times*, and *Entrepreneur* and has given countless radio interviews, assuring our planet's people that "You can easily create the life you deserve."

Mark is the recipient of numerous awards that honor his entrepreneurial spirit, philanthropic heart, and business acumen. He is a lifetime member of the Horatio Alger Association of Distinguished Americans, an organization that honored Mark with the prestigious Horatio Alger Award for his extraordinary life achievements.

You can reach Mark at:

Mark Victor Hansen & Associates, Inc.
P. O. Box 7665 • Newport Beach, CA 92658
phone: 949-764-2640 • fax: 949-722-6912
www.markvictorhansen.com

Who Is
Wendy Walker?

Wendy Walker is a former commercial litigator who has been a stay-at-home mom for the past eleven years. She began writing several years ago and her first novel, *Four Wives*, was released in February, 2008, by St. Martin's Press and will be translated into Italian and Dutch. Her second novel will be published by St. Martin's Press in the fall of 2009, and *Four Wives* will be released in paperback in March, 2009. In addition to editing and contributing to *Chicken Soup for the Soul: Power Moms*, Wendy has contributed to *Chicken Soup for the Soul: Teens Talk Middle School* and *Chicken Soup for the Soul: Teens Talk Getting into College*.

As an attorney, she worked in private practice both in New York and Connecticut, and served as a *pro bono* lawyer at the ACLU. While attending Law School at Georgetown University, where she graduated *magna cum laude*, she spent a summer in the Special Prosecutions Division of the U.S. Attorney's Office for the Eastern District of New York.

Wendy obtained her undergraduate degree from Brown University with a double major in economics and political science. Her junior year was spent at the London School of Economics. Upon graduating *magna cum laude*, she worked as a financial analyst in the Mergers and Acquisitions department of Goldman, Sachs & Co. in New York.

As a young girl, Wendy trained for competitive figure skating at facilities in Colorado and New York. She now serves on the board of Figure Skating in Harlem, an organization committed to the development of underprivileged girls which she has supported since 1997. She lives in suburban Connecticut and is busy raising her three sons and writing her third novel.

Visit Wendy and learn more about the women writers and entrepreneurs from *Chicken Soup for the Soul: Power Moms* at: wendywalkerbooks.com!

Acknowledgments

Over the past several months, I have had the privilege of reading stories about the journeys women take through motherhood. These stories made me laugh, cry and feel more than ever the incredible bond that this experience creates. I am grateful to each and every one of the women (and men) who took the time to share their intimate life stories. And while only a small number could be chosen for this book, every contributor helped to shape its pages and the messages it holds. Thank you!

My heartfelt gratitude goes out to Amy Newmark, my publisher, for taking a chance on a fiction writer and having faith in my vision for this book. Her bright spirit and enduring sense of humor made this project a labor of love. Also to D'ette Corona, my assistant publisher, who put up with my novice questions and meticulously managed the nuts and bolts of this very complicated process—a huge thanks to you!

And to the rest of the team at Chicken Soup for the Soul, Bill Rouhana, Bob Jacobs, Barbara LoMonaco, Kristiana Glavin and Brian Taylor, thanks for making this company so wonderful.

My family and friends have offered tremendous love and support during this project, and always. Juliet Kerr picked up the pieces around my house (and my life) with her usual efficiency and enthusiasm. And my brother, Grant Walker, was there for my kids at every turn. I could not have done this without them.

To my three beautiful boys who taught me everything I know about being a mother and who are the daily confirmation that the choices I've made have been good ones—I love you guys.

And, finally, to my beloved grandfather, Charlie Biamonte, who passed away in December. I will miss you dearly.

~Wendy Walker

Chicken Soup for the Soul

Improving Your Life Every Day

R eal people sharing real stories—for fifteen years. Now, Chicken Soup for the Soul has gone beyond the bookstore to become a world leader in life improvement. Through books, movies, DVDs, online resources and other partnerships, we bring hope, courage, inspiration and love to hundreds of millions of people around the world. Chicken Soup for the Soul's writers and readers belong to a one-of-a-kind global community, sharing advice, support, guidance, comfort, and knowledge.

Chicken Soup for the Soul stories have been translated into more than forty languages and can be found in more than one hundred countries. Every day, millions of people experience a Chicken Soup for the Soul story in a book, magazine, newspaper or online. As we share our life experiences through these stories, we offer hope, comfort and inspiration to one another. The stories travel from person to person, and from country to country, helping to improve lives everywhere.

Share with Us

We all have had Chicken Soup for the Soul moments in our lives. If you would like to share your story or poem with millions of people around the world, go to www.chickensoup.com and click on "Submit Your Story." You may be able to help another reader, and become a published author at the same time. Some of our past contributors have launched writing and speaking careers from the publication of their stories in our books!

Your stories have the best chance of being used if you submit them through our website, at

www.chickensoup.com

If you do not have access to the Internet, you may submit your stories by mail or by facsimile. Starting in 2010, submissions will only be accepted via the website. Please do not send us any book manuscripts, unless through a literary agent, as these will be automatically discarded.

Chicken Soup for the Soul
P.O. Box 700
Cos Cob, CT 06807-0700
Fax 203-861-7194

Chicken Soup for the Soul®

Divorce *and* Recovery

101 Stories about Surviving and Thriving after Divorce

Jack Canfield,
Mark Victor Hansen,
Patty Hansen

Chicken Soup's first book on divorce is wonderfully uplifting and filled with stories and poems from men and women who have been there and successfully navigated the divorce and recovery process. Heartfelt stories provide support, inspiration, and humor on all the phases of divorce, including the initial shock of the decision, the logistics of living through it, the inevitable self-discovery, and the new world of dating and even remarriage.

978-1-935096-21-4

*C*heck out our

Chicken Soup for the Soul® Empty Nesters

101 Stories about Surviving and Thriving When the Kids Leave Home

Jack Canfield,
Mark Victor Hansen,
Carol McAdoo Rehme,
Patricia Cena Evans

This book provides support during a very emotional but exciting time for parents. These heartfelt stories about gazing at surprisingly clean bedrooms, starting new careers, rediscovering spouses, and handling the continuing, and often humorous, needs of children, will inspire, support, and amuse parents. They'll nod their heads, cry a little, and laugh a lot, as they recognize themselves and their almost grown-up children in these stories.

978-1-935096-22-1

other great books!

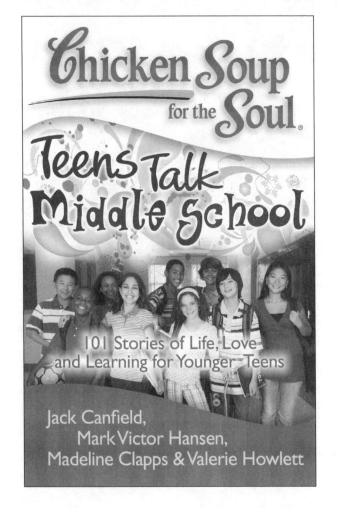

This "support group in a book" is meant for middle school students ages eleven to fourteen. The stories provide emotional support, humor, and inspiration for the young teens making their way through the tumultuous middle school years, and cover regrets and lessons learned, love and "like," popularity, friendship, tough issues such as divorce, illness, and death, failure and rising above it, embarrassing moments, bullying, and finding something you're passionate about.

978-1-935096-26-9

Check out our

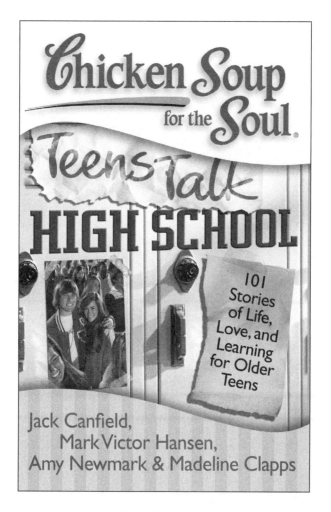

This book focuses on issues specific to high school age kids, ages fourteen to eighteen, covering topics of interest to older teens such as sports and clubs, religion and faith, driving, curfews, growing up, self-image and self-acceptance, dating and sex, family relationships, friends, divorce, illness, death, pregnancy, drinking, failure, and preparing for life after high school. High school students will find comfort and inspiration in the words of this book, like a portable support group.

978-1-935096-25-2

other great books!

www.chickensoup.com